T0361794

Industrial Policy

With the advent of Thatcherism in the UK and Reaganomics in the USA, 'industrial policy' had become something of a discredited notion in the 1980s. The emphasis had shifted to programmes of deregulation, de-nationalization, and tax reform.

The essays in this challenging and vigorous collection, first published in 1989, sprung from work that had been conducted in the USA, notably at the Harvard Business School, on reappraising the role of the public sector in industrial management. This American work suggested ways in which public sector and other bodies might have revitalized industrial life.

This book is ideal for students of business and economics.

Industrial Policy

USA and UK Debates

Edited by
Grahame Thompson

Routledge
Taylor & Francis Group

First published in 1989
by Routledge & Kegan Paul Ltd

This edition first published in 2015 by Routledge
2 Park Square, Milton Park, Abingdon, Oxon, OX14 4RN
and by Routledge
711 Third Avenue, New York, NY 10017

Routledge is an imprint of the Taylor & Francis Group, an informa business
Introduction © 1989 Grahame Thompson
Chapter 2 © Routledge & Kegan Paul 1987
Chapter 3 © Routledge & Kegan Paul 1984
Chapter 4 © Routledge & Kegan Paul 1986
Chapter 5 © Routledge & Kegan Paul 1987
Chapter 6 © Routledge & Kegan Paul 1986

The right of Grahame Thompson to be identified as editor of this work has been asserted
by him in accordance with sections 77 and 78 of the Copyright, Designs and Patents Act
1988.

All rights reserved. No part of this book may be reprinted or reproduced or utilised in
any form or by any electronic, mechanical, or other means, now known or hereafter
invented, including photocopying and recording, or in any information storage or
retrieval system, without permission in writing from the publishers.

Publisher's Note
The publisher has gone to great lengths to ensure the quality of this reprint but points
out that some imperfections in the original copies may be apparent.

Disclaimer
The publisher has made every effort to trace copyright holders and welcomes
correspondence from those they have been unable to contact.

A Library of Congress record exists under LC control number: 88030361

ISBN 13: 978-1-138-82984-8 (hbk)
ISBN 13: 978-1-315-73756-0 (ebk)

Industrial Policy

USA and UK Debates

Edited by
Grahame Thompson

Routledge
London and New York

First published 1989 by Routledge
11 New Fetter Lane, London EC4P 4EE
29 West 35th Street, New York NY 10001

Introduction © Grahame Thompson 1989
Chapter 2 © Routledge & Kegan Paul 1987
Chapter 3 © Routledge & Kegan Paul 1984
Chapter 4 © Routledge & Kegan Paul 1986
Chapter 5 © Routledge & Kegan Paul 1987
Chapter 6 © Routledge & Kegan Paul 1986

Printed and bound in Great Britain by
Biddles Ltd, Guildford and King's Lynn

All rights reserved. No part of this book may be reprinted or
reproduced or utilized in any form or by any electronic,
mechanical, or other means, now known or hereafter invented,
including photocopying and recording, or in any information
storage or retrieval system, without permission in writing from
the publishers.

British Library Cataloguing in Publication Data
Industrial policy : USA and UK debates.
   1. Great Britain. Industries. Policies of
government. 2. United States. Industries.
Policies of government.
   I. Thompson, Grahame, *1945–*   II. Economy
and Society
338.941

Library of Congress Cataloging in Publication Data
Industrial policy : USA and UK debates / edited by Grahame Thompson.
   p.   cm.
Bibliography: p.
Includes index.
   1. Industry and state—United States.   2. Industry and state—
Great Britain.   I. Thompson, Grahame.
HD3616.U471456   1989 338.941—dc19   88-30361

ISBN 0-415-03800-6

Contents

Notes on contributors

Allin Cottrell teaches in the Department of Economics, Elon College, North Carolina.

Tony Cutler teaches at Middlesex Polytechnic, London.

Colin Haslam teaches in the Department of Business Studies, North East London Polytechnic, London.

Grahame Thompson teaches economics at the Open University, Milton Keynes.

Andrew Wardlow, *John Williams*, and *Karel Williams* are at the Department of Economics, the University College of Wales, Aberystwyth.

1
Introduction

1

The term 'industrial policy' is likely to be approached with some caution in the late 1980s. With the advent of Mrs Thatcher's government in the UK and President Reagan's administration in the USA, the idea of a centrally organized and state orchestrated industrial policy suffered an almost total rejection in the search for market orientated responses to the decline of both economies. The emphasis shifted to programmes of deregulation, denationalization, tax reform, and limited and selective assistance to the high-technology elements of the industrial structure only. Previous forms of more widespread industrial support have been condemned in both countries as representing one of the main contributory factors leading towards that decline rather than as a possible remedy for it.

It was in this context that *Economy and Society* set about a re-appraisal of the notion of industrial policy by publishing the series of articles reprinted in this volume. The initial stimulus for this interest came, perhaps surprisingly, from work being conducted in the USA and within the heartland of corporate managerialism at that time, namely the Harvard Business School and other leading US business institutions. As is argued in the chapters below, this work presented a refreshingly open analysis of not only the shortcomings of the *dirigiste* option so despised by the New Right but also of the New Right's own much favoured non-interventionist and market-led position. Sometimes by implication, but more often in terms of explicit argument, the American authors suggested novel ways in which public and other bodies might need to become involved with managing industrial decline if the two economies were ever to re-establish a robust manufacturing capability. The characteristics of these arguments, the criticisms that can be levelled against them, and the lessons if any they hold for the UK, form the main thrust of the analyses offered in the chapters below. In the rest of this intro-duction some of the main points at issue in this debate will be high-lighted and what the chapters have to say about them outlined.

2

The rapid de-industrialization of the UK economy in the 1970s and early 1980s is well known. In Chapter 2 this process is reviewed in the context of the US economy. While perhaps not quite so dramatic or extensive as in the UK case, the American economy has gone through a period of relative decline demonstrating many of the tendencies symptomatic of de-industrialization: a fall in productivity; loss of jobs in the manufacturing sector; import substitution and decline in exports leading to a severe negative balance of payments on the trading account; loss of international competitiveness; offshore substitution of economic activity, and the like. For the Americans, used to being the powerhouse among trading nations, a severe loss of confidence ensued, particularly amongst business-related interests. The result was a surprisingly open, widespread, and often robust debate about the causes of this decline and of possible remedies for it. This debate forms the focus for Chapter 2.

Whilst led by academics, this debate also involved politicians, labour organizations, business journalists, employers' groups, departments of government, independent 'think tanks', and more besides. Chapter 2 discusses the contribution of all of these, and also attempts to document the results of the debate in terms of concrete action taken at the federal level and, perhaps more importantly as it turned out, at the state or local level.

One interesting feature of the debate was its eventual foundering on the generally recognized impossibility of organizing a centrally directed and federally led national industrial recovery programme, as had been proposed by some of the early advocates of an industrial policy. Here the political constraints were highlighted as undermining the credibility of such suggestions in the US context. As is emphasized in Chapter 2, many of these political constraints are likely to be equally binding in the UK. Thus one of the most important issues associated with the idea of an industrial policy under contemporary conditions, in either country, concerns the political conditions for its successful implementation and, what is of equal importance, its successful continuation and development. So often in the past rather unrealistic policies have been proposed and initiated, involving the creation of a new range of institutional mechanisms to conduct those policies.[1] Inevitably this generated not only political opposition to the high-profile campaigns waged to try and secure those novel institutions and their policies, but also an administrative opposition as those parts of the existing bureaucracy whose scope and powers were perceived to be being undermined brought their own kinds of pressure to bear. Thus one of the lessons of the debate, as argued in the chapter, is to pay heed to the kinds of solution proposed in the US for facing this dilemma.

Another point raised in Chapter 2 that forms a key link between this chapter and a number of others in the book involves the emphasis given within the industrial policy debate to the character of managerial practices and of the 'managerial function' in US manufacturing industry. If we can characterize the US discussion as negatively invoking the idea of a centrally run and state-led approach to industrial policymaking, then it could alternatively be characterized as positively invoking a central concern with managerial practices. The debate developed a battery of critical assessments of American managerial procedures and calculations. This distinctive feature posed the opposition between management conceived as a strategic and universalistic practice and management centred on the improvement of technical and productive efficiency at the operational level. Put briefly, the American authors drew attention to the undesirable consequences of the former with respect, first, to causing industrial decline and, then, in trying to reverse it. Subsequently they began to explore the implications of transforming the traditional emphasis by developing the idea of a managerial practice designed explicitly to re-enhance the 'manufacturing function'. Perhaps not unexpectedly, a focus for this re-appraisal has been to initiate a re-examination of US management education, particularly the nature of MBA programmes.[2]

This critique of American (and by implication UK) management practices did not go unchallenged, however. For instance, in the context of the argument that the problems of the US economy were (and still are) macroeconomic in character rather than ones involving issues of industrial structure and microeconomic adjustments, it was pointed out that American businesses worldwide had not suffered the decline they had on the geographical mainland of the USA. Lipsey and Kravis (1985), for instance, argued that American owned and managed firms maintained or even increased their share of world exports over the period of the 1960s and 1970s, though those operating solely from the mainland lost world share. The shift of production 'offshore' was mainly a consequence of the decline in competitiveness of domestic-based manufacturing enterprises. American multinationals increased their comparative advantage, they argued. Thus the problem identified here was the relatively high US domestic cost profile, itself attributed to US monetary and fiscal policy, through effects on exchange rates and prices, and US wage and productivity behaviour. Macroeconomic adjustments were called for, it was suggested, rather than adjustments to American managerial practices. These were still healthy, if residing abroad. Chapter 2 reviews and criticizes other similar macroeconomic suggestions as a response to the decline in US competitiveness.

A final point to make about this second chapter involves the discussion undertaken there of the role of corporate tax moves in the US which have been introduced as something of a response to the industrial policy debate. One of the main policy responses at the federal level to the decline in the competitiveness of manufacturing industry, associated with the argument about the lack of both quantity and quality of US investment, was to initiate a sweeping 'supply-side' reform of corporate (and personal) tax rates. This culminated in the 1986 Tax Reform Act which reduced corporation tax from 46 per cent to 34 per cent, but which at the same time removed a number of tax incentives to investment (the investment tax credit and some depreciation allowances were made less generous and minimum corporation tax requirements were tightened up). These and other minor changes were designed to increase the tax burden on companies by about $120bn over the five years 1987–92.

Such a 'supply-side' approach followed a similar set of moves initiated by the British government in its 1984 budget. Main rate corporation tax was reduced from 50 per cent to 35 per cent over the period 1984 to 1987 and a range of investment allowances reduced or eliminated. In both countries this rearrangement of the incentives to invest was predicted on the intention of improving the quality of investment in the first instance. The problem this has thrown up, however, is an old one. Investment incentives are all very well but they tell us little about the changes in *ex-post* investment that are actually likely to emerge. This remains an empirical matter. In the UK, for instance, contradictory evidence has been presented as to whether the post-1984 budget tax burden on the company sector overall would have increased or decreased. The Treasury argued that it would decrease (Treasury and Civil Service Committee, 1984) and this was supported by the independent analysis of Levis (1986). However the influential Institute of Fiscal Studies (see Devereux and Mayer, 1984), supporting King (1985) and Kay and King (1986), present evidence that it would increase. Depending on which one of these is the case, incentives to invest will either be enhanced or reduced.[3]

But this is not the end of the story because independently of these issues, which only affect the incentives to invest, there remains the question as to whether a rearrangement of incentives is enough or of any significant practical importance in the actual calculations made by firms in their decision to invest. As suggested above, this remains an empirical problem. But this is itself open to dispute, and not easily settled. For instance, on the one hand, those US economists supporting a basically neoclassical approach to the analysis in this

area, where it is the 'cost of using capital in any period' that determines the downward sloping investment function, have found the
recent Reagan supply-side moves to have enhanced the level of
investment in the US economy (Sinai *et al.*, 1983; Shapiro, 1986).
On the other hand, those working within a more Keynesian inspired
framework, often where 'animal spirit' expectations drive an
accelerator-type model, have found little if any enhanced investment
resulting from the tax moves (Bosworth, 1985; Mansfield, 1985).[4]

Summing up on the evidence overall, King (1985, p. 253)
suggests: 'In the current state of knowledge it would be unrealistic to
pretend that the impact of the changed incentives on the level of
investment is easy to predict. Econometric studies of the determinants of investment behaviour have been inconclusive.' If this is
the case, why use so much space discussing the issue here? The
reason for dwelling on it is that so much has been invested on both
sides of the Atlantic in just these incentive mechanisms when very
little hard evidence exists to justify optimism on this count. The
whole 'supply-side' programme for generating better quality investment in the US and UK may thus founder. As Chapter 2 points out,
corporate tax incentives remain more or less the only serious
industrial-policy-type move made by the Reagan administration,
and similar comments could be made about Mrs Thatcher's governments in the UK.

One of the main protagonists in the US debate about industrial
policy was Robert Reich. Reich, a professor of public administration
at the Kennedy School of Goverment, Harvard University, and
someone close to the Democratic Party's policymaking machine,
produced a string of books and articles in the early 1980s advocating
an industrial policy (of sorts) for the USA. These writings are
reviewed in outline in Chapter 2. In Chapter 3 a more thorough
assessment of this position is undertaken. It takes the form of a
review of an early book Reich produced with Ira Magaziner, another
influential figure in the debate. In this book – *Minding America's
Business* – they set about trying to explain the poor manufacturing
performance of the American economy.[5] As Chapter 3 argues,
Magaziner and Reich draw on a critique of enterprise calculation
originally developed in the *Harvard Business Review*; return on
investment (ROI) calculations figure prominently here. These, it is
argued, have biased capital outlays towards short-term and top-up
replacement investment, to the detriment of long-term strategic
investment designed to secure market share. The logic of ROI
calculations is a patching defence of existing process technology and
product lines. Chapter 3 goes on to discuss other aspects of
Magaziner and Reich's argument, particularly the way they characterize the possible role of government and the manner in which

institutional constraints operate in their account. On both counts, Chapter 3 takes a critical stance. It argues, for instance, that the institutional arrangements for the raising of capital to finance investment is a major problem more or less ignored in *Minding America's Business*. Second, the government cannot pick winners in quite the instrumental fashion that perhaps Magaziner and Reich would like. Finally the chapter points to some important discrepancies between enterprise and state calculation in respect to economic matters, most notably in the case of employment practices and their consequences, which it suggests are also largely ignored in the book.

Many of the criticisms levelled at dominant American practice by Magaziner and Reich, and the criticisms made of their own book in Chapter 3, are brought to bear in the subsequent chapter. Chapter 4 takes the form of a detailed economic appraisal of three of the UK's major state-run industries – coal, steel, and cars. It charts the progressive operational retreat of these industries over the period since 1970 and tries to assess the reasons for this. Specifically, it examines the extent to which the initial strategic investment miscalculations in the industries were caused by an uncritical reliance on the net present value return-on-investment criterion, and the extent to which the subsequent contractionary retreat was propelled solely by profit and loss considerations. One important additional feature introduced into this analysis is the critique of investment decisions based upon expected economies of scale. The chapter argues that these figured strongly in the plans of all three industries but that they were never in a position to reap the promised benefits. Two points are crucial here.

The first is that unless some attention is paid to solving marketing difficulties, perhaps in the manner of some form of 'protection of the market', very large-scale 'green-field' site investment becomes a high-risk affair and one probably doomed to fail. Without a secure base market it becomes impossible to push the demand curve out along the declining average cost curve. Rather the demand curve begins to be pushed back up the average cost curve and a disorderly retreat ensues.

Second, there is a problem of the kind of process technology embodied in investment. This raises an issue pursued in the following chapter, but it concerns the nature of contemporary developments in the productive structure more generally. Put simply, is there still scope for large-scale mass-production technology in an era of increasing demand fragmentation and market differentiation? But even if these are the dominant market trends, there still remains the issue of what is the appropriate process technology to deploy when considering strategic investment. Chapter 4 argues that a miscalculation in this area has been more responsible for the problems besetting the three industries than financial miscalculation *per se*.

An issue thrown up by the American industrial policy debate – originally almost as a side issue in fact – is developed in Chapter 5. As discussed in Chapter 2, and as was again posed just above, the question of the future of mass production has hovered around the edges of the debate. In this chapter it is placed centrally on the agenda by a review of Michael Piore and Charles Sabel's book *The Second Industrial Divide: Possibilities for Prosperity*. The thesis of this book is that contemporary transformations in the whole nature of mature capitalism are rendering the 'Fordist' model of large-scale mass production, perhaps the quintessential embodiment of the modernist project in economics, a redundant organizational form. Instead it is 'flexible specialization' that heralds the new (perhaps post-modernist?) era of productive structure. Chapter 5 argues that too much is built on this one fundamental distinction. Piore and Sabel construct an elaborate regulatory apparatus that they say is necessary to support mass production, the centrepiece of which is the Keynesian demand management framework. With the demise of mass production this framework must be re-thought and trans-formed, they suggest.

The Second Industrial Divide presents a long and interesting historical sketch of the various phases of capitalist industrial organ-ization. Chapter 5 takes issue with a good deal of this. Involved here is a fundamental, almost epistemological, issue. Has mass produc-tion ever been the characteristically typical and dominant organ-izational form that Piore and Sable insist upon? And if so what exactly is it? Fundamental questions indeed.

In opposition to the conceptions of the book, Chapter 5 argues that there has never been a single mass-production form of technology, let alone an exclusive economy of mass production. Rather a complex pattern of overlapping productive forms has existed. What is true of the past also informs the present, it is suggested, and this leads to a critique of the centrality given to flexible specialization in Piore and Sabel's account of the present transformation. Whatever one makes of these criticisms, *The Second Industrial Divide* remains a suggestive and even provocative book. In the UK it has stimulated some interesting work on new forms of work organization under a regime of 'flexible specialization' (Tolliday and Zeitlin, 1987) and with respect to industrial rejuven-ation (Hirst and Zeitlin, 1989).

The final chapter in this collection is somewhat different in character to the others. Chapter 6 takes a more macroeconomic look at the possible consequences of one particular policy proposal designed to increase domestic investment in the UK economy. It examines the Labour Party's idea of taxing the earnings derived from overseas investments of UK residents. This is part of that Party's attempt to provide a means for restricting the outflow of investible money capital overseas without placing any physical restrictions on it. It has been tied to the further idea of creating a National Investment Bank (NIB) to encourage domestic industrial and manufacturing investment, particularly its quality. The tax on overseas revenues would be used to finance the NIB.

Clearly this kind of proposal has been an element in the wider industrial policy debate conducted on both sides of the Atlantic, so it is entirely appropriate that it should be assessed here. In Chapter 6 two macroeconomic models are used to examine the approach and a cautious endorsement is given to its likely effectiveness. This very much depends on the particular economic circumstances being faced by a government that might launch such a tax. The assessment of Chapter 6 thus differs from the usual economists' diehard defence of the free flow of capital when dealing with these matters (e.g. Budd, 1986, and Chrystal and Dowd, 1986, on the NIB issue).

3

The chapters of this book interpret industrial policy to be particularly concerned with the manufacturing sector of the economy. The problem is seen as one of encouraging a renewed capability of the US and UK economies to operate effectively at a world level with regard to manufacturing. There are a number of reasons for this emphasis.

In the first place it is manufacturing that has traditionally produced a high value-added output. This in turn has allowed relatively high-waged jobs in the economy. The service sector, by contrast, is typified by low value-added and low-waged jobs. Thus if the objective is to maintain a high standard of living in an economy, we need to encourage high value-added content production in the manufacturing sector.

Secondly there are some very undesirable international payment consequences of the decline in manufacturing capability of the two economies. In the US case this has led to a startling reversal of its balance of payments position and, with it, a dramatic unsettling of its domestic financial markets, a roll-on effect into the international sphere, and a further destabilization of the foreign exchange markets. In the UK case the economy has only been able to sustain existing levels of consumption because of the beneficial effects of North Sea oil production. As the oil runs out towards the closing years of this century, a revived manufacturing sector is the only one likely to provide the necessary compensation on the balance of payments account. The arguments of the chapters in this book suggest that neither macroeconomic policies nor a reliance on the automatic adjustment of the market alone will be sufficient to revive this vital sector in either economy.

Notes

1. See Cowling (1987) for a recent example of this.
2. A parallel development is desperately needed in the UK. For a comprehensive historical account of the way UK management education largely adopted American practice, and of its undesirable consequences, see Armstrong (1987).
3. The justification offered for the UK corporate tax moves are discussed in Thompson (1986, Chapter 7), and Thompson (1988) discusses these and the recent American moves in greater detail.
4. A more developed critique of neoclassical conceptions of investment determination is given in Bosworth (1984) and in Blume *et al.* (1981).
5. As pointed out in Chapter 2, Magaziner subsequently went on to help formulate the ill-fated 'Greenhouse Compact' which proposed an industrial policy for Rhode Island.

References

Armstrong, P. (1987) *The Abandonment of Production Intervention in Management Teaching Syllabi: An Historical Analysis*, Industrial Relations Research Unit, University of Warwick.

Blume, M.E., Crockett, J.A., and **Friend, I.** (1981) 'Stimulation of capital formation: ends and means', in Watcher, M.L. and Watcher, S.M. (eds), *Towards a New US Industrial Policy*, University of Pennsylvania Press, Philadelphia.

Bosworth, B.P. (1984) *Tax Incentives and Economic Growth*, Brookings Institution, Washington DC.

Bosworth, B.P. (1985) 'Taxes and the Investment Recovery' *Brookings Papers on Economic Activity* 1, Brookings Institution Washington DC, pp. 1–45.

Budd, A. (1986) 'Do we need a National Investment Bank?' *National Westminster Bank Quarterly Review*, August, pp. 36–48.

Chrystal, K.A. and **Dowd, K.** (1986) 'Two arguments for the restriction of international capital flows', *National Westminster Bank Quarterly Review*, November, pp. 9–19.

Cowling, K. (1987) 'An industrial strategy for Britain: the nature and role of planning', *International Review of Applied Economics*, vol. 1, no. 1, pp. 1–22.

Devereux, M.P. and **Mayer, C.P.** (1984) *Corporation Tax: the Impact of the 1984 Budget*, Report Series No. 11, Institute of Fiscal Studies, London.

Hirst, P.Q. and **Zeitlin, J.** (eds) (1989) *Reversing Industrial Decline*, Berg Publishing, Leamington Spa.

Treasury and Civil Service Committee (1984) 'The company tax measures – a note by HM Treasury', Appendix 10 of *The 4th Report of the Treasury and Civil Service Committee: The 1984 Budget*, HCP 341, April, HMSO, London.

Kay, J.A. and **King, M.** (1986) *The British Tax System*, Oxford University Press.

King, M. (1985) 'Tax reform in the UK and US', *Economic Policy*, November, pp. 220–38.

Levis, M. (1986) 'The 1984 Budget: the impact on corporate tax payments, *National Westminster Bank Quarterly Review*, May, pp. 28–42.

Lipsey, R.E. and **Kravis, I.B.** (1985) 'The competitive position of US manufacturing firms', *Banca Nazionale del Lavoro Quarterly Review*, 153, June, pp. 127–54.

Magaziner, I.C. and **Reich, R.B.** (1982) *Minding America's Business*, Harcourt, Brace, Jovanovich, New York.

Mansfield, E. (1985) 'Public policy towards industrial innovation . . . an international study of direct tax incentives for research and development', in Clark, K.B., Hayes, R.H., and Lorenz, D. (eds), *The Uneasy Alliance: Managing the Productivity-Technology Dilemma*, Harvard Business School Press, Boston.

Piore, M.J. and **Sabel, C.F.** (1984) *The Second Industrial Divide*, Basic Books, New York.

Shapiro, M.D. (1986) 'Investment, output and the cost of capital', *Brookings Papers on Economic Activity*, vol. 1, pp. 111–64.

Sinai, A., Lin, A. and **Robins, R.** (1983) 'Taxes, savings, and investment: some empirical evidence', *National Tax Journal*, vol. XXXVI, no. 3, pp. 321–45.

Thompson, G.F. (1986) *The Conservatives' Economic Policy*, Croom Helm, London.

Thompson, G.F. (1988) 'Private sector investment: the interventionist temptation?' Unit 11 of the Open University course D345 *Economics and Government Policy*, Open University Press, Milton Keynes.

Tolliday, S. and **Zeitlin, J.** (1987) *The Automobile Industry and its Workers: Between Fordism and Flexibility*, Polity Press, Cambridge.

2
The American industrial policy debate: any lessons for the UK?

Grahame Thompson

Abstract

In this chapter an assessment of the industrial policy debate that went on in the US roughly between 1980 and 1985 is conducted, very much in the context of its lessons for the UK. The argument is that this debate can help re-focus wider issues of industrial policy with a pertinence to other countries than the US. In particular it opens up the rather more political constraints and conditions that surround the establishment of any robust industrial policy. The paper assesses the course of the US debate, the way that debate has fragmented in a policy context into issues of renewed international competitiveness for the US economy, into tax reform, and into state-initiated policy. Finally this debate is used to try and provide an analytical framework in which the articulation of industrial policy to other policy areas can be more profitably discussed.

1 Introduction

It is fashionable nowadays, particularly in the USA, to dismiss the debate about 'industrial policy' that went on in America roughly between 1980 and 1985 as a dead issue.[1] America will not introduce any new initiatives or programmes that can be characterized as an 'industrial policy' it is argued, and indeed what is more there is no *need* for such initiatives or programmes anyway.[2] In fact it is this latter position that has been the most influential and the one seen as instrumental in undermining much of the credibility of the debate, at least amongst economists. But in addition to this there has been a rather more political argument against industrial policy which has had considerable impact. The point here is a slightly different one, in that this argument stresses, in the first instance at least, the political difficulty of organizing an industrial policy rather than whether or not one is justifiable. From this position it is a question of the feasibility of such a policy in the American context rather than its desirability.[3]

Below I deal with this range of arguments in greater detail, but one preliminary point it serves to register is the importance of political considerations in shaping the character of the US debate. Even those centrally involved in arguing for a positive and more developed industrial policy have tended to be political scientists or experts in public and business administration rather than economists (though economists have not altogether been absent). From the start therefore the debate has had a heterogeneous style and involved a wider set of considerations than might be found in comparable British or European debates. As is argued below, this is one of its strengths which gives it an interest and significance somewhat beyond purely US considerations.

It may seem strange that the United States of America should have been the host to a debate about industrial policy at all, given its well known antagonism towards governmental intervention in the economy. But one point the debate has served to highlight is the actual degree of intervention going on in the economy in a name other than that of industrial policy.[4] As has been pointed out by almost all commentators, the government does have an implicit industrial policy – one largely operated via the federal tax system, the Defense Department, and via such bodies as NASA. But the stimulus for a more overt discussion, and in the context of this of arguments for the creation of a range of new federal institutional mechanisms to conduct a more developed and coordinated policy, came from two related sources. One was the increasing integration of the US economy into the world division of labour during the 1960s and 1970s, which manifested itself in increasing import penetration and relative loss of competitiveness on the part of US exporters. The other was the advent of at least a perceived process of 'de-industrialization' of the American economy and a spiriting abroad of investment finance to the detriment of domestic jobs. These twin developments, all too familiar in the UK context, shook the confidence of American business in the 1980s and galvanized first the proponents of an industrial policy and then those critical of such policy suggestions.

As of summer 1986 it is probably fair to say that the notion of an industrial policy conducted at a national level in the US is indeed no longer seriously contemplated. In a way then it was not so strange that such a debate arose in the first place but that it could have been sustained for so long, and as argued below to have produced such a useful set of analyses with implications for countries other than the US. In addition it would not be fair to say that the industrial policy debate has totally collapsed or that it might not prove quite telling in the future. It is suggested below that this debate has now fragmented rather than disappeared altogether. It has fragmented into precisely those areas where it was probably always in fact located, with one notable exception. It is around the tax system and in terms of trade orientated measures to promote 'international competitiveness' that arguments about 'industrial policy' are still being conducted in the US. These are areas where there has always been at least some industrial policy purchase. But the exception here, and something that is genuinely new in the debate, is its fragmentation into state initiatives and programmes. If industrial policy is alive and relatively well in the US it is at the state or local level that this robustness is located. The national arena proved an over-ambitious and too general level at which to pitch a politically serious industrial rejuvenation programme, given the diverse economic conditions facing different states in the USA. Major problems of readjustment tend to be locationally specific and differentially specific to particular sectors. This makes for a diverse response, one probably better handled at a state level. However, there still remains a problem at the national level, even though perhaps the conditions necessary to address this at a national level are not yet present. So much here depends upon what happens to the US economy over the medium term. But if as seems likely the present 'recovery' does not solve major structural problems and, what is probably more important, persuade Americans to readjust their expectations about the performance of the economy, then a lot of the ideas floated but dismissed in the recent debate may well reappear as more pressing and politically feasible. I return to this towards the end of the chapter.

The plan of the rest of this chapter is as follows. In the next section some of the underlying constraints on the economy are discussed to present a background to the subsequent analysis. This is followed by a brief history of the rise and fall of the industrial policy debate and some of the more important positions and points that arose within it. The 'dispersion' of the debate forms the focus of the next section, which is followed by a step back from the particularities of the debate to look at industrial policy more generally. Here an attempt is made to provide an analytical framework for talking about industrial policy under contemporary conditions. Finally perhaps the main point of the paper is discussed in the concluding sections where the implications of the debate are assessed for the UK in particular, and where some comment is made about the future prospects for industrial policy in the US itself.

2 Problems of the economy

The American economy is experiencing something of a cyclical recovery from the stagnation and depression of the early 1980s.

Real GNP has grown by approximately 4.5 per cent per annum since 1982 and industrial production by 7.6 per cent per annum (1982–5). This relatively buoyant nature of the economy has made it difficult to sustain much interest in 'industrial policy'. Thus it is precisely because the economy is growing rapidly that industrial policy seems irrelevant. However, this could mask some deeper

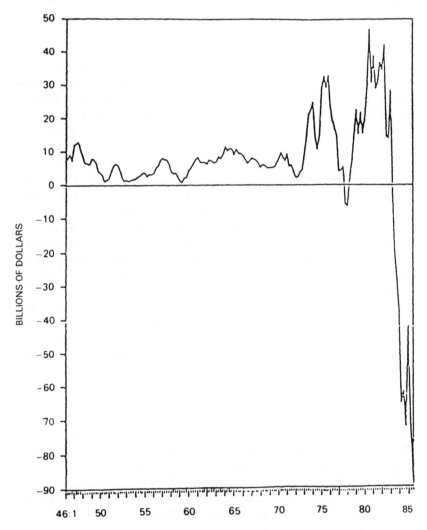

Source: Joint Economic Committee US Congress (1986) *The American Economy in Transition: From the Second World War to the 21st Century,* p. 26.

Figure 2.1 The US trade balance on current account, 1946–85 (billions of US dollars).

underlying trends in the US economy – which might be termed
structural – and which demonstrate longer-term problems of decline
and adjustment. For instance Figure 2.1 shows the current account
trade balance on goods and services over the period 1946 to 1985.

On the basis of this measure of the overall trade balance (which
includes 'invisibles'), the economy seems to have entered a sustained
period of deficits only since about 1983 and this has caught public
attention in the US. It is estimated that the current account deficit was
running at something over $160bn in 1986. But from the point of
view of competitiveness of the economy the narrower merchandise
trade account is perhaps a better indicator of long-term trends than

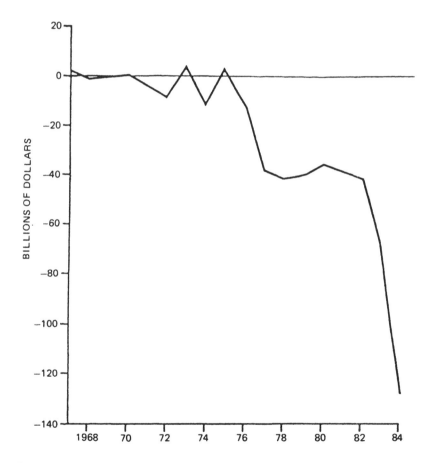

Source: President's Commission on Industrial Competitiveness *Global Competition: The New
Reality,* US Government Printing Office, Washington, Vol. II, Chart 6, p. 13.

Figure 2.2 US merchandise trade balance, 1967–84 (billions of US
dollars).

is the overall balance. This is shown in Figure 2.2 for the period 1967–84. Between 1893 and 1970 this measure of the trade balance had been positive in the US. It turned negative in 1971 for the first time and except for 1973 and 1975 has declined ever since.

Traditionally the US has relied on a significant positive balance on its agricultural trade account to cushion the overall balance and help accommodate temporary deficits on other elements of its trade account. But agriculture itself has entered a difficult phase and is in something of a decline. The agricultural net trade balance peaked in 1981 at $26.6bn. In 1984 it was down to $18.5bn and was predicted to be about half this much — near $9bn — in 1985/6 (Government Printing Office, 1986). Thus the ability of any agricultural surplus partly to offset a growing deficit on the manufacturing trade account is likely to be severely limited in the future, and anyway it would not have been enough to compensate for the large deficits that emerged in the early 1980s. Thus there is a major and growing problem for the American economy in terms of its ability to sustain present consumption levels via running balance of payments deficits. Clearly this raises questions of the trends in international competitiveness of the economy.

The competitiveness of an economy can be a rather elusive concept since there are a number of ways in which it can be defined and measured. For the purposes of this discussion international competitiveness is defined by unit labour costs (wage rates divided by productivity) corrected for exchange rate changes (where the currencies involved are weighed according to their relative importance in the trade of the country concerned). Clearly there are a number of separate issues submerged within this single measure – notably exchange rate movements, domestic real wage changes, and productivity changes – but these are discussed separately later. Figure 2.3 shows measures of relative unit labour costs so constructed for manufacturing activity only. The period 1962 to 1984 is divided into two sub-periods for convenience.

In part (a) exchange-rate-corrected unit labour costs were on a downward trend for the US (shown by the dashed line), though there was also some strong cyclical variation involved. This phase lasted until approximately 1980. From then on, as part (b) shows, exchange-rate-adjusted unit labour costs were on an upward trend. This latter period is associated with a substantial dollar appreciation, itself fostered by macroeconomic policies involving the federal budget deficit and high interest rates. It was during this latter period that deficits on the overall trade balance began to appear in earnest, as shown in Figure 2.1. These deficits have largely been put down to the sustained currency appreciation. As we shall see later, it is such an explanation that led to the emphasis on macroeconomic manage-

(a)

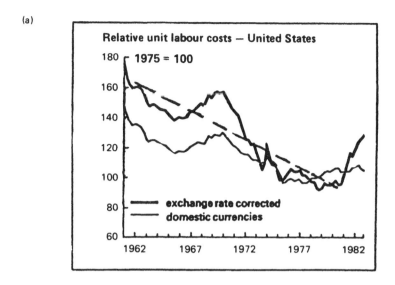

(b)

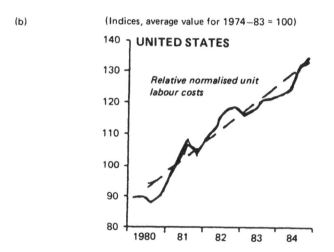

Source: (a) HM Treasury, *Economic Progress Report*, No. 158, July 1983; and (b) *IMF World Economic Outlook*, June 1985, Chart II–12.

Figure 2.3 US international cost competitiveness, 1962–84.

ment as the appropriate tool for rectifying the problem of loss of competitiveness embodied in these trends rather than to the introduction of any new industrial policy initiatives. Clearly it would be silly to suggest that the rapid appreciation of the dollar during this period had no effect on the emerging trade deficit. But to concentrate solely on exchange rate changes as both an explanation for this

Grahame Thompson

and, perhaps more importantly, as providing a remedy via devaluations of the currency, is to miss some longer-term problems.

These can be broached in connection to part (a) of Figure 2.3.
Over the period to 1980 the economy was becoming more cost
competitive according to this measure. Indeed, as is shown in part
(a), even non-exchange-rate-adjusted unit labour costs were also
'improving' over most of this period. But whilst the economy was
becoming more internationally cost competitive in terms of manufacturing activity, its merchandise trade account was rapidly going
into deficit. In fact over a similar period America's two main
economic rivals, Japan and Germany, were becoming less internationally cost competitive. In addition they were increasing and

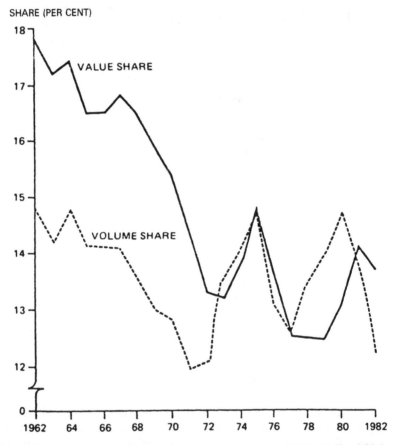

Source: President's Commission on International Competitiveness (1985), vol. II, exhibit 1,
p. 176.

Figure 2.4 US share of world manufacturing exports, 1962–82.

maintaining respectively their share of world trade in manufactures, while the US was losing its share.[5] This loss of share in world manufacturing trade is shown in Figure 2.4 for the USA. If a narrower definition of world manufacturing exports is taken to look at only the percentage of industrial country, high technology exports then the US would again show a declining trend.[6]

Looking now at the other side of the trade account – at imports – the period of the 1960s and 1970s heralded the full-scale entry of the US into international trade mechanisms and in particular the

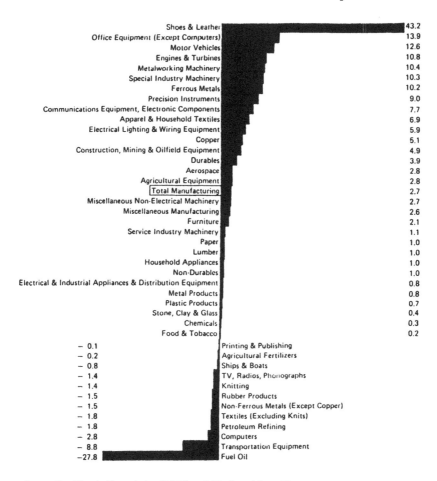

Source: President's Commission (1985), vol. II, chart 10, p. 18.

Figure 2.5 Change in import penetration of US industry, 1982 versus 1972: percentage point change in US import/output ratio. Note: Import/ Output Ratio = US Imports ÷ US Domestic Production.

advent of import penetration.[7] This is demonstrated in Figure 2.5, where the sectoral changes in import penetration are given between 1972 and 1982. (Note that this encompassed something of a transitional period for the economy in terms of its international competitiveness, as pointed out earlier.) It should be clear from Figure 2.5 that there has been a growing problem of import penetration of the American economy over this period, particularly in crucial areas like motor vehicles, machine tools, and electrical engineering sectors, though the economy has shown resilience in areas like transport equipment and computers.

Two general points are worth stressing from this presentation. In the first place it is important to note the way in which problems associated with domestic US manufacturing activity and its international competitiveness began to emerge well before the currency appreciation of the early 1980s and its accompanying current account deficit. Second, we need to explain the seemingly paradoxical trends in increasing international competitiveness of US manufacturing activity at the same time as export share was declining and import penetration developing. How can one account for this latter feature?

Here we need to draw a crucial distinction between cost (or price) competitiveness and non-price competitiveness. Overall competitiveness will be a combination of these two. The US economy may have been becoming more cost/price competitive over the period of the 1960s and 1970s, but was it maintaining its non-price competitiveness? By non-price competitiveness we mean to stress the quality aspects of traded goods which may not be reflected so much in their price. These would include the design, the delivery dates, and after-sales service, performance and durability, the reliability and continuity of supply, the role of effective marketing, and the like. Increasingly it is these features of commodity exchange that are becoming important in consumer purchase decisions, rather than simple reliance on the lowest price of comparable commodities.[8] We return to a fuller discussion of the implication of these issues below, but here it will be germaine to point out their link to productivity. Clearly some of these disadvantages can be overcome via price adjustments. In the case under discussion of international cost/price competitiveness, this could be achieved by devaluations of the currency. But experience elsewhere (in the UK in particular) demonstrates that trying to increase competitiveness through continual exchange rate adjustments, rather than by attending to the productivity-linked quality issues, is a recipe for longer-term decline.

Thus one of the other underlying problems associated with the decline in the economy's competitiveness concerns the issue of

Table 2.1 Growth of labour productivity* in manufacturing, selected developed countries 1960–80 (annual percentage change)

Measure period	US	Canada	France	Germany	Italy	Japan	UK	Eight European countries**	Eight European countries plus Canada and Japan
1960–80	2.7	3.8	5.6	5.4	5.9	9.4	3.6	5.4	5.9
1960–73	3.0	4.5	6.0	5.5	6.9	10.7	4.3	5.9	6.4
1973–80	1.7	2.2	4.9	4.8	3.6	6.8	1.9	4.2	4.7

Notes: *Output per hour.
**France, Germany, Italy, UK, Belgium, Denmark, Netherlands, and Sweden.
Source: Lawrence, R.Z. (1984) *Can America Compete?*, Brookings Institution, Washington, DC (adapted from Table 2-9, p. 32).

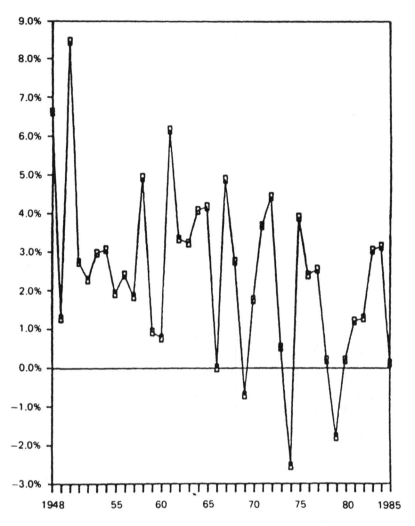

Source: Joint Economic Committee US Congress (1986) *The American Economy in Transition*, p. 25.

Figure 2.6 Yearly changes in US productivity (output per hour) 1948–85.

productivity. The US is still the most productive advanced industrial economy, at least in terms of traditional measures like output per operative hour. Where the problems arise is in terms of comparable growth rates of productivity. Table 2.1 indicates the relevant figures. The US has consistently achieved lower growth rates of productivity than other industrialized countries. In addition, as Figure 2.6 demonstrates, its productivity growth rates look to be on a downward trend – though again there is considerable cyclical variation. But over the longer periods 1960–73 and 1973–80 output growth per operative hour declined from 3 per cent per annum on average to 1.7 per cent per annum on average. For 1985 productivity growth was running at just above zero (*Business Conditions Digest*, US Department of Commerce, April 1986).

Some of these trends are perhaps not that surprising given the enormous productive lead the US economy had built up during the interwar period and immediately after the Second World War. Given the aspirations for growth and development elsewhere it might be expected that an older and more mature economy like the US would have to yield something on share of traded goods and on productivity growth. Trying to account for the decline of the latter has proved arduous and not altogether convincing.[9] However, the point to emphasize at this preliminary stage is that a failure to address properly both the causes of such long-term changes and to provide appropriate policy action to try and remedy them is likely only to store up problems for the future.

As will be argued later, there are a range of other more structural issues implicated in this loss of competitiveness, but here we have concentrated upon two of the most obvious and generally recognized. In addition, as will again become clear later, appropriate policy does not imply a return to the situation of the 1950s for the US economy. That would be both impossible and, one might add, undesirable from the point of view of the rest of the world.

3 The debate: positions and arguments

This section looks at the course of the industrial policy debate in the US – and the stress is upon the debate, since that is more or less what it amounted to. The arguments tended to be intellectual ones, and for reasons outlined below and already hinted at above, their impact on actual policy or institutional change has been minimal if non-existent. But this is not to suggest that the debate has lacked policy proposals. Far from it: they have proliferated, as we shall see.

The de-industrialization of America

Perhaps the earliest explicit formulation of a problem or set of problems to which the industrial policy debate was addressed condensed around the term 'de-industrialization'. The rundown of manufacturing activity, in particular the loss of manufacturing jobs, was stressed by Bluestone and Harrison (1982) and Magaziner and Reich (1982). Such claims were echoed by both the US labour movement (e.g. UAW, 1983, and AFL-CIO, 1983) and by certain business related interests (The *Business Week* Team, 1982). Whilst all these parties shared a similar conception of the problem, they put forward somewhat different prescriptions as to how it could be tackled.

The shared conception was one of significant, and for the American economy a new and sharp rundown of its manufacturing base, particularly in 'traditional' sectors like steel, footwear, and textiles but also in newer industries like auto-production, colour television manufacture and in sensitive areas like the machine tool industry and semiconductor development.[10] Loss of jobs in the north-eastern 'rust-belt' or 'smoke-stack' sectors formed the main focus of attention, but along with this went a feeling that increased unemployment more generally was consequent on a loss of dynamism associated with low domestic investment, offshore substitution of production, lack of job creation in new high-tech industries, and a switch to low-wage service activity. Anyone familiar with the UK discussion of 'de-industrialization' should recognize this list of features and there is little need to dwell on it further.[11]

As far as prescriptions were concerned, here a wide range of suggestions were involved. As might be expected, that position which established the flavour and terms for a good deal of the subsequent critical assessment of the industrial policy debate came from the organizations of the labour movement and the radical left of the Democratic Party. The UAW, other unions and the AFL-CIO, for instance, proposed a range of new institutional mechanisms to develop a balanced and co-ordinated industrial policy. In particular two major new institutions would be created: a National Industrial Policy Board (NIPB) supplemented by a new Reconstruction Finance Corporation (RFC).[12] The NIPB would concentrate on reorganizing industrial sectors and regions that needed particular help – whether these be in decline through lack of growth or because of exceptionally rapid growth. Thus both older sectors and industries would be involved, in the 'smoke-stack' states, and newer emerging high-tech ones in the economically developing 'sunrise' states. The Board would promote the diffusion of new productive technologies within new industries and the development and application of advanced productive technologies domestically. In this the Board would be aided by a National Civilian Technology Administration (NCTA) with specific responsibilities to finance and encourage R & D. The NIPB would pay particular attention to interdependencies between industries. It would organize and lobby for targeted tax treatment and specific trade policy actions, regulate other industries in the interests of overall industrial strategy, approve mergers and acquisitions, and support worker training and re-training. In this way the NIPB would have to work closely with other federal agencies to act as a focus for a wide range of interventionist policies and programmes. The RFC would support this Board by providing funds for some of the activities envisioned. It would make long-term loans or take equity stakes in companies restructured under the Board's programmes. In addition it might lend to local authorities as intermediaries in the reconstruction proccss, oi fur the development of necessary infrastructure investments. The Corporation should work with criteria based upon a 'desirable social return on investment' and not simply on short-term profitability criteria, while the Board would develop its strategy with the use of 'social accounting' – looking at overall social costs and benefits rather than just at the private profit and loss statement.

These somewhat radical suggestions, in the US context, to change the criteria for public modes of calculation were to be parallelled by the manner in which the NIPB was to be established and run. Its activities would have to be subject to the scrutiny of Congress in the normal manner (largely because it would have to be financed by it) but in addition the idea was for such a body to be supported by, and in effect directed by in terms of policymaking, a widely representative public advisory board to include consumers, environmentalists, academics, civil rights, and other group interests. These would advise the board, which would in turn bargain with the government and the employers/management to establish both the general direction of the economy and the industrial strategy concomitant upon it. Thus for all intents and purposes macroeconomic policy would itself be at least co-ordinated with the reindustrialization strategy and probably subordinated to it.

This set of proposals put forward by the union movement has been described in some detail because it acted as something of a touchstone against which the arguments of other participants in the debate can be measured. It presented a kind of a base point around which criticisms and differences developed within the debate – from those both for and against an industrial policy. It also represented the most comprehensive and radical suggested institutional challenge to the existing arrangements for economic policymaking in the US.

If anything as comprehensive in scope as this existed elsewhere it was probably embodied in the proposals put foward by Bluestone and Harrison (1982), though these differed in emphasis and were somewhat critical of the implications of the unions' suggestions. If the AFL-CIO represents the more 'traditional' left's response, then Bluestone and Harrison represented the 'New' left's response, though this is complicated by the adoption early on in the debate of some of the AFL-CIO type proposals by interests more closely associated with business and management. In particular the new RFC idea was supported by The *Business Week* Team (1982,

p. 133) and in a series of influential articles written by the Democratic investment banker Felix Rohatyn (collected together in Rohatyn, 1983) amongst others. In fact these authors were suggesting the adoption of an RFC more or less at the same time as the AFL-CIO proposals were being formulated.

The 'first' RFC was originally established in 1932 by President Hoover as an independent agency designed to lend money to various economic organizations where it was thought the public interest would be served by their survival and rejuvenation rather than demise (Weil, 1983). Its pump-priming role was re-confirmed and expanded under the auspices of Roosevelt's National Recovery Administration, established by the National Industrial Recovery Act of 1933. During its existence (it was wound up in 1953 under the shadow of collusion and bribery charges) it lent $40.6bn to industry, railroads, and banks. Amongst other things it helped finance the development of synthetic rubber production and the establishment and reorganization of aluminium production in the US. The Corporation proved a success in a period of extreme economic dislocation, also producing a financial return on taxpayers' money (Rohatyn, 1983, p. 130).

In the early 1980s a number of bills were introduced in Congress in effect to establish a new RFC.[13] Even though these came to nothing, the sentiment behind them continued to influence the early industrial policy debate strongly. But the form of the RFC proposed by Rohatyn and the like, as embodied in the proposed Congressional bills, differed somewhat from the idea behind the New Left's approach. As proposed, the 1980s RFC would have been an embodiment of a new 'corporatism' it was claimed. It was this critique of the corporatist overtones of both the traditional labour left's proposals and the practical manifestation of the RFC in Congressional bills, embodying a liberal-democratic and managerialist strategy, that formed a focus for the New Left's position.[14] The most likely outcome of a new RFC and of the NIPB-type proposals, the New Left argued, would be a big business/big government alliance to restructure industry from the top down and largely at the expense of labour interests. Even if organized labour were present in genuine negotiations, as the AFL-CIO hoped, there was a suspicion that a deal would be struck by the parties concerned which would again largely ignore the 'real interests' of the wider working class and 'new movement' groups. This critique of 'corporatism' is a well rehearsed feature of the Marxist left and it need not detain us any longer at this stage.

In place of this 'corporatist solution', the vision of the New Left was one loosely associated with increased 'democratization'. 'Re-industrialization with a human face' is the title of Bluestone and

Harrison's concluding chapter, where their proposed programme is spelt out. Amongst other things this would involve an emphasis on the production of useful goods and services (the UK Lucas Aerospace Combine's plan systematically to convert from defence to 'social need' production is appealed to here), where profitability would be a secondary criterion. 'Planning agreements' (again UK inspired) should be negotiated to develop 'sunrise' industries, where new enterprises of a combined public/private nature would be promoted, along with workers' co-operatives, and genuine workers' ownership (rather than 'stock ownership plans' current in the US, which invest control, if not ownership, in original administrators, it is argued — Bluestone and Harrison, 1982, pp. 258–61). For 'sunset' industries there should be systematic and extensive public monitoring of corporate investment and disinvestment decisions by government agencies, unions, and community bodies — in particular to make sure disinvestment was truly necessary. New legislation should also be introduced to require proper prior notification of impending planned closures, and to provide adequate severance pay, job replacement measures, and redeployment compensation. It was argued that any increase in productivity would require more, not less, job security. All this was to be done in the context of creating a more hospitable, interesting, and less authoritarian working environment, in which genuine accountability and democratic planning would stand instead of 'corporatism'. It was recognized that a good deal of this would go against existing trade union sentiment and organization.

In focusing on the concept of 'de-industrialization', the union movement, the New Left, and even the concerned business interests were naturally drawn to look at problems of the older established industries and their readjustment, rather than at the emerging new-tech sectors. These latter were not ignored, but they did not figure as a central element in either the analysis offered or in the cluster of policy proposals suggested. In addition, because the 'problem' to which the analysis was directed was seen to represent a general societal tendency – something thought to inhabit and organize the very structuring mechanisms of the industrial/social system as a whole – rather vague and general sentiments tended to be paraded as a solution. This is not to deny the quality of Bluestone and Harrison's work on job loss and disinvestment in the sectors or regions they focused upon, nor that some of their prescriptions have a relevant purchase. In addition the labour movement's insistence on institutional change is understandable. But the political realities of these suggestions were more or less ignored. They were clearly too general and comprehensive to be achieved in the American context, something returned to below.

A kind of interim position between the massive and comprehensive change envisaged by Bluestone and Harrison and the AFL-CIO, and positions which argue that nothing much needs to be changed anyway (which are discussed below) was occupied by Magaziner and Reich's early work. They quite astutely avoided the term 'de-industrialization' altogether, though they discuss a similar process. They were also more concerned with problems in high-tech sectors and in advanced-tech sectors. Here is an important difference which is not always clearly established. 'High tech' refers to innovative and creative R & D-based activity, involving the development of new generic product possibilities, whereas 'advanced tech' concerns the deployment of such innovations and developments to enhance the productive capacity of already established product lines, or to the adaptation of these to a renewed and dynamic productive environment. In the first case very long-term horizons are needed, whereas in the latter the medium-term reorganization of existing product and process technologies forms the main focus. In addition the employment consequences of each could be quite different. High tech is unlikely to generate many new jobs in the manufacturing sector – it relies on educationally intensive activity and small-scale production. Advanced tech, on the other hand, looks towards the application of new technology not only to existing product sectors, but also to the development of new high-volume markets. In this case job creation (or perhaps preservation) is more strongly involved in the manufacturing sector. These trends are discussed again later. Magaziner and Reich looked to mainland Europe and Japan for indications of the kind of industrial policy suggestion to make in the context of the US. 'Organized domestic economic development' is their key term – assisting the restructuring and growth of domestic productivity rather than merely subsidizing production for export or looking to macroeconomic adjustment mechanisms to create 'competitive advantage'. But for this to operate effectively, well-established labour market policies and regionally balanced growth would be necessary, which would involve the development of well-defined and longstanding participation from management, labour, financial institutions, and the government.

In an attempt to engender such a 'new consensus', a range of policy areas and proposals would have to be included, they suggested. But these are rather vaguely identified in their book and few specific or detailed suggestions are worked out. Advanced notification of shutdowns is one suggestion, re-training programmes another. Enhanced civilian orientated R & D activity, financed by the government and possibly backed by a new agency, is strongly recommended. Linkage industries with strong interdependencies like steel, autos, and microchips are identified for special consideration.

They also note the inadequacy of American capital markets in terms of providing loans for high-risk business, for long-term lending, and for small businesses of a venture capital type. The only explicit institutional change is suggested in this context. A government subsidized lending institution to fill the need for high-risk capital would be created, which would enter into partial funding agreements with companies developing new products promising substantial international competitive success (Magaziner and Reich, 1982, p. 353). This criterion of international competitiveness forms the focus for other suggested changes, namely in export insurance cover, assistance for small business exports, and with overseas marketing.

In general Magaziner and Reich see industrial policy as a measure of national co-ordination – a dynamic interaction between government and industry in which government plays a supportive role to ensure industries' competitiveness, rather than an intrusive one of over regulation or control (p. 362). In true liberal tradition, it is for the government to support private industry in its struggle for renewed international competitiveness – to help it reorganize and re-adjust. But the 'radical' element in the US context involved the comprehensiveness of the problems to which the proposals were addressed and the quest for a co-ordinated and coherent approach in terms of policy mix. This, along with an emphasis on accountability and the development of a new range of industrial management competencies to be systematically installed within the administrative bureaucracy, provided a fertile ground for conservative criticisms which were launched at this and similar proposals.

Reich supported the general thrust of these arguments in a series of articles and books appearing in the early 1980s,[15] which were influential in the debate within the Democratic Party over its strategy for the 1984 presidential election. The Democrats saw 'industrial policy' as an alternative to the Republicans' emphasis on 'supply-side economics', and adopted much of the Magaziner and Reich type arguments and proposals as part of their electoral programme. In so doing, however, they subtly changed its emphasis in an attempt to reconcile a desire for economic growth with the Democrats' traditional emphasis on social justice and 'community values'. In fact such a change was partly registered in one of Reich's later books, *The Next American Frontier*.[16] Here Reich sets up the problem of two characteristic American cultures or 'ideologies' – that of business, with its emphasis on the values of individual enterprise; and that of the realm of government, with an emphasis on civic values. Each of these sees the other as its antithesis. Those holding to American civic values see the world of business as one propelled by fear and greed, while those wedded to the realm of business and economics look upon the governmental sphere as one characterized by irresponsibility and profligacy.

But these are false choices, or 'myths', he argues. The real choice is between either shielding the US from a changing world economy or adapting it to engage in the new realities of international competition. The problem then is two-fold. One is to change these ideologies and re-focus them on the latter choices. The other is how to reconcile the ideologies in that very process of change and reformulation. Here the Democrats' schism between an acceptance of the particular capitalist vision or path of economic growth and development, and their perceived need to re-focus traditional US civic values of democracy, accountability, and redistributive justice, are brought into sharp relief.[17]

The problem for the Democrats, imposed in part on their minds by the success of 'Reaganism', is thus inflected into a search for a new coherent ideology to address what is seen as the main choice facing the US economy and society in the coming decades – protectionism or renewed competitive vigour. But the emphasis on the need to change ideology above all else should be treated with caution. It may over-estimate the impact of the ideological shift wrought by 'Reaganism' in the first place (rather than focusing upon the details of what Reagan has actually done to the economy),[18] and also leads to a parallel focus on the need for an alternative comprehensive 'ideological readjustment' at the expense of developing a detailed and institutionally robust set of policies precisely to adapt the economy to those new realities. If ideologies and values are the products of the interstices of economic and social existence, as located in institutional mechanisms and processes, then it is just these that need to be addressed in the first instance. Nobody is going to be persuaded by ideological argument alone.

While it would be unfair to suggest that Reich in *The Next American Frontier* ignores policy proposals – he in fact largely reiterates and expands those suggested in the book written with Magaziner – these are now organized around a new 'vision' for the economy that hopes to reconcile the two competing cultures discussed above. This vision involves the era of 'human capital' combined with flexible systems of production. Reich here slightly pre-figures Piore and Sabel's (1984) analysis of the displacement of mass production as the paradigm of western industrial organization with a new flexible specialization system (fss), akin to the craft production of previous eras. Since I wish to discuss this idea of flexible specialization systems more fully below, I leave for later exactly what it involves. Suffice it to say at this stage that for Reich, fss displaces the manner in which work is organized in the factory – replacing rigid hierarchical chains of authority with more collaborative, participatory, and egalitarian forms. But more importantly, this new organization of work will rest on a new organization of society (Reich, 1983, p. 246). It will need to be supported and sustained by a broader public framework which will integrate economic growth with the development of human capital. In this way the schism will be closed by the vision of a revised productive and societal formation.

To some extent these rather more 'programmatic' elements to the industrial policy debate, whilst running parallel to it, represent a marginal and tangential element, though a very interesting one. *The New American Frontier* operated rather in this manner for Reich himself, since it was followed by a more concrete and specific analysis of the lessons to be learned for industrial policy from one particular episode in recent US economic history (Reich and Donahue, 1985). The rescue of the Chrysler corporation from bankruptcy in 1979 was the culmination of a series of explicit 'bailouts' in the 1970s – Conrail, Lockheed, New York City – and pre-figured others – Harley Davidson, International Harvester, First National Bank. Each of these involved a new kind of federal assistance – large amounts of money clearly and explicitly directed at a single troubled firm (or in the case of NY at a city authority). Rather than the traditional American technique of tariff protection, general expenditure programmes, tax relief, etc., which affect all firms indiscriminately within a sector, locality, or industry, Chrysler was granted a huge $2.5bn package of re-adjustment assistance. This was accompanied by an explicit oversight and meticulous supervision by government agencies, which insisted on austerity measures and, what is more, achieved them. Reich and Donahue ask what could be learned from this episode in terms of institutional adaption and change? What was learned by the actors in the drama — the banks, management, unions, the federal government – and what more general lessons does it have for industrial policy?

In the first place the banks learned how to co-operate in dealing with large bailouts. While banks in the US are by law not allowed to become true investment banks, they are increasingly being drawn into this kind of activity, and Chrysler and the other examples only went to help establish criteria by which banks could operate to help with necessary financial re-adjustment. But it also put the banks into a different relationship with government. The major obstacle to further development along these lines they argue, however, remains the institutional inability or reluctance of banks to intervene in a counselling capacity before a crisis emerges.

Second, management learned a new set of skills – what are described as 'trimming down skills', i.e. how to manage a decline and retrenchment and, what is more, to accept outside interference in their own prerogatives. Management skills in a firm (as well as with respect to a national economy) have traditionally been geared up to growth and are quite unsuited in most part to situations of decline or structural re-adjustment. The usual US management–government relationships are described as ones of 'brokering' which were suppressed in the bailout situations, it is suggested.

In the third place the federal government learnt the advantages of putting explicit conditions on help provided to the private sector. In fact public involvement actually increased the private commitment to the rescue because the provision of public money was made contingent on private sacrifice. Whether or not this lesson will endure is another matter, however, as we shall see later.

Finally, and perhaps most ambiguously, they ask: what did labour learn? Labour was put into a position by the rescue of something akin to a 'shareholder', but without sanctions. It shared the risk and rewards by changing work practices and remuneration packages. In particular it initially entered into profit-sharing arrangements, sacrificing the indexation of wages. Subsequently this experiment collapsed, however, when workers voted for immediate wage rises in 1982, surrendering their profit-share advantages. This is indicative of the more general trend in profit-share deals made by ailing companies (e.g. Eastern Airlines). As soon as the immediate crisis is over, workers in particular vote down the innovation and return to 'free collective bargaining' arrangements. Whilst 'profit sharing' in various guises is being heavily promoted in the US (and in the UK) as a mechanism for overcoming stagflation and unemployment (see Weitzman, 1984, in particular), the conditions of its implementation and chances of sustained survival have been less well thought through. In the Chrysler case, however, the main shortcoming on labour's part as far as Reich and Donahue are concerned was its failure to press for job security. The unions did not seem to raise this as an issue – they were only interested in short-term remuneration conditions. In fact it was jobs that gave in the Chrysler rescue – wage levels, the government's stake, shareholder, and creditor positions were all defended by contract, covenant and law. In consequence Reich and Donahue make the interesting and important point that perhaps there is little difference between rescue and bankruptcy as far as jobs are concerned. In both cases similar levels of employment might actually emerge *post facto*, while in the rescue case shareholders in particular are cushioned.

This short history of Reich's changing position within the debate has been sketched to make a more general point about its overall trajectory. He moves from a position stressing the need for a comprehensive and co-ordinated federally-led industrial policy to one where it is a more modest set of lessons for the parties involved that can be learned from a very particular restructuring episode. In this latter work it is management practices that are stressed rather than government initiatives. In a way this paralleled the course of the larger debate itself over the early 1980s and, as will be argued near the end of this chapter, presents its own lessons to be learned in the UK context.

Reich's insistence upon the crucial role of productivity, R & D and investment more generally to the rejuvenation of American industry has been echoed by others close to the Democratic Party, notably Thurow (1983 and 1985). Thurow has pointed to the low savings ratio in the American economy as a major source of its low investment record. In 1983 the net personal savings ratio was 5 per cent for the US, compared to 13 per cent for Canada, 14 per cent for Germany, 21 per cent for Japan, and 23 per cent for Italy (11 per cent for the UK). This is largely attributable, it is suggested, to the tax deductibility of many income and expenditure items in the US tax code. In particular, offsetting deductions on personal borrowing tends seriously to depress what is a reasonable gross savings ratio. The clear implication of this is to reform the tax system. Thurow favours a move away from income tax to an expenditure tax system as the best way to improve the savings ratio, but such a long-term and radical change looks unlikely in the near future. In the meantime he proposes restrictions on consumer credit, tax advantages for bonus payments (since these are thought to enhance savings),[19] and the liberalization of individual retirement accounts (IRAs) so that any amount of money could be located in these accounts and gain the tax advantages associated with them.[20] In addition, measures to reduce the $200m annual federal budget deficit are proposed as a necessary adjunct to increased private savings as a means for raising the level of investment. Tax increases would be involved here, at least initially, in an attempt to eliminate the deficit.

Along with a number of other economists and the Reagan administration itself, Thurow also proposes a sweeping reform of corporate taxation. Since this represents an important and complex area, and also raises more general issues of the character of industrial policy, these and other proposals involving taxation are discussed later. As far as industrial policy measures in the more restrictive sense are concerned, Thurow sees R & D spending as a crucial area and proposes a civilian ministry of technology or an industrial research-and-development foundation, along the lines of Japan's MITI, and also points to the absence of genuine investment banking in the US with a suggestion for the establishment of a 50 per cent public/50 per cent private participation. Reconstruction Finance Corporation along the lines already discussed above. These are his main suggestions for institutional changes.

Thurow's general aim would be to reach a 25 per cent investment rate of GNP within ten years and to improve dramatically America's productivity record, which he sees as the main problem facing the economy. But unlike the advocates of industrial policy discussed earlier, he would not tie industrial policy explicitly to a job creation objective. This is a distinguishing feature of his argument and something that rather breaks with a lot of conventional wisdom in the industrial policy field. Thurow has been mainly associated with the encouragement of new advanced-tech and high-tech industries where immediate job prospects are uncertain. He is against 'bailout' industrial policies of the Chrysler type that concentrate upon propping up declining sectors or industries.[21] Thus for Thurow industrial policy must be above all else a forward-looking policy rather than backward-looking one. The implications of this in the UK context are taken up later.

The emphasis given to increasing the savings ratio by Thurow as a pre-requisite for increasing investment raises a more general theoretical issue, however. This can be expressed via the usual Keynesian accounting identity:

Private Savings + Public Savings = Domestic Investment + Net Foreign Investment

In a normal Keynesian fashion this must hold *ex-post* so that investment is thought to be highly constrained by the level of savings (public and private). Since the government is a net dis-saver when running up a budget deficit, this adds to the perceived need for budgetary reform to increase savings and investment.

There are a number of issues that arise in the context of this equation. In the first place there is a tendency to ignore the composition of the expenditure side of the federal budget. For instance not all the deficit is used to finance consumption but may be used to finance investment expenditure itself. This is perhaps less the case in the US, where the federal government is relatively inactive on the public investment front, but it could be an important aspect of UK budget deficits for instance. However, it points to the need to scrutinize closely that which the deficit is used to finance. One way of increasing investment in an economy may be to increase public investment by running up a larger budget deficit. Clearly this then raises issues of how the expenditure is to be financed, e.g. by taxation or by borrowing, and the wider economic consequences of either of these. The argument in the US is that the budget deficit has in fact been financed by borrowing which in turn has forced up interest rates and this has had the effect of choking-off private investment because of the high cost of capital it implies for private industry. Here is a case of the 'crowding-out effect'. But the point still remains that there is no necessary reason why budget deficits should imply lower investment in an economy, or why they should in principle be detrimental to overall investment. It all depends upon what use the money so raised is put to and how it is raised. A marginal unit of government expenditure may be more investment intensive than a marginal unit of private expenditure – as has traditionally been the case in the UK.

Second, the equation disguises a further means by which investment might be financed, notably by borrowing from abroad. Clearly this would be represented in the equation by the net foreign investment variable, but emphasizing the question of financing investment from abroad highlights the way domestic investment may not be strictly constrained by domestic savings. The conventional response to this is to say that while this may be the case in the first instance, in the long run domestic savings must respond to 'pay for' the borrowing abroad. Here then is a case not of an *ex-ante* disequilibrium but an *ex-post* equilibrium. However, the implications of this are quite important. Savings do not constrain investment *ex-ante*. What constrains investment *ex-ante* are issues of the demand for loans and how they can be financed. In a developed, financially sophisticated economy this means that it is the form of the financial system that fundamentally constrains the level of investment, not savings as such, plus the determinants of the demand for investment (i.e. the state of 'expectations' as well as the rate of interest and profitable potential, broadly speaking). Clearly this is not to suggest that savings are unimportant with respect to investment. They generate financial flows within the system which are indeed 'lent on' to potential investors. But it is to suggest that savings are not the fundamental *ex-ante* constraint on investment. Indeed savings would 'adjust' to finance the investment that has actually taken place (investment creates incomes out of which savings eventually emerge; thus investment and savings are always brought to equality by accounting convention).

A third point to make with respect to the savings=investment identity is that experience has shown there is not much that public bodies can do to increase the savings ratio in an economy. By contrast, public bodies can and have done a lot to increase investment levels in economies.[22] Thus the emphasis should be upon measures to increase investment in the first instance, not the savings ratio.

To sum up on these points, they add up to a criticism of Thurow's insistence on public policy directed towards increasing the savings ratio as the primary means by which the government might help to increase the level of investment in the economy. Rather, the points made above show the crucial role of the organization of the financial system and its mode of financing investment. In particular this helps bring into focus the typical modes of financial calculation and institutional mechanisms that articulate industrial and financial capital in the US, something not altogether ignored by Thurow, as pointed out above when discussing his suggestion for a new investment bank. But the problem is somewhat wider than this since the creation of an investment bank may not of itself change these modes of calculation. Let us look at this in a little more detail, since it has some wider implications.

Many authors have pointed to the short-term nature of American financial calculation. It is often claimed that the US has one of the most developed and efficient capital markets. The problem is that 'efficiency' is not an absolute concept, but is only measurable with respect to a definite pertinence. Its capital market may be efficient in terms of the ability to relocate capital quickly to where it is likely to earn the highest short-term profits, but it may be inefficient in terms of the longer-term aim of developing a stable manufacturing capability. Because of the 'over-developed' nature of the stock market, corporate goals are highly dependent upon share performance. Given that there is no direct way in which the link between particular product-market strategies and stock price appreciation can be measured, management's efforts to maximize shareholder wealth tend to be evaluated by financial criteria like return on investment (ROI) levels and consistent quarterly and annual growth in earnings per share. In most companies executive compensation plans also depend upon the growth or level of these measures, dampening the incentives for longer-term 'non-financial' objectives to emerge. One of the most influential mechanisms developed to

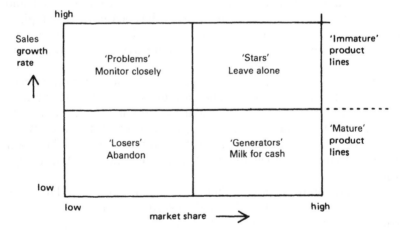

Figure 2.7 Sales growth and market share matrix for cash management.

enhance the capacity of management in its quest for short-term profitability has been the so called 'cash-management' technique, codified by the Boston Consulting Group (originally affiliated to Harvard Business School — Bluestone and Harrison, 1982, pp. 150–3). This emphasizes cash management within the firm over the commitment to any particular product line. Mainly addressed to large diversified firms with many branches and product lines, the aim is to generate the largest cash-flows from the 'portfolio' of activities undertaken. Even nominally profitable but low growth and market share product lines could be abandoned to concentrate upon those with higher market share and growth potential, it is argued. But as Figure 2.7 demonstrates, where the classic matrix representation of strategic choices is sketched, the mature high market share/low growth rate sectors might themselves be 'used' to provide cash for development of other sectors with higher growth of sales potential. The problem here is that unduly high ROI objectives attached to each product line in an attempt to generate the required cash-flows internally can mean a number of potentially robust sectors might be either abandoned or run down. In emphasizing the short-term nature of managements' objectives, the longer-term and careful assessment of existing product lines potential is underemphasized. Relative 'disinvestment' is the result.

All this is as a consequence, it is claimed, of the need to provide institutional investors with enough confidence in profit/earnings measures for continued investment in the company's stocks. It is overlaid by an increasing rate of stock turnover (on the NYSE this rose from 12 per cent in 1960 to 51 per cent in 1983, with typical individual company rates such as 67 per cent for Xerox, 98 per cent for Tandy, 137 per cent for Digital Equipment Corporation, and 223 per cent for American Airlines in 1982 – Ellsworth, 1985, p. 173).

Other familiar disadvantages associated with the US financial system stemming from its institutional characteristics are the high cost of capital relative to competitor countries. This is shown in Table 2.2. It should be clear from this table that the cost-of-capital disadvantage experienced by US firms is something that emerged well before the early 1980s and the budget deficits of the Reagan administrations. It is more of a long-term structural feature of the US system, asssociated with the leverage characteristics of American firms. The absence of close liaisons between banks and industrial concerns is partly responsible for the low debt-to-equity ratio of American industry – it relies more on share capital than debt capital, and this in turn raises the overall cost of capital (other things remaining equal, like risk) since interest on debt is a deductible expense. Also other governments intervene in the financial system to

Table 2.2 Cost of capital – estimated weighted average after tax

	1971 (%)	1976 (%)	1981 (%)
US	10.0	11.3	16.6
Germany	6.9	6.6	9.5
Japan	7.3	8.5	9.2

Source: Ellsworth (1985), exhibit VI, p. 176.

reduce risks associated with financial leverage. In addition the integrated organizational links between financial institutions and industrial firms have traditionally led to the demand for lower typical return-on-investment criteria, and with it the ability to re-invest resources in projects with longer time horizons and lower acceptable prospective returns.

All these features add up, then, to a systematic disadvantage for US manufacturers in terms of the incentive to invest (and, in as much as they are duplicated in the UK, for British manufacturers as well – see Thompson, 1986b, for a discussion of this). As we shall see, traditional investment criteria themselves as applied by US companies (and British companies) have also been the subject of a thoroughgoing critique, but we leave this for the discussion of attempts made to upgrade the capital stock in the face of rapid technological change.

The work discussed so far has mainly concentrated on capital investment issues. But behind this lurks the real objective of all these approaches. This can be summed up in terms of the need to make the US economy more competitive and particularly internationally competitive. As we shall see, this has been taken up explicitly by the government in its response to the industrial policy debate, but it was pre-figured by clarion calls for more 'international competitiveness', particularly by business orientated interests. Indeed these probably represented the main focus for this overall approach and offered the most strident arguments for its adoption. Besides the *Business Week* Team already mentioned – who also endorsed the early arguments about 'de-industrialization' and the need for a 'new' RFC – the business case for a national industrial strategy along the lines of re-stimulated competitiveness has been most strongly argued by Phillips (1984). (See also Labor-Industry Coalition for International Trade, 1983.)

Phillips pitched his arguments explicitly against the high-tech 'new liberals' of the Democratic Party (which he variously describes as 'Atari-Democrats' or 'lemon-socialists') and places his own analysis squarely in the framework of what is characterized as a 'pragmatic business orientated moderate conservatism'. He is thus against the traditional liberal interventionists (AFL-CIO) and the free market conservatives (supply side economics school), as well as the high-tech progressives. Other elements like the New Left and the New Right he thinks are unimportant in the debate. The political project of his book was to promote a business and conservative interest in 'industrial strategy' where the liberals had dominated so far. The nature of the position is described as a kind of 'conservative interventionism' – a nationalistic business assertiveness over trade policy along with *ad hoc* interventionist measures to stimulate domestic economic efficiency. Basing himself on what various business organizations had called for, he rejects protectionism – perhaps the main 'conservative' measure current in trade policy – and any ideas of a national industrial development bank (RFC), or the idea of the government picking product or industrial winners and losers. Rather than *free trade*, which he suggests no longer commands a definable majority coalition in the US, the agenda is being set by *fair trade* (at least amongst large companies). This is the main affirmative principle current in US business circles, he suggests, that is not a simple protectionist one. In this the thrust of the policy should be towards *reciprocity*, with tougher trade policy and trade law enforcement. The principal concern here is with the targeting by foreign governments of key industries for maximum assistance which creates an 'unfair' trading pattern with the US. If the US were playing on a 'level-field' then it could easily out-compete other countries and regain the number one competitive position. Indeed this is the explicit objective – to be the principal nation again as far as economic strength is concerned.

To this end it is suggested there should be new trade reciprocity legislation to limit access to the US market for trading partners not allowing US products equal access to their national markets. Existing trade laws should also be fully enforced and there should be close monitoring of foreign industrial policies and non-tariff restraints. Pressure should be brought to bear here to combat the unfair trading consequent upon such foreign industrial targeting practices. All this should become the responsibility of a Department of International Trade and Industry. This would centralize and co-ordinate the information gathering and legislation proposing activity at present shared by the Commerce Department and the Office of the US Trade Representatives. It would also act as a counterweight to the Treasury and the State and Defense Departments.

In addition there should be a revision of anti-trust laws to allow companies to co-operate in the development of new technologies,[23] there should be expanded credit facilities for companies involved in international trade (an expansion of the Export-Import Bank concept), and more tax breaks for internationally orientated business. Targeted tax and export reliefs are proposed, with new safeguards against technological transfer and espionage. US lobbying abroad should be increased and made more effective, while restrictions should be placed on US domestic lobbying by overseas governments and companies. A range of other federally supported measures to increase export performance are also proposed, involving domestic capital formation measures via tax advantages, R & D support, and, more tentatively, labour retraining and security advantages. (These later elements are suggested mainly for political reasons rather than economic ones – Phillips, 1984, p. 106.)

Such a set of nationalistic ('mercantilist') orientated measures, along with a commitment to 'tripartitistic' gestures, would meet the growing sentiment of big business it is claimed, while heading off conservative 'protectionism' on the one hand and 'liberal-democratic' calls for full blooded interventionism on the other. As we shall see, this scenario has had some purchase on the actual course of policy formation by the Reagan administration.

But Phillips has not been the only advocate of 'increased competitiveness'. As suggested above in one way or another, it has been endorsed by nearly all the advocates of industrial policy.[24] What marks the Phillips position out is its insistence on a return almost to the pre-1960s position, though to some extent this is a sentiment carried by all those advocating a renewed vigour of American international competitiveness.[25] It is usually tempered, however, with a recognition that the US must at least re-adjust to a situation in which it will have to be just one amongst a number of dominant but highly competitive nations (Scott and Lodge, 1985, p. 4). In this case it is more a matter of keeping up with competitors than of beating them.

Perhaps the main analytical point to emerge from the 'industrial policy as renewed international competitiveness' appoach is the attack it levels against the notion of comparative advantage. There is a growing recognition that competitiveness is more and more a matter of organized strategies in which governments lead and less and less a product of natural endowments. Thus it is increasingly government actions which are actively shaping the outcomes of international trade. In this way such interventions permanently alter the terms of international competition and irrevocably change the very structure of the market – they do not simply 'distort' an otherwise efficient market (Zysman and Tyson, 1983). Both the Heckscher-Ohlin and the Ricardian theories of international trade, which still dominate traditional trade theory, postulate mutual gains from free trade to the trading partners, it is claimed. Thus here the competitive problems of individual industries in international trade are the market consequences of changing patterns of comparative advantage. This assumes fixed technology and fixed factor endowments, something that in a dynamic environment are no longer exogenously determined but rather increasingly and decisively endogenously determined. Endowments and technologies can therefore be quite different in form and character between nations or firms, even for the production of essentially the same goods or services. Exactly what technologies are promoted and adopted, and what the factor intensities of different countries' endowment are, can be the direct consequence of deliberate national governmental policies.

> To understand [how this can come about] . . . it is necessary to distinguish between the notions of comparative advantage and competitive advantage. Comparative advantage refers to the relative export strength of a particular sector compared to other sectors in the same nation and is usually measured after adjusting for market-distorting government policies. For the purposes of our discussion, competitive advantage refers to the relative export strength of the firms of one country compared to the firms of other countries selling in the same sector in international markets. According to this interpretation, the competitive advantage of the firms of a particular country in a particular sector may be the result of that country's absolute advantage in that sector. In contrast to the usual notion of absolute advantage, however, the notion of competitive advantage allows for the presence of economic policies that help or hinder the international performance of different firms. Thus the competitive advantage of the firms of a particular country in a particular market may be the result either of real absolute advantage or of policy-induced and hence distorted absolute advantage. Indeed, policy-induced advantage can become real absolute advantage over time. (Zysman and Tyson, 1983, p. 28)

Thus a nation can create its own 'comparative advantage' by the efforts of its industries or governments to establish competitive advantage in any market. 'Comparative advantage' must be understood, as a consequence, as the cumulative effect of both company capacities and governmental policy choices, rather than simply the effect of given endowments in an undifferentiated capital and labour resource. These initially given endowments are not unimportant, only increasingly rendered secondary by government policies, in the highly advanced industrialized economies. Where this is the case markets can be manipulated, 'imperfections' created, and there need no longer be automatic mutual gains from trade.

Such gains would have to be 'negotiated into' trade arrangements.[26]

A broad range of commentators on the industrial policy debate have recognized these elements in the problem of the decline of American manufacturing capacity since the 1950s, and called for a response similar to those proposed by Phillips, i.e. aggressive counter measures (e.g. Zysman and Cohen, 1983; McKenna, Borrus, and Cohen, 1984; Wolff, 1985, amongst others; and most importantly in a policy context the President's Commission on Industrial Competitiveness, 1985).

One problem this discussion has highlighted is whether increasing competitiveness is at heart a zero-sum game. If the US increases its competitive position internationally, is the resultant improvement in its trade position at the expense of some other party? Clearly with the simple theory of comparative advantage, both parties to trade automatically gain. But if this theory no longer holds (if it ever did) then things are more problematical. To say the least, any gains from trade are likely to be ambiguous with respect to their effects across nations. The President's Commission decisively rejected this, however (pp. 7–8, vol. 11), arguing along traditional lines that both parties will gain from the consequential growth of overall economic activity. But while this may be true in terms of absolute levels of income relative to the previous position, even in a growing environment one country's relative gain in competitiveness against another's must mean that the other's position is partially undermined. With zero or small overall growth this position could be even worse and become zero sum at the limit. This has important implications for international trade since a policy environment in which all countries strain to achieve renewed competitive advantages can only mean some winners and some losers. In principle also there seems no reason why some of these strategies should not be negative-sum even. Thus the pursuit of a competitive policy by both trading partners might actually lead to a lower overall growth for both of them. The alternative would be a more managed or negotiated system of international exchange. Whilst in fact a great deal of international trade is already conducted in this manner, foregrounding it as an explicit aim rather than the achievement of dominance in a competitive sense would seem a more sensible course to follow.

For instance the Multi-Fibre Agreement (MFA) is described as a 'workable but imperfect solution' to the problem of international trade in textiles and apparel in a careful and sensible analysis of its operation in the US context (Nehmer and Love, 1985, p. 248).[27] They point to the difference between 'consumer interests' and 'producer interests' in international trade and make the point that too much emphasis is given to consumer interests in these matters. The

MFA provides a solution to the equitable allocation of negative structural adjustments more fairly among those countries that are less competitive. But it also stimulated the US's own textile industry, which has become more internationally competitive within the context of the MFA rather than less as predicted. Expanding this concept to other areas of trade problems, thereby encouraging the selective management of trade on a more multilateral basis, is recommended.

Whatever the precise arguments adopted about how American manufacturing might stimulate its international competitiveness, all the approaches discussed above stress their opposition to something called 'protectionism'. This is seen as the universal tendential mechanism against which 'competitive re-adjustment' needs to be pitched. It is used as a catch-all term to characterize that which should not be done – embracing anything from the overt unilateral imposition of tariffs or quotas on the one hand to the introduction of an all-embracing industrial policy on the other, and anything thought 'undesirable' in between. But the crucial point to recognize is that the positive measures suggested in opposition to this are themselves protectionist in character. They must be if they are to be effective. Thus the real issue – if one believes that there is a competitiveness problem – is not undifferentiated 'protectionism' *versus* the rest but the form of protectionism that is to be introduced. What have been discussed so far are in fact different forms of protectionism.

However, there is a position which in essence does reject any form of protectionism (though as we shall see even this cannot be an absolute rejection). Such a line was developed by the Brookings Institution in a series of very influential publications emerging during the heart of the industrial policy debate in 1983–4 (Schultze, 1983; Rivlin, 1984; Lawrence, 1984) In effect these (along with the Reagan victory in the 1984 election) more or less killed off the debate, at least amongst economists who from then on generally adopted the line developed in these analyses.[28] The Brookings position was probably initiated in response to what it saw as the most likely trend to emerge from the industrial policy debate, namely outright protectionism of the traditional conservative kind (i.e. tariffs but particularly quotas[29]). In effect the Institution argued that the US does not have a long-term competitiveness problem in the sense of either difficulties in re-adjusting its industrial structure or the inadequate incentives to export and the capacity of overseas nations to penetrate the US economy's home demand with targeted strategies. Rather the problem is a macroeconomic one which can be solved by macroeconomic management tools without the need to resort to an industrial policy, or 'protectionism' and stridently nationalistic trade policies.

The initial attack of the Brookings Institution was upon 'de-industrialization'. Lawrence argued that the US was not experiencing a general structural process of decline in its manufacturing sector. In fact quite the opposite. Its manufacturing base was adjusting adequately and relatively robustly. Rather its competitiveness problem was the result of temporary adverse macroeconomic conditions, particularly the rapid appreciation of the dollar in the early 1980s (cf. Rivlin, 1984). This was in turn caused by the federal deficit which had to be financed by offering high interest rates. This encouraged overseas financial investment in the US to purchase federal debt, forcing up the exchange rate, which in turn caused domestic investment in manufacturing industry to be choked off because of the high cost of borrowing. Growth generally would be impaired by this process, it was argued, despite the fact that the US economy turned in a dramatically better growth performance than it had done for many years after 1982. In fact the Brookings Institution had a point here in that the growth experience during the early 1980s has been a rather unbalanced one – led by consumer spending, real-estate appreciation, and the like, rather than by a thoroughgoing increase in underlying manufacturing investment and productivity. In addition their attack upon 'de-industrialization' hit home. Too much emphasis was given to the systemic nature of the decline in manufacturing employment and to the rundown of industries in a number of north-eastern states by the initial advocates of the de-industrialization thesis.

However, the Brookings analysis under-estimates the longer-term nature of the trends in productivity and loss of competitiveness as outlined in the opening section of this chapter. As Thurow (1985) has pointed out, it is possible to maintain international competitiveness by devaluation of the currency, but without attending to the underlying causes of this – i.e. the relatively low growth in productivity – it can only be achieved at the expense of declining living standards. The implication of the Brookings position is for continued devaluations to maintain competitiveness in the face of declining relative productivity (itself partly the consequence of the inadequate level and quality of investment), or massive increases in overseas borrowings to finance potential balance of payments deficits. Both of these have severe limits and imply declining relative living standards, something those familiar with British economic history should well recognize. What is bizarre, however, is that more or less the same arguments as the Brookings Institution has advanced in the US against the need for an industrial policy are being deployed in the UK for an economy undergoing a similar process of long-term economic decline. There is no need for a comprehensive or even a selective industrial policy (in the UK), it is argued, since macroeconomic adjustments can produce the necessary conditions for renewed growth and competitiveness.

In the US (as in the UK to some extent) it is the budget deficit that is seen as the problem, and what is needed are measures to eliminate this. The debate is then over how best to achieve this (i.e. tax increases as advocated by Brookings, or cutbacks in spending as advocated by the Reagan administration — plus 'supply-side' tax reform to stimulate growth and savings, see below).

Whilst any industrial policy initiatives would seem to be unnecessary or ruled out by this kind of approach – indeed they would be positively detrimental to the market-inspired adjustment envisaged – they do in fact creep back in a rather *ad hoc* manner, at least for Lawrence (1984). Thus familiar policies to enhance the take-up of new technologies by industry and to promote R & D activity are endorsed. Information gathering and dissemination, and 'market failure' ameliorations can be instituted. In addition unfair trading practices can be focused upon and temporary measures, some quite draconian, developed to deal with them (Lawrence, 1984, Chapter 6; Rivlin, 1984, pp. 133–56). All these go, however, to promote a market-led adjustment – they are part of the provision of a flexible environment in which private decision-takers respond positively. The Brookings view is one of a fundamental symmetry between an economy's response to a decline and to an upward growth trajectory. One is simply the reverse of the other. There is no conception of the fundamental asymmetrical relationships involved here – that losing ground in a decline is easy and fast relative to the enormous effort needed to recoup those losses for rebuilding the economy.[30]

4 The dispersion of the industrial policy debate

The above discussion has painted a picture of the main constituents of the debate within the US roughly between 1980 and 1985. In this section we concentrate on where that debate has ended up. This involves both a discussion of some of the policy initiatives actually pursued as well as around which issues the debate is still continuing, if in a muted form.

4.1 International competitiveness and trade policy

The Reagan administrations have taken trade policy very seriously. The President's Commission was a crucial document in this respect. It set out the problems clearly and developed a politically acceptable philosophy to respond to these:

Improving competitiveness is best achieved by actions that

increase productivity and facilitate the working of market forces. Such policies aim to *improve the context* for competition rather than intervene in it. The Commission *rejects active Government participation in the development of specific sectors.* (President's Commission on Industrial Competitiveness (1985) vol. II, p. 29 – emphasis added)

It argued that competitiveness is a complex category involving four key indicators: labour productivity, real wage growth, real returns on capital employed, and the position in world trade. On all four counts the US was found wanting, and the Commission suggested a range of low level institutional changes and *ad hoc* policy initiatives akin to those already discussed above around the international trade and competitiveness issue. The Commission also strongly confirmed the direction of 'gaze' for American trade policy – towards the Pacific Rim countries and Japan in particular. The US is relatively uninterested in the Atlantic and European countries as far as trade problems are concerned. It does more trade with Taiwan, South Korea, Singapore, Hong Kong, Malaysia, and Japan than with all of Europe combined, and trade with these countries is predicted to be double the size of European trade by 1995 (pp. 9–10). Table 2.3 also confirms the fears about productivity growth differences between the US and these countries.

In fact a lot of this concern about the Pacific Rim has turned into rather crude anti-Japanese sentiment in the US. Outright protectionism is very popular and, despite the exhortations of the authors quoted above, gathering pace amongst congressmen and the public alike. The Reagan administration has taken up the ideas of strengthening the US resolve in asserting a 'fair-trade' policy and stressing

Table 2.3 Productivity growth in newly industrializing countries (real GDP per employed person)

Country	Period	Annual changes (%)
Taiwan	1963–82	5.6
Korea	1963–82	5.3
Mexico	1960–80	3.6
Singapore	1973–82	2.9
Malaysia	1973–82	2.2
Japan	1960–83	5.9
USA	1960–83	1.2

Source: President's Commission on Industrial Competitiveness (1985), vol. II, adapted from Tables 2 and 3, p. 111.

reciprocity agreements in an attempt to head off more full-scale protectionist moves (see Government Printing Office, 1986, Chapter 3). Bilateral political negotiations have been underway with a range of countries, notably Japan, Korea, and Canada, to establish 'fair-trade' conditions and orderly marketing agreements over a range of goods (for instance semiconductors with Japan and timber products with Canada). Thus the administration hopes to establish specific criteria of protection for a limited range of products, and apply discriminatory and time-dependent measures to these. Whether this will be sufficient to offset the more strident measures being promoted by Congress,[31] and to deter other countries' 'subsidization' of their exports, remains to be seen, but seems unlikely.[32]

4.2 Tax policy as industrial policy

Tax reform is perhaps the other main area in which there have been active policy initiatives that impinge directly on industrial issues. This remains one of the main planks of President Reagan's 'supply-side' approach. While he has adamantly refused openly to sanction tax increases in the face of the mounting government debt, he has pressed strongly for tax reform measures and introduced two major initiatives. The first of these was embodied in the 1981 Economic Recovery Tax Act and the second, proposed by the President in May 1985, passed through Congress in the summer of 1986 (Government Printing Office, 1985a).

The principal sources of federal revenues are the personal income taxes, social insurance tax, and the corporation tax. In 1984 these yielded about 91 per cent of total federal receipts. The personal income tax accounted for 48 per cent of this, social insurance taxes 41 per cent, and corporation tax 11 per cent (Government Printing Office, 1985b, p. 77). The hidden story of American tax history over the postwar period, however, has been the massive increase in the importance of social insurance taxes and the decline of corporation tax (Bradford, 1986, Table A7, p. 355). The reform movement was heralded by the 1977 Treasury document *Blueprints for Basic Tax Reform* (Bradford, 1984). It laid out two possible 'tax models' – a 'comprehensive income tax' approach in which the distinction between corporate and individual taxes would disappear, and a consumption tax ('cash flow tax') which would have the same effect, and where savings would not be taxed. As might be expected neither of these two models has much hope in terms of legislative enactment but they have acted as a touchstone for the tax policy debate in the US.

Any radical reform of the tax system would involve serious alter-

ation of both personal and corporate taxes. Since as yet a break with
the distinction between these has not emerged, and corporate
taxation is still the main mechanism directed at investment and
industrial policy issues, we concentrate upon this in the following
discussion.

In 1984 the federal government collected some $60bn from
corporate income tax, but it gave away some $80bn to corporations
in the form of 'tax expenditures' (Sub-Committee on Economic
Stabilization, 1984, p. 3). Whilst not always intentional in effect, the
tax code targets specific activities, industries, sectors, and even firms
for preferential treatment. This is a disguised way of conducting
industrial policy – of implicitly 'picking winners' – and has major
efficiency consequences.

Table 2.4 Effective post-ACRS tax rates by asset type

Asset type	Effective tax rate (%)
1 Autos	6.10
2 Office, computing and accounting equipment	7.50
3 Trucks, buses, and trailers	7.10
4 Aircraft	5.50
5 Construction machinery	5.30
6 Mining and oilfield machinery	5.10
7 Service industry machinery	5.10
8 Tractors	5.00
9 Instruments	10.00
10 Other equipment	4.70
11 General industrial equipment	9.70
12 Metal working machinery	4.10
13 Electric transmission/distribution equipment	23.60
14 Communications equipment	4.00
15 Other electrical equipment	4.00
16 Furniture and fixtures	3.80
17 Special industrial equipment	3.60
18 Agricultural equipment	3.50
19 Fabricated metal products	17.30
20 Engines and turbines	30.70
21 Ships and boats	3.00
22 Railroad equipment structures	25.00
23 Mining exploration, shafts and wells	8.80
24 Other	45.60

Source: Sub-Committee on Economic Stabilization (1984), Figure 10, p. 49.

The Economic Recovery Tax Act of 1981 reduced the corporate tax burden by replacing the system of numerous asset depreciation classes with a new accelerated cost recovery system (ACRS). This contained only three capital recovery classes in which all new capital investment was to be placed for depreciation and tax purposes: light equipment written off over three years; other equipment over five years; and business structures over ten to fifteen years. Despite differences in economic lives, therefore, actual tax/depreciation lives were codified according to this schedule.

A number of consequences resulted from this move. In the first place the tax revenue from corporations fell dramatically between 1980 and 1982, and would have continued to fall if Congress had not exacted another bill in 1982 (the Tax Equity and Fiscal Responsibility Act) which repealed some tax advantage provisions of the 1981 Act (Sub-Committee on Economic Stabilization, 1984, pp. 13–14). Secondly the Act created incentives to invest in assets with shorter lives since these gained the main tax advantages. But

Table 2.5 Industrial impacts of ACRS

Industry	Reduction in the required pre-tax return attributable to ACRS (%)
Motor vehicle	43
Petroleum refining	42
Tobacco	37
Glass, cement, and clay	36
Paper and pulp	36
Primary metals	35
Fabricated metals	35
Rubber	35
Printing and publishing	34
Food	34
Logging	34
Textiles	32
Leather	32
Transportation and equipment	31
Wood products and furniture	30
Machinery and instruments	30
Chemicals	30
Apparel	28
Electrical machinery	28

Source: Federal Reserve Bank of Atlanta, *Economic Review*, May 1982.

one of its major effects was to benefit the real estate and utility industries. The biggest tax break of all went to real estate, shortening the depreciation life from forty years to fifteen years, providing huge write-offs of office building and other real estate and encouraging tax sheltered real estate investment in shopping centres, apartments, and office building, instead of in industrial capacity. Table 2.4 shows the variable post-ACRS tax rates on different types of equipment assets. However despite reductions in tax on different types of structures these still attracted the highest post-ACRS tax rates. Table 2.5 shows the estimated percentage reduction of tax on different industry sectors.

Both of these tables would need to be supplemented by the 'taxable capacity' of sectors or firms to determine the overall burden of the tax. Some industries and firms are much more profitable than others, or have tax credits which they can use to offset their tax liability. In general it has been argued that those industries not subject to foreign competition, e.g. real estate, public utilities, or less subject to it, e.g. 'domestic' orientated industries, services generally, were the ones to gain the most from the 1981 Act's provisions, precisely the opposite to that thought necessary by the 'increased international competitiveness lobby' (Sub-Committee on Economic Stabilization, 1984).

What the 1981 Act did not address are the amazing proliferation of tax concessions existing for corporate bodies that have developed over the years to cope with special problems and interests, and in attempts to 'fine tune' the economy. These exist for a broad range of activities – domestic and foreign investment, exporting, R & D, small businesses, energy conservation, hiring disadvantaged workers, etc; for specific sectors – oil and gas, other minerals, timber, agriculture, construction, finance, maritime industries, railroads, amongst others; and the largely unintended effects for particular firms – a large number of well known and profitable firms pay no tax because of the way they manipulate the tax laws. It is these that have been largely responsible for the growing tax expenditures and declining tax take of the corporate sector.

Some of these well-entrenched tax advantages for companies became the object of the 1985 tax reform package proposed by the President. This represented a very major reform initiative — something most commentators thought could not pass through the legislature without drastic amendments. It initially proposed to broaden the tax base by cutting out a lot of the tax advantages to borrowing and other exemptions for tax liability, and a reorganization of the company taxation system. In particular here the basic corporation tax rate would be cut from 46 per cent to 33 per cent and tax advantages to real estate would be curtailed plus those to a number of most favoured sectors like oil and gas, mineral extraction, transportation, and communications. There would also be a 'minimum corporation tax', payable to all profitable companies. Second, other marginal tax rates would also be reduced – paid for in part by the widening of the tax base. Connected to this would be a simplification of the tax system, particularly the personal tax system. The income tax for instance, presently organized into fifteen taxable brackets ranging from 11 per cent to 50 per cent, was to be codified into just three rate bands – 15 per cent, 27 per cent, and 35 per cent. All this was to be 'revenue neutral' so that any overall tax increase was ruled out (see Government Printing Office, 1986, pp. 89–91).

By and large this package – with a number of other provisions designed to increase investment and productivity – was enacted more or less in full in September 1986. On the corporate tax side this was set at 40 per cent for 1987, after that it would be graduated up to 34 per cent. One of the main investment incentives was also eliminated (the 'investment tax credit' which had allowed companies to reduce their tax bill by 6–10 per cent of the cost investment). All in all these two measures were estimated to increase companies' annual tax bill by an extra US$25 billion over the next five years. Together with a range of other measures the tax reform overall was designed to shift $120 billion from personal to corporate and other taxes over this period. No party in this debate was prepared to argue openly for tax increase or for the maintenance of a more progressive personal income tax schedule; despite attempts in both the Congress and the Senate to link tax reform with the budgetary process, the sentiment in the US is for tax reductions rather than tax increases. In fact the President has the Democrats in a tight political corner on this score – just hoping that they will openly declare for tax increase. In the face of the Democrats' desire at least to maintain welfare spending in the context of a large budget deficit and the Gramm-Rudman Act,[33] the Democrats have only two political options that differentiate them from the Republicans – to propose tax increases or to suggest a reduction in the defence budget. Both of these could spell a political disaster for the Democrats and they are thus caught in a position of meekly supporting the Reagan administration's tax reform and budget moves in a rather moribund political stance.

But what can be said more generally about the tax reform moves proposed and subsequently enacted? Here it is necessary to raise the issue of whether tax incentives are the main problem from the point of view of increasing productivity and investment. Table 2.6, for instance, shows an early estimate of the likely consequences of the Treasury's proposals for tax changes on new investment in various industrial sectors. Under this reform proposal agriculture, manufacturing, and trade investment experience a tax reduction while the

Table 2.6 Effective tax rates on new investment

Industry proposal	Current law (%)	Treasury (%)
Agriculture	44	40
Mining/oil & gas extraction	26	33
Construction	35	40
Manufacturing	45	40
Transportation	27	39
Communication	23	39
Electric/gas utilities	31	38
Trade	50	40
Services	36	39
Overall	41	39

Note: Includes equipment, structures, and inventories, and reflects both corporate and personal taxes (but does not consider individual rate reductions). Assumes after-tax real return to creditors is 3.25 per cent and tax rate is 25 per cent; assumes cost of corporate equity is 7 per cent (before persona taxes), dividend return is 4 per cent, and stockholder tax rates is 35 per cent. Financing is assumed to be one-third debt. Inflation rate is set at 5 per cent.
Source: Sub-Committee on Economic Stabilization (1984), Figure 13, p. 79.

other areas show tax increases. This would seem a sensible aim, though it does not signal the likely total tax burden since this depends upon the age mix of the capital stock in each industry.

But there is a more fundamental problem which involves whether there is any confirmed link between tax rates on investment and the quantity of investment, or on the growth record of productivity and GNP. While tax incentives may encourage the redistribution of investment between differentially rated sectors, there is little evidence that it increases the overall quantity of investment, let alone its quality. It is the quality of investment, of course, that is so important for productivity growth. In fact international comparison shows that simpler and more neutral tax regimes are coupled with overall tax rates that are higher than those prevailing in the US (King and Fullerton, 1984). In addition there seems to be no correlation between these investment tax rates (or tax levels more generally) and capital formation, or between either of these and productivity or economic growth rates (see Blume *et al.* (1981) and Bosworth (1984) Chapters 2 and 6 for convenient summaries of the lack of evidence). At best it is only between 22 per cent and 25 per cent of productivity growth that can be attributed to investment anyway, and whether the marginal changes in tax rates envisioned are going to affect investment is also questionable given the small impact these changes are going to have upon the overall after-tax cost of capital. Bosworth for instance suggests that causation is more likely to work in the opposite direction, in that higher output and growth is likely to stimulate investment rather than *vice versa* (Bosworth, 1984). Thus the emphasis given to investment incentives in the context of productivity growth may be misplaced. Even the effectiveness of incentives to R & D investment have been found to have only a marginal impact on this crucial area, if any impact at all (Mansfield, 1985). Increasingly it is towards the conditions of labour organization that attention is being directed in matters of productivity, something the measures outlined in this section more or less totally ignore. But it is not the incentive to supply labour arguments as dependent upon personal tax rates which is being invoked here – this is not ignored in the current tax reform debate. Rather it is the conditions and modes of labour organization and control at the work place, plus the 'security' aspects of employment and redundancy conditions that are being stressed (Walton, 1985). If productivity is to be increased, the quality of the investment must be increased rather than simply its quantity, and this emphasizes a range of management practices at the level of the firm – something we return to below.

4.3 Industrial policy at the state and local level

The third major area into which industrial policy has fragmented is into state and local governmental initiatives. The states in particular have stepped in to fill a vacuum created by the absence of any co-ordinated national response to industrial restructuring problems. This also involves something of a political rejuvenation for state governments and for state governors who have led the way in promoting industrial re-adjustments for their states. This has had the effect of propelling governors more into the forefront of political activity in the US and may have sparked a 'new federalism' in American politics more generally (Anton and Reynolds, nd).

Every state in the Union provides some kind of fiscal and investment incentive for businesses, to try and attract them into its area. These fall into a number of different categories. Perhaps the most comprehensive in terms of coverage are those associated with small or medium-size business (Disman, 1983). Here it is often a case of state subsidies to lower taxes or interest rates, or of providing funds for employee training. In addition a number of states have enacted legislation ahead of various federal initiatives to help set up local enterprise zones. By 1983 nineteen states had done this, and others were contemplating similar moves (Revzan, 1983, p.31). By and large these kinds of initiatives involve measures which alter the commercial environment within the state and for particular types of businesses. They often also involve specifically directed incentives to innovative or venture-capital firms. In this connection a good many quite innovative mechanisms of locally based finance for investment have grown up within the states, linking up local banks and savings institutions with prospective businesses under state guarantee, or directly involving the states issuing 'development bonds' themselves to finance their own activity (Disman, 1983, pp. 14–15).

A second type of state activity in this area, usually running in parallel to that described above, involves infrastructure development (Zorn, 1986). This does not mean simply the traditional activity of building transport and social infrastructures but of specifically targeting particular urban areas, for instance, and laying a ground-work of factory buildings and providing expertise and training in business skills and the like. Again quite innovative mechanisms of finance and co-operation have been developed here (e.g. Zorn, 1986; A. Alfred Taubman Center, 1985, pp. 4–9).

On quite a different scale to these efforts, at least in terms of their public impact, has been a third type of state backed initiative. Here either at a state-wide level or with respect to a particular designated area, usually associated with universities, state or local governments have tried to provide a comprehensive generator of economic activity often based upon the stimulation of high-technology firms. Examples that come to mind are areas like the 'Research Triangle' in North Carolina (University of North Carolina at Chapel Hill, Duke University) which was originally set up as far back as the early 1960s (Vogel, 1985); 'Silicon Valley' in California (around Stanford University); 'Route 128' in Boston, Massachusetts (MIT, North-eastern University); Austin, Texas (University of Texas at Austin); and a number of others. In addition other states have set up or tried to generate comprehensive and strategic state-planned high-tech development packages which have gone further than merely provid-ing the 'right conditions for the market to work'. Of particular interest are the so-far successful Pennyslvania 'Ben Franklin Part-nership' and Massachusetts efforts with its Technology Develop-ment Corporation, and the highly unsuccessful attempt to establish a state-led industrial policy for Rhode Island – the 'Greenhouse Com-pact' developed by Ira Magaziner – which collapsed in June 1984.

All of these approaches cast the relevant authorities in a new semi-entrepreneurial role, rather than as simply providers of subsidies or a better commercial environment, but they have gone about their activities in quite different ways and with different objectives in mind. The Ben Franklin Partnership, begun in 1983, is mainly organized around job preservation and job creation. It is only secondarily a technology development programme. The state enters into co-operatively financed projects, often based around universities, in which it at most matches private finances but usually provides one-third. The focus for these projects is advanced technology rather than high technology, and they are directed at problems arising from already established local industries and businesses (Lang, 1985).

The Massachusetts Technology Development Corporation is one of a number of new institutions created by the state government to develop and finance mainly new high-technology ventures in the state. Unlike many other state's initiatives it can hold a portfolio of investments (in 1985 some thirty firms) and is heavily involved with seeking out and initiating projects (Hodgman, 1985). It takes a very active and 'strategic' role in the state's economic development. Massachusetts has in fact transformed itself from a declining state in 1975, when it had 12 per cent unemployment, into one of the strongest economic states of the Union with effective 'full employment' in 1986 of only 3 per cent unemployment. In 1975 the state's budget was $600m in deficit while in 1985 it was $950m in surplus. In the mid-1970s the state was suffering from the decline of its basic manufacturing capacity in textiles and shoes: in 1986 it is the home of one of the most dynamic regions for high-technology developments and has achieved a well balanced recovery over the state as a whole. During this period it has moved from a state 'boosterism' approach to one stressing the active orchestration of public economic activity. However, it is recognized even by the Governor's Office of Economic Development (from which this information is drawn from interviews) that national economic decisions have driven the state economy, particularly defence initiatives and private decisions, with the state itself 'playing a small though important role at a largish margin'.

Perhaps the most celebrated attempt by a state government to take a large-scale and comprehensive attitude to the re-industrialization of its economic base was the Rhode Island 'Greenhouse Compact'. Salutary lessons have been drawn from this for the industrial policy debate in the US. The Compact proposed to spend $750 millions over a seven-year period to create 60,000 new jobs. It was written down in a document of over 1,000 pages. A high profile campaign was initiated to prepare and present the plan, in which local financial and business interests, and eventually labour organizations, combined with the state's economic development bodies, to back and legitimize the plan. Over 800 meetings were held statewide to discuss the plan in the closing stages of its presentation, after a decision had been made to seek voter support in a referendum on the project. An unprecedented publicity campaign was initiated to explain its character and objectives.

When the vote finally came, however, it was unexpectedly and heavily rejected by a margin of four to one. It had included many of the proposals of a broad industrial policy agenda – targeted subsidies for industry, education and training programmes, business 'green-houses' for high-tech research and development, and incentives for the investment of a venture capital type. It was presented as an answer to many of the ills of the state's economy – a declining manufacturing base, contentious labour relations, poor business and social climate, low average wages. But the Compact was perceived by voters as something that would benefit 'someone else' rather than themselves (Carroll *et al.*, 1985; Anton and West, nd). They were suspicious of the 'elite-group' promotion of the project. The emphasis on high-tech and higher wages gave the impression that those already living and working in the state might be 'left behind' by new business and their imported employees. A further negative feature of the campaign was the failure to involve locally elected representatives directly in the endorsement process. Both Democratic and Republican candidates for governor publicly supported it but state representatives and senators kept a discreet distance from the whole process, sensing its likely demise at the hands of voters.

But perhaps above all else the project was rejected because of the manner in which it was presented to voters in terms of its finance. The referendum was directly about the finance of a $750 million project for about one million state residents, via tax increases. This led to a highly personal calculation of costs and benefits in which voters thought they would be the ones bearing the direct and immediate cost, while banks, big business, 'politicians', and colleges would be the ones reaping both the short-term and long-term benefits (Carroll *et al.*, 1985, p. 112; Anton and West, nd, p. 11).

The lessons to be drawn from this and the other state-led initiatives are that they can be successful if handled correctly and sensitively. Indeed in the US context (and as UK experience has shown as well) the 'local' level is probably the one at which most can be achieved in terms of more traditional industrial policy agenda. Evolving specific initiatives to meet the local diversity of circumstances is to be recommended against a rigidly centrally planned and directed approach. But there are major problems here also. One is the zero-sum character of a good deal of the attempts to attract businesses with reliefs and subsidies. Whether this produces any net additional activity is still open to question in the US. Second, the national economic environment is crucial to the success of state or local initiatives, as the Massachusetts examples would demonstrate. Third, and perhaps most importantly, the 'institutional' mechanisms by which these kinds of initiatives are best handled is a crucial element in their success. Both the Ben Franklin Partnerships in

Pennsylvania and the Massachusetts state-initiated approaches have relied upon what might be termed a 'discreet' and non-flamboyant public style of presentation. By and large these and other of the more successful initiatives have attached themselves to existing parts of the administrative machinery of state government rather than attempted to establish totally new and independent bodies, which might compete with the existing machinery. This has secured their acceptance within the bureaucracies concerned and made them less likely to face politically inspired attacks from the outside. In addition these successful initiatives have conducted their business in an open but discreet manner, paying careful attention to their public image, not drawing undue attention to themselves, being modest in their objectives and claims of success, maintaining a bi-partisan political style as much as possible, and so on. In this way a relatively politically robust set of institutional mechanisms has emerged and become established. One thing they have not done is to subject themselves not directly by tax increases but by floating 'development bonds' within the normal activity of state finance. What this than just the topic under direct consideration, and are an unstable way of gathering support, particularly for such contentious issues as 'industrial policy'. The mistake in RI was less one of offering a 'corporatist' solution to the state's industrial problems – it is difficult to see how an industrial policy could not be initiated and developed by some 'elite' body – but rather one of presenting this to the electorate in a 'take it or leave it' package with a discreet (tax based) financing clause attached. All the other initiatives have financed themselves not directly by tax increases but by floating 'development bonds' within the normal activity of state finance. What this does demonstrate, however, is the major problem of finance for any locally based industrial policy, something particularly problematical in the UK context where the fiscal and financial independence of local authorities is being eroded by central government.

One final comment to make in this section concerns a rather general issue about industrial policy that is raised by this discussion of the more political conditions for its successful implementation. 'Industrial policy', whether considered at a local, state-wide, or national level, is always a very contentious political issue. Why is this? Part of an answer will be provided in the next section where we analyse the way industrial policy becomes articulated with a range of other policy areas. As we shall see it tends to occupy a crucial and central place within a complex matrix of possible policy initiatives – all of which are of a sensitive political character. But another level at which this can be discussed involves what one might term the 'legacy of liberalism' in a broad ideological sense. Within the industrial policy field this legacy is three fold. Broadly speaking it sanctions three types of intervention – subsidization, regulation, and nationalization. These are the main mechanisms by which liberal democracies have conducted their industrial policies. Note, however, this presumes that what is to be affected by any interventions is already established prior to the attempt to regulate it, subsidize it, or nationalize it. Where 'industrial policy' has had great difficulty is to establish new economic activity. Robust mechanisms within liberal democracies to carry out this kind of 'intervention' are very difficult to come by (in the UK the NEB tried this but largely failed). As we have seen, only Massachusetts in the examples quoted above has come anywhere near to this and then only in a very weak form associated with limited new-technology firms.

The problem then is that industrial policy is always 'pregnant' with the possibility of the public authorities initiating this kind of activity. It is written into the nature of 'industrial policy' that it should identify gaps in the productive structure and seek to fill these, not simply to subsidize, regulate, or nationalize some already existing activity. But when this is the case industrial policy is as a consequence always close to a form of 'socialistic' practice. It embodies the seeds of a type of economic function that exceeds the legitimate bounds of the liberal tradition, and this is what makes it so politically sensitive.

5 Industrial policy: what is it?

In this section we step back from the analysis and description of the particularities of the American industrial policy debate to try and assess industrial policy more generally. It is perhaps surprising how little explicit reflection has been conducted on this from those involved with the debate. As a result 'industrial policy' tends to be left either as a rather vague and general term, or something that encompasses a very broad range of adjustment mechanisms. For instance Chalmers Johnson, while one of the few to have focused on the matter, is typical of the former tendency when he defines industrial policy to mean 'the government's explicit attempt to co-ordinate its own multifarious activities and expenditures and to reform them using as a basic criterion the achievement of dynamic comparative advantage for the American economy' (Johnson, 1984, p. 77). Clearly this could involve almost any form of government activity or expenditure, as could an approach suggested by Lodge and Crum (1985, pp. 479–502), which calls for something that is strategically 'holistic', 'coherent', 'flexible', and 'balanced' to enhance US competitiveness.

On the other hand Zysman and Tyson (1983) develop a comprehensive discussion of industrial policy involving a range of aspects –

sectoral-specific policies, aggregate policies, market promotion, protectionism, regulation – covering a number of types of industrial change – growth, transition, and decline – which, whilst again refreshingly open, is also too wide ranging to be that analytically useful.[34]

In a way these ideas are both too comprehensive about industrial policy at the same time as they are not quite comprehensive enough. For instance they do not even capture the full diversity of objectives that have adhered to the American policy debate as discussed above. But they do have the virtue of highlighting how industrial policy is one of those rather unusual areas of potential economic policy activity around which a very broad range of issues crystallize. Indeed, this is one of the main problems with industrial policy. It seems to attract too many potential objectives. It becomes over-burdened with policy initiatives and is continually drawn in to solve problems that either are not within its purview in the first place or which it just cannot be properly developed to address. Industrial policy is thus typified by too many objectives and not enough instruments, and it is continually 'over-determined' by other policy areas.

For instance Figure 2.8 shows the array of policy areas that have traditionally been articulated with industrial policy, both in the US and in other countries, notably the UK. Thus industrial policy can be called upon at times to solve employment problems, problems of regional imbalance, defence policy issues, social welfare issues, and housing policy amongst others. In addition tax and fiscal policy can substitute for industrial policy, as can domestic and/or international competitiveness and trade policy, educational and training policy, or even financial policy. Thus policies associated with the reorganization of the financial system in an attempt to increase investable money capital for industry can stand in for industrial policy proper. What tends to happen with industrial policy therefore is that it gets fused together with this range of other policy areas and/or it gets substituted by other policy areas, or a combination of the two of these. This makes unravelling what is the specific domain of industrial policy rather difficult, but quite necessary. It is necessary because only in this way can the particular limited role of industrial policy and its legitimate arena of operation be analytically separated from these other aspects. This is important if strategic consider-ations of the way industrial policy is to be re-articulated to these other areas, and to which ones, are to be more clearly made. Thus the issue is not one of the total divorce of industrial policy from the other areas specified. That would be impossible since industrial policy will inevitably be articulated to other problems and issues. It is rather to suggest its prior analytical separation and subsequent analytical re-articulation according to some strategic calculation.

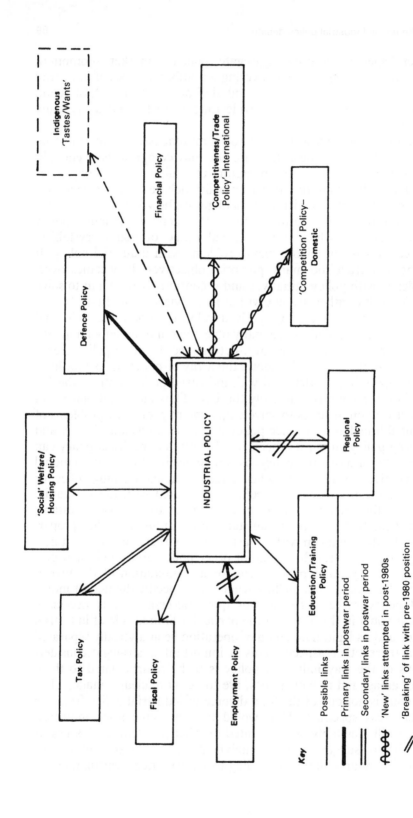

Figure 2.8 The primary level: industrial policy and other policy areas.

This articulation of industrial policy with other policy areas, which is not just a mere 'co-ordination' of them, is termed the primary level in Figure 2.8. But we also need a more limited specification of the elements involved with industrial policy in a narrower sense. Here it is suggested emphasis should be given to the conditions of production and marketing involving issues of the structure of industry, technology, use of the capital stock, managerial efficiency, etc. Appropriate policy to address these issues is termed industrial policy at a secondary level, broadly speaking. But then any specific industrial policy actually operative would involve objectives associated with these areas in combination with some other policy area(s) illustrated in Figure 2.8. For instance, UK industrial policy has traditionally been directed towards solving the problem of employment and to meet defence policy requirements. In a sense then it has been 'over-determined' by these twin policy objectives. It has continually been 'overtaken' by the need to prop up employment in declining industries, usually working indirectly through regional policy programmes, and the needs imposed upon it by Britain's rather unique defence policy posture. Attempts at 'modernizing' British industry, for instance, in an attempt to articulate it to an international competitiveness objective, or to enhance trade policy, or even to revamp the domestic competitive environment, have largely failed. Thus this industrial policy has involved aspects of both the primary and secondary levels in a specific complex combination.

Turning now to the US we would have first of all to put industrial policy heavily under a question mark in terms of Figure 2.8. The issue needs to be posed, as indeed it has been in this chapter, whether the US has even had a proper industrial policy in the sense outlined briefly above. The 'industrial policy debate' could be seen as in effect an attempt to develop such a policy arena in the US. Thus in the case of the US, as we have seen, a rather surrogate industrial policy has operated alternatively via the tax system and trade/international competitiveness policy. The US has not been able to develop any distinct institutionally located industrial policy instruments and hence construct an industrial policy arena, at least at the national level.

Thus in the centre of a Figure 2.8 drawn specifically for the US, we would probably place 'tax policy' rather than 'industrial policy'. But just as with the case of the discussion of the UK and industrial policy, the US has been characterized by an 'over-determined' tax policy. The tax code has been burdened with meeting too many objectives – raising federal revenues, creating an equitable personal tax system, helping with the amelioration of 'welfare' hardships, addressing housing policy issues, standing in for industrial policy on investment, and so on. With too many objectives and not enough independent instruments, a thoroughly complicated system emerges which can fail to achieve any of its objectives properly. A similar over-complex industrial policy emerged in the UK, where attempts were made to address too many issues through the limited number of independent policy mechanisms made available to it.

Thus industrial policies need to be pared down to address a limited set of issues. In doing so, however, the specifically industrial policy initiatives may well come into conflict with other quite legitimate and desirable policy objectives. For instance, supposing one breaks the traditional link between industrial policy and employment policy, as was suggested above was the implication of Thurow's (1985) position in the US debate; in this case industrial policy would not necessarily be directly articulated to employment policy goals.

Indeed it may well mean the displacement of labour and the creation of more unemployment in the first instance. In addition this might create added welfare problems. Should we then abandon the particular industrial policy adopted or try to ameliorate its effects by attaching additional constraints upon it? In doing so the policy itself is likely to be weakened and even rendered moribund or collapse – as so often has been the case in the UK when attempts have been made at a radical modernization of the industrial structure for instance. The argument here would be to avoid this course but rather to develop independent instruments to address these added policy issues in their own right and within their own domain, so to speak. This is what is meant by the necessity of analytically separating these issues out beforehand. Thus, though more unemployment might be initially created by an industrial policy, that unemployment would need to be 'taken care of' or addressed by a different set of policy instruments than industrial policy ones. Similarly with welfare objectives. Indeed it is suggested that industrial policy is not the legitimate domain explicitly to address these issues – it has to be confined to areas where it has some purchase.

The UK is in a rather more fortunate position with this respect than is say the US. This is because it already has well established and comprehensive programmes installed in these other areas, as well as a tradition of industrial policy initiatives.

This argument is not one supporting a simple 'trickle down' conception of industrial policy. With such an approach the beneficial consequences of industrial restructuring in terms of growth and new employment opportunities are assumed eventually and 'automatically' to reach those initially adversely affected since they will also benefit – if in the long run. In the meantime they must cope the best they can.

The argument here on the other hand is to calculate these potential costs and benefits quite carefully and to provide appropriate amelioratory policies within the other affected domains concerned. The impact of industrial readjustments are likely to be multi-dimensional – and not all of these effects can be addressed by industrial policy alone. It is not useful or legitimate either to attach them to industrial policy or to expect industrial policy to 'solve' them.

This discussion also allows us to press an alternative idea about exactly what industrial policy might be articulated with in the long-term. The discussion above has offered a critique of traditional conceptions of industrial policy in terms of its often implicit and unrecognized over-determined character. Putting things somewhat simply, there have been two main cases. The first of these has articulated industrial policy directly to employment goals and defence policy broadly speaking. The second has articulated it to the 'trade policy/international competitiveness/domestic competition' complex. It is with this latter case that the US and particularly the UK are at present toying. But neither country has so far been able firmly to establish this latter complex, and indeed in the US in particular the industrial policy/defence policy sub-complex looks set for renewed vigour with the Reagan Star Wars initiative. Clearly those arguing for a 'renewed international competitiveness' are pressing for some form of the latter main complex to be robustly established in the US. But the problem here is one outlined above about the near zero-sum character of this approach if pushed to the limit. So is there an alternative?

In the upper right-hand part of Figure 2.8 an articulation between industrial policy and something called 'indigenous tastes and wants' is suggested. This refers to a first-instance possibility only in as much that it would necessarily have to be secondarily supported by some form of an international competitiveness link as well. By 'indigenous tastes and wants' is meant those demands originating from domestic populations which arise from deeply entrenched social and cultural trends.[35] It means identifying such trends, the demands that are likely to arise from them, and then developing one's industrial policy to meet those demands. But this is not quite the same as the 'tending to the front yard' approach suggestion by Gordon (1986) and mentioned above (see note 25). Gordon would emphasize social needs of the domestic population, whereas the idea behind 'tastes and wants' is wider than this. It is neutral as to whether these are 'needs' or 'wants'. 'Needs' implies some mechanism which calculates these for a population and then provides them in an administrative fashion. 'Wants' expresses rather something that can arise without a socialized calculation in this sense and which can be demanded in the form of market-type relations. Thus the approach here is to stress the fact that indigenous 'tastes' and 'wants' can and will quite legitimately arise as market demands do, and will have to be met in the context of those demands. They are not calculated for a population but by it, as the consequential basis of social and cultural trends. However, this is not to deny the pertinence of the 'social needs' approach either, which would also have its place. It is only to recognize it as playing a secondary role for the foreseeable future within the overall pattern of the determination of social consumption. The problem then is to anticipate the demands likely to arise in the future which are themselves predicated on underlying social relations and the likely trends in their characteristics. In a sense this is what many societies do or try to do already, but what is being suggested here is to bring this to the forefront in a more conscious manner and directly articulate it to industrial policy. A prioritized set of likely long-term culturally specific developments and their economic consequences might then be installable within mechanisms of industrial assessment.

The last few paragraphs have strayed somewhat from industrial policy itself in an attempt to specify one of its likely relationships to another discrete policy/social domain. Let us now return to industrial policy at a secondary level, in the context of Figure 2.9. Here three core elements of industrial policy are characterized – strategic investment, process technology, and market 'protection'. These have been emphasized as the three main areas by Williams *et al.* (Chapter 4 of this book). The point here is that any industrial policy should aim at a satisfactory balance between all three features, they argue. It is little use providing massive strategic investment resources, for instance, while directing these at the wrong process technology or effectively forgetting about 'protecting' the market in some satisfactory way. In fact Williams *et al.* argue that this is just what has happened in the UK recently with steel, coal, and cars.

Protecting the market is put in inverted commas to indicate that

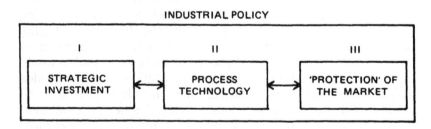

Figure 2.9 The second level: industrial policy elements.

this need not imply traditional outright 'protectionism' as criticized above. It means that some attention must be given to the long-term demand pattern — and to safeguard this as well as possible — if a supply is to be provided via large amounts of strategic investment. It is little use undertaking massive investment in new or upgraded facilities while leaving the demand to take care of itself via totally free market arrangements. There are a number of ways in which the market can be protected which do not necessarily involve tarriffs or quotas – e.g. long-term contractual agreements, privileged buying, other orderly marketing arrangements, 'value-added' agreements, and so on.

One other important element in industrial policy – something often ignored by commentators or relegated to a very secondary position – is the issue of appropriate process technology (element II in Figure 2.9). In the US context recently this aspect has received considerable attention so it will be worth reviewing this discussion before drawing out some further implications for the UK.

6 The organization of production and industrial policy

The single most important explanation for the world wide decline for US manufacturing competitiveness is management's view of the *manufacturing function*, its role, and how that ought to be carried out. Thus restoring that competitive edge requires a basic change in philosophy, perspective, and approach. (Wheelwright, 1985, p. 27, emphasis added)

It is with the idea of the 'manufacturing function' that Wheelwright and other progressive professors of business administration have been trying to develop a renewed emphasis on industrial restructuring in the US. They argue that the problems of US manufacturing firms are not fundamentally the result of foreign competitive pressure, high labour costs, or too much government interference, but rather of crucial weakness in US management practices, and these problems are not uniquely American (Abernathy *et al.* 1983; Lawrence and Dyer, 1983; Hayes and Wheelwright, 1984; Clark *et al.*, 1985).

For these authors it is the 'American modern management approach' which constitutes the problem. This encompasses contemporary organization and control theory, financial portfolio management, and the 'marketing concept', amongst other things. These in turn emphasize analytical detachment and strategic elegance over 'hands on' experience and well managed line operations, short-term results rather than long-term goals and capabilities, and the management of marketing and financial resources at the expense of manufacturing and technical resources.

Organizational and control theories promote the adoption of a number of relatively autonomous profit centres as the ideal management structure. While this might be a flexible approach, and one capable of responding quickly where responsiveness to changing consumer needs and product differentiation is at a premium, in an environment of steady or rapid economic growth it becomes unsuitable for periods of major product or process change. Under these circumstances emphasis shifts to R & D management within the firm, since existing products and assets can be quickly rendered obsolete. But managing R & D does not sit easily with the profit centre approach. It tends to be a separate and autonomously organized activity, not clearly integrated with the profit centre management structure, and this just at a time when it needs to be foregrounded and closely integrated with the other aspects of the business. In addition the assessment of profit centres (and even R & D activity) tends to be solely on the basis of financial results where 'bottom line' rates of return on capital invested press for a short-term 'payback' environment.

This unsatisfactory character of financial forms of calculation is re-inforced in times of stagnant growth and rapid technological change by the overriding commitment of firms to improve their rate of return on investment (ROI). This can be achieved either by increasing profits – which is a difficult and long-term process – or by reducing investment, which is easier and short-term in character. The result is a tendency to go for the latter response, i.e. to delay replacement investment, replace with less expensive (or less productive) investment, or to replace with a rapid payback type of investment. This compounds manufacturing problems.

Such tendencies are encouraged by management development, promotion, and evaluation procedure, it is argued. Management personnel have increasingly been drawn from financial, accounting, and legal experts who have little 'hands on' experience in marketing, production, or engineering. These are increasingly trained in 'strategic skills' designed to cut through the complexities of messy problems while standing aloof from the nitty-gritty details of line management and detailed engineering production problems. In addition, management expectations and aspirations are propelled by a 'fast track' mentality, in which quickness and decisiveness are the key to success, switching around within and between organizations being the mode of gaining promotion, and short-term bonuses on year-end performance are central to recognition and remuneration.

All of this is overlaid by the manner in which the vertically integrated, multi-divisional, diversified conglomerate form of manufacturing organization has arisen and developed over the long-boom phase of economic growth. This has meant management becoming increasingly exercised in looking for acquisition opportunities, fighting off unwelcome merger attempts, or divesting unprofitable business lines that do not fit. Most of the conglomerate businesses so formed have developed for financial reasons rather than for productive ones increasingly awkward productive fits have emerged where there is little possibility of serious and efficient linkages between different parts of the business, and where management skills become ones of 'brokering' between the various parts of the business, or of a purely corporate portfolio exercise akin to financial management (Scherer, 1986). In this situation the quality of corporate debt deteriorates – control is bought by increasing debt (the issues of 'junk bonds') – as does the quality of productive output. It leads to an approach suggesting there is little need to invest, build, or develop anything oneself. Given enough capital and good financial management, anything can be bought and any problem divested. There is no need to invest in internal proprietary process development, for instance, or to develop and sustain a small number of highly focused product lines.

As far as the 'marketing concept' is concerned, this suggests that new products and ideas should only flow from consumer analysis and should be tested exhaustively for consumer reactions before being introduced. It tends to lead to imitative designs of a minor product differentiation type. The problem here is that enthusiasm for product innovation is dampened by this outlook. It becomes too risky and time consuming, and possibly requires a fundamental re-organization of the whole productive process, which is seen as too disruptive.

Against these systems, and of what amounts to an essentially 'static optimization' and hierarchical perspective in terms of work form and technology management, is pitched the idea of a 'dynamic' and evolutionary perspective on the 'management function'. Firms need to develop as central to their activity a thoroughgoing concept of their manufacturing strategy and let this 'lead' their other functions. Indeed Hayes has suggested that the usual 'rationalistic' manner of conceiving a production strategy needs to be re-thought in this context. Instead of a planning process ordered in the form of 'ends–ways–means', i.e. where objectives (ends) are determined first, followed by the conception of the strategic 'methods' or processes required to meet those goals (ways), and then the assembly of the resources necessary to implement the chosen strategy (means), what is needed is a 'means' based process which leads the 'ways–ends' elements. Where the world of competition is non-predictable, upsetting any clear logical path that might be drawn across it, 'static optimization' to meet clearly defined goals in a classic top-down hierarchical fashion will not work. Rather the investment in the development of productive capabilities along as wide a front as possible is suggested, allowing the technological and organization strengths of the firm at the 'bottom-end', so to speak (i.e. its 'means'), dictate more the exploitation of innovative ideas and products that might arise there. This should then be grafted on to a flexible and discontinuous planning process that integrates these initiatives into a strategic conception of the 'line of business' in which the firm is located, but one which also allows it to evolve dynamically to meet competitive challenges as they emerge (Hayes, 1985). This is the task set up by highlighting the 'manufacturing function'.

In mounting this challenge Hayes and his associates have also developed a critique of two of the most widely held conceptions in management decision-making, namely the central importance of economics of scale and discounted cash flow (DCF) techniques for making investment decisions. Rather than economies of scale, Hayes and Wheelright (1984) stress various forms of diseconomies of scale. These are:

1 distributional diseconomies which arise because of the increasing cost of distribution to dispersed customers as production becomes more concentrated – total delivered cost may increase, as can the time taken to deliver, which itself undermines competitive advantage and a flexible response;
2 bureaucratic diseconomies arising from increased size and difficulties of management;
3 diseconomies of confusion which emerge in the context of increasing number of products, processes, and specialists within a given plant; and finally
4 diseconomies of vulnerability to risk — multi-plant operation increases the possibility of interruption of supply if one plant becomes inoperational for some reason.

In opposition to these is introduced the idea of a 'minimum economic size' of plant; the smallest plant unit that is competitively and operationally viable.

With respect to DCF techniques, the argument here is that these cannot adequately deal with strategic investments which involve either the strong likelihood of retaliatory moves by competitors, or which imply an interdependent chain of further investments, or which have hidden 'soft' investment consequences like necessary programming and working capital implications (Hayes and Garvin, 1982; Malpas, 1983; Myers, 1984). In addition Kaplan (1986) suggests the DCF has inhibited American manufacturers from installing 'computer integrated manufacturing' (CIM) systems in attempts to gain strategic competitive advantage, because it is biased towards short-term marginal adjustments of an incremental investment type.[36]

Alongside this critique of management practices has emerged a more general concern with the future of mass-production technologies as a whole. For instance, in an influential book Piore and Sabel (1984) argue that the interruption of the long boom at the end of the 1970s heralded the demise of mass-production techniques as the paradigmatic form of production process technology, installing a new paradigm instead which they term 'flexible specialization'. Such 'flexible specialization' represents a response to the increasing demand for product differentiation by consumers and the growing interdependent character of national economies, which in turn produces a fragmentation of domestic markets. With 'small batch' or 'niche' demand resulting, firms are being forced to abandon their previous mass-production strategies and develop new more flexible production systems that can adapt to the rapidly changing patterns of demand that emerge, it is claimed.

In fact there are two somewhat different ways in which 'flexible specialization' is discussed in the literature. On the one hand flexible specialization is seen to involve the break up of large firms or plants where previously mass production had thrived. It is small and medium-sized firms that most adequately fit the new flexible production regime, it is suggested, and what is more these firms are increasingly linking together within local areas to form networks of interdependent and complementary productive systems. Piore and Sabel cite the Emilia–Romagna region of Italy as a prime example of this new 'paradigm', though this is also generalized to include parts of Southern Germany, Denmark, and the Lyon area of France.

But secondly there is a different way in which flexible specialization is discussed. This revolves around the introduction of 'flexible manufacturing systems' (FMS) into factory production but where these are not as yet seen as necessarily implying any abandonment of mass-production, though they may still lead to the production of relatively small batch but standardized products. Such flexible manufacturing systems integrate a variety of functions such as loading, unloading, storing parts, changing tools automatically, and the data processing activities of manufacturing processes, into co-ordinated production centres. These centres are increasingly being controlled by computers to produce small or medium-sized, totally automated production lines. They are designed to provide diversification of parts and assemblies in batches.

To a large extent these two different senses of 'flexible organization' are run together in Piore and Sabel's analysis to provide their idea of flexible specialization. Thus it is small firms employing specially adapted FMSs, linked together at a local level via familial, ethnic, or contractual ties to form a set of robust interdependencies, that represent the new paradigmatic form of production organization. Added to this are some additional new production operation systems like 'materials requirement planning', 'just-in-time' process organization, and 'optimized production technology', which enhance the flexibility requirement.

Suggestive though this idea of 'flexible specialization' is, it is problematical on at least three major counts. In the first place, as was briefly mentioned above, FMS need not imply the break up of the large factory or the end of mass-production of standardized components or products. Flexible manufacturing systems are rapidly being introduced into European production (UN Economic Bulletin for Europe, 1985), but still within the context of large plants producing relatively standardized commodities. They allow for 'batch production' and are hence flexible in this sense but do not imply any necessary undermining of mass-production technology as such. Product differentiation and variation can be introduced via minor design embellishments which can easily be incorporated into FMS technology. In addition a good many of the peripheral flexible operating systems attached to FMSs are not peculiar to it. They can be introduced into production processes of an older and quite conventional type, e.g. 'just-in-time' stock processing, and work-in-progress control mechanisms in the context of 'Fordist' mass-production technologies.

Second, it is not clear that the emphasis on 'flexibility' and the presumed end of 'standardization' is anything but a temporary response to the economic recession of the late 1970s and early 1980s. There are for instance some clear economic and social advantages of the relative standardization of components and commodities with long production runs. Continual and frequent changes in the internal production process of a firm can have detrimental effects on its labour force, on its productivity, and on its financial position. Such disruption puts strains on the labour force, it can mean lower productivity, and it increases the uncertainty of the business environment and consequently increases financial risk. It also has disadvantages for consumers as well in terms of ease of use and maintenance of products. The pressure for 'flexibility' may therefore be worth resisting.

In addition, any tendency observed towards product differentiation and 'niche' production by firms could represent just a defensive response to the slowing down of growth or stagnation of markets over the last ten years. Under such circumstances a desperate search for sales ensues in which the characteristics of variation and differentiation take on a particular significance in both producers' and consumers' eyes. As adjustments are made, however, and as a more steady pattern of growth emerges (even if still quite modest by postwar standards) the advantages of standardization for both producers and consumers could re-emerge. To promote 'flexible specialization' at the expense of standardized mass production as the general mechanism of economic organization could therefore lead to a weakening of competitive position in the long term.

Finally there is a problem of the evidence for the argument about 'flexible specialization' displacing 'mass production' in the advanced industrialized countries. While there exists some indication that in Italy the small-firm sector is increasing in importance relative to large production facilities (Zanetti, 1983; Weiss, 1984), it is not at all clear that such tendencies are very far advanced in other countries. Certain small areas or even regions of Germany, France and Denmark may indicate the process, but their significance in terms of overall GNP is not established. In addition one reason for the demise of the large-firm sector and of 'mass production' has been the rundown of manufacturing capacity in a number of the industrialized countries, which has traditionally been the main sector for mass-production and large companies, rather than because of any 'indigenous' increase of the small firm/flexibly organized sectors within manufacturing. Furthermore, as mentioned earlier, the trend in the US as well as in the UK over recent years has been for a 'merger-movement' creating even larger diversified holding-company type conglomerates rather than a break-up trend resulting in smaller firms.

In considering any lessons to be learned from this discussion of American responses to the decline of the 'manufacturing function', we should, as a result, perhaps place more emphasis on the former set of arguments with respect to 'management practices' than on arguments about 'flexible specialization'. Crucial to this is the way the factory itself is organized and run.

However, there are in addition some more traditional issues about the progressive rundown of critical parts of the manufacturing base such as machine tool production which are important. Table 2.7 shows the production and trade position of the ten most important producers of machine tools in 1985. It is clear that the US has a major trade problem here but also increasingly a production problem in that American home production is growing more slowly than is Japan's, Germany's, and that of other countries, while its consumption is increasing roughly at the same rate. This relative decline in the American industry has been partly attributed to the Pentagon undermining its efficiency via the manner it distributed defence contracts to industrial firms. In its contracts with machine

Table 2.7 Most important machine tool producers and their trade position
(1985 US $millions-estimates).

Country	Production	Trade		
		Exports	Imports	Surplus (deficit)
Japan	5,269.7	2,098.9	222.5	1,876.4
West Germany	3,123.1	1,899.8	591.4	1,308.4
Soviet Union*	3,015.0	193.7	1,291.1	(1,097.4)
US	2,575.0	455.0	1,725.0	(1,270.0)
Italy	1,056.4	611.9	193.5	418.4
Switzerland	954.7	832.8	174.7	658.1
East Germany*	789.3	750.2	118.7	631.5
UK	722.9	335.6	343.1	(6.5)
France	468.0	228.3	350.0	(121.7)
People's Republic of China**	453.3	34.2	136.7	(102.5)

*Country with controlled currency whose official rate may not represent real
values.
**Rough estimate from fragmentary data.
Source: Adapted from 'Japan widens machine-tool gap', *American Machinist and
Automated Manufacturing*, February, 1986, p. 89.

tool producers, for instance, it assigned cost a 'weight' in the overall
selection criteria of only 15 per cent. As a result, costs escalated
(Melman, 1983, p. 5). US manufacturers also responded to the
introduction of numerically controlled machine tools by de-skilling
their labour force rather than preserving this element and using it to
enhance productivity.

However, perhaps the main element to re-emphasize in this
debate is to recognize that it is not so much the introduction of new
automated machinery into factories that is the key to solving the
problem of the 'manufacturing function', but rather the close attention focused upon how the complex production process is organized
as a whole (Blumenthal and Dray, 1985). 'Automation' as such is no
solution. More important are elements such as the detailed
relationships between design and manufacturing within the more
general R & D process (Westney and Sakakibara, 1986), or the
organizational links between manufacturers and systems development firms within the semiconductor industry for instance (Borrus,
Millstein, and Zysman, 1983; Ferguson, 1983).

7 Lessons for the UK and conclusions

Inasmuch as the UK displays many of the features of the US economy discussed above, the discussion and criticism of the various remedies promoted in the US debate are as appropriate to the UK as they are in the US case. Indeed in emphasizing various elements of the US debate the analysis has already been half looking over its shoulder at the UK economy and its similar set of problems and proposed remedies. In this concluding section, however, a number of particular features of 'industrial policy' which are both of a more general interest and of specific import in the UK situation are focused upon for final comment, plus one or two other issues only peripherally mentioned so far.

Perhaps the main point to emphasize from the above analysis – something already highlighted in the American context – is the likely political constraints on any industrial policy initiatives. While the UK has operated an industrial policy of varying emphasis over the postwar period, the political robustness of this has been quite suspect. In an atmosphere of likely heightened political tensions of the late 1980s careful consideration must be afforded this aspect. Under these circumstances the launching of a very high profile set of new institutional proposals to address 'industrial decline' is unlikely to be successful in the long run. New national 'planning' and 'co-ordinating' bodies, as have been proposed by all sides in the American debate, are unlikely to be implemented there or, one might add, in the UK either.[37]

This is not an argument for doing nothing substantial however. It is quite possible to change the ways a number of existing institutions function that are already associated with industrial policy – like the DTI, NEDO, the MSC, and Treasury, even the Bank of England – without adding an additional layer of bureaucratic departments on to this administrative machinery. First priority should thus be given to adapting existing institutions or adding new elements to these rather than to the wholesale creation of 'alternatives'.[38] Associated with this is the need to keep careful control over the style and manner of presentation of any industrial policy so as not to make too many grandiose claims or be seen to undermine too many vested interests. Vested interests need to be attacked and radical initiatives taken, but these should be managed within the context of existing administrative arrangements as far as is possible.

One notable exception to this is likely to be Labour's National Investment Bank idea. Already far advanced in the planning stage, this is set to occupy a central place in Labour strategy. But even here caution needs to be exercised in terms of its likely effectiveness and robustness. In the US, while the proposed new RFC is presently in abeyance, it could easily be revived. This could be made more likely under conditions of a continually deteriorating economic performance where other policy suggestions have been more or less exhausted, and would be more politically acceptable if introduced by a conservative Republican administration. Neither of these two conditions is totally ruled out by present trends.[39] Thus the US too could end up with an industrial development bank similar in conception to the UK's.

One other issue of intense debate in the US around industrial policy concerns whether it is possible to 'pick winners' as implied by such a policy. Those against industrial intervention have argued that it is impossible for administrative personnel to decide on what are going to be the successful product innovations of the future, and support industries or sectors producing them. Even some of the strong advocates of industrial policy like Thurow and Harvard Business School professors have taken this position, arguing instead for what amounts to more of an emphasis on 'creating the right environment' or 'reforming management education'.

But this issue cannot be ducked. Advocating any kind of industrial policy implies some discrimination between those industries, sectors, firms, or products which are to be supported in some way and those not so favoured. And it means trying to 'create' winners rather than simply 'picking' them. This cannot be avoided. It is not to be expected, however, that all those sectors or products supported will prove to be successful. Some 'losers' will inevitably also be created. The objective must be to develop a 'portfolio' of projects where the successes outweigh the failures.

There seem no reasons why properly trained and recruited public servants cannot foresee market trends and identify potentially successful projects, even though they may have been somewhat indifferent at this in the past. Judged against the dismal record of British management's efforts in this respect, their attempts are probably as good if not better. More important are the criteria by which any industrial policy might be organized. Given the rather desperate state of British manufacturing and the fact that political caution is likely to be of the essence in the medium term, a number of possibilities present themselves.

Accepting that some satisfactory long-term strategic calculation has been made with regard to the articulation of industrial policy and other policy areas, as discussed in section 5, those sectors with high value added have often been advocated for special treatment. However high value added is not necessarily the correct criterion to apply, since it can lead to an emphasis on sectors like oil and gas, basic chemicals, or other mineral extraction (these demonstrate the highest value added in the US and the UK). Rather criteria like 'high income elasticity' or 'rapid technical progress' would seem more appropriate, though perhaps also more difficult to measure and assess. Accepting this, however, the next step might be to go to 'best practice' firms in those sectors or product ranges identified and see what they want from an industrial policy. Thus the emphasis would be on tailoring any policy in the first instance to the requirements of such firms, but using proposed public assistance as a lever to get firms to do things they might not at present be contemplating, or indeed might be resistant to.

Second, protecting the market must be taken seriously. Here selective tariffs may prove necessary but developing cartels can be seen as an alternative to this. As is argued elsewhere, within the European context cartels are developing in a number of areas to cope with the problems of stagnant demand and intense price competition (Thompson, 1986a, Chapter 7). Public policy could be brought to bear here (as indeed it already has with sectors like steel) to promote a negotiated 'allocation' of the market between producers and help eliminate excess capacity. The usual economists' reaction of horror to these trends is an inappropriate response under the circumstance. A more sensible approach is to advocate a careful monitoring of these trends (which are happening anyway), to set time limits over which they might operate, and even to encourage their organization where it seems necessary and appropriate (see Bower and Rhenman, 1985).

Another way of protecting the market is to institute 'domestic content agreements' with producers of key imported products. In a peculiar way the UK is in a strong position with respect to moves such as these precisely because import penetration is so high. The UK still represents a large market for items such as motor vehicles or domestic electrical and 'white goods'. Overseas based producers might then be persuaded to adopt such content agreements to protect their relatively lucrative existence within the UK markets.

A final issue to raise here is perhaps the most difficult and intransigent from the point of view of industrial policy. This concerns the 'process technology' elements of Figure 2.9's discussion of industrial policy. As the subsequent discussion of the American debate indicated, most of the problems have to do with managerial practices which are rather beyond any easy public regulation or re-formulation. Clearly some institutional re-organization is possible which could affect this area. Probably the most obvious would be some drastic change in the form of management education, but this can only be a long-term project. Meanwhile British industry is likely to be stuck with very poor quality management, which has shown itself virtually incapable of developing a robust 'manufacturing function'. At present the trend is towards production/design deals and joint venture liaisons with more efficient and progressive foreign based firms. But as a recent survey of American motor car manufacturer's attempts at this has shown, it can lead to all the high value added and technically progressive elements being conducted abroad rather than in the home country itself (Reich and Mankin, 1986). The result is simple assembly operations being increasingly conducted within the USA (and the UK), with little prospect of developing and driving forward with new product innovations in these areas.[40] A major problem then, and one around which an intense national debate needs to be organized, is what can be done to enhance the 'manufacturing function', conceived in terms of management practices, for the British economy.

Acknowledgement

This paper was written while I was a Research Associate at the Centre for European Studies, Harvard University, Cambridge, Massachusetts. I would like to thank the Centre and its staff, particularly Peter Hall, for the hospitality offered me in the US. Also thanks are due to the Open University Overseas Travel Committee and the Faculty of Social Science Research Committee for partly financing this research. Vivienne Brown and Lawrence Harris kindly commented on this paper, for which I also thank them. Any remaining errors of fact or interpretation are of course my own.

Notes

1. Such is the flavour of Norton's (1986) recent somewhat idiosyncratic survey.
2. This is the line most strongly advanced by the Brookings Institution, among others. See Schultze (1983), Rivlin (1984), and Lawrence (1984) in particular.
3. Typical arguments can be found in Badaracco and Yoffie (1983), Heclo (1986), and in Russell (1986). Political constraints are also stressed in Allen and Rishikof's (1985) useful review.
4. The Congressional Budget Office found that government aid to business amounted to $132 billion in 1984. This did not include $140 billion spent by the Defense Department on procurement, nor a further $110 billion subsidy to medical and housing services (Lodge and Crum, 1985, p. 46). However a survey by Anton for 1984 revealed $500 billion being spent by the federal government to promote private sector development activity (not including housing and defence spending), and $50 billion by state governments (A. Alfred Taubman Center, 1985, pp. 2–3).
5. These seemingly paradoxical results are confirmed by the UK's position. It was also losing its share of world trade at the same time as it was becoming more internationally cost competitive, rather like the US. See Thompson (1987) for an explanation of this, and below in this text.
6. President's Commission on Industrial Competitiveness (1985), vol. II, Chart 9, p. 15.
7. See Magaziner and Reich (1982) Chapter 2, for a summary of the evidence. Overall import penetration increased from 7 per cent to 22 per cent during the 1970s (Krieger, 1986, p. 130).

8. Such an emphasis on changes in the quality attributes of American products *vis-à-vis* their foreign counterparts has been stressed by Abernathy *et al.* (1983) to account for the demise of the car industry in particular. See also Hayes and Wheelright (1984) for a more generalized approach centrally involving this aspect.

9. For a useful summary of the arguments involved see Bosworth (1984) Chaptei 2, and Thurow (1985).

10. The problems American industry has had in competing in a range of industrial markets are well documented in Zysman and Tyson (1983), Lawrence and Dyer (1983), as well as in Magaziner and Reich (1982).

11. For a thorough review of Magaziner and Reich's book, which also deals with a wider set of issues associated with industrial policy in the US, see Williams, Chapter 3 in this book.

12. It is interesting to observe how the more radical proposals of the UAW were tempered by the AFL-CIO in the process of agreeing on a general labour movement approach. For instance the UAW suggested a National Strategic Planning Board and a National Strategic Development Bank (UAW, 1983). The names of these were changed when they appeared in the AFL-CIO document, to National Industrial Policy Board and Reconstruction Finance Corporation (AFL-CIO, 1983). In the American context these later names are clearly more comfortable (though still quite radical in spirit), particularly as there had been an RFC during the Roosevelt 'New Deal' administrations (see below). However this was not the end of the matter. When the AFL-CIO's 1983 'White Paper', referred to above, was rendered into a public statement by the Industrial Union Department, the names had again changed to Council of Industrial Competitiveness and Bank of Industrial Competitiveness respectively (actually spelt Competitivemess in the Report – AFL-CIO, 1984, p. 39). Thus, although the essential message in terms of what these organizations might do stayed much the same, the names used to describe them moved; in effect from 'Planning' to 'Competitiveness' (or mess!). As we shall see later, this change prophetically paralleled a change in the terms of the wider debate on industrial policy.

13. The most important of these was introduced in February 1981 and would have created a US Revitalization Bank as a wholly-owned government bank authorized to issue obligations and provide loans and loan guarantees to qualifying business enterprises and local governments. It was proposed to be dedicated to helping cities regain their financial health, and to aid businesses to modernize and expand to provide more employment and improve productivity. It would have begun with capital of $5 billion subscribed by the US Treasury and would have been able to issue obligations up to five times its paid-in capital (Weil, 1983, p. 1,007).

14. Bluestone and Harrison (1982) pp. 210–14; Bowles, Gordon, and Weisskopf (1983) pp. 208–20; Watkins (1981).

15. Reich (1982a), (1982b), and (1983); and in Kantrow (1983).

16. Such a reconciliation has been a constant theme in the writings of prominent Democratic intellectuals during the early 1980s. Besides Reich (1983) see Thurow (1983 and 1985) and Kuttner (1984) in particular.

17. The kind of analysis which emphasizes problems at a cultural level – of 'ideologies' and 'myths' – is also stressed by Lodge (1984) in the context of American industrial policy.

18. See Ferguson and Rogers (1986) for a discussion of the continuity in basic American values despite the Reagan election victories. These authors, however, by concentrating upon 'ideologies', under-estimate the changes actually wrought in American institutions and society by 'Reaganism'.

19. Tax advantages for bonus payments were a feature introduced by the UK Conservative government in their 1986 Budget. This move was associated with the attempt to encourage a 'share-economy' (see Weitzman, 1984, Chapter 7, for a justification of this).
20. In 1985 IRAs were restricted to an investment of $2,000 maximum tax-deferred contributions per person per year, but their future was in balance in 1986 as new tax legislation was passing through Congress. See below in the text where this reform is discussed more fully.
21. These points are most explicitly made in an exchange of views on industrial policy between Bluestone and Thurow (see *Working Papers* (1980) and also *Working Papers* (1983) which contains an interview with Harrison and Blue-stone).
22. This point is made well by Bosworth (1984) pp. 180–5.
23. At present US competition policy does not allow such co-operative agreements common in other countries – though it tends to turn a blind eye to them when they have occurred.
24. For instance, 'when it comes to international competition, America wants to be a winner with a standard of living second to none. To win America has to compete, but also has to co-operate' (Thurow, 1985, p. 323).
25. This position has been rightly criticized by Gordon (1986), who instead advocates a 'tending the (American) front yard approach' – i.e. attending to the domestic needs of the population first and foremost. See below in the main text for further discussion of this approach.
26. This outline of the deficiencies of traditional trade theory would need to be tempered somewhat for a more thorough treatment. In the first place it is not altogether proper to link only natural endowments to comparative advantage as this is only one possible source of competitiveness for different countries in the traditional theory. This also tends to be more 'dynamic' in character than suggested, where technology in particular is conceptualized as a factor of production subject to change and augmentation. Finally the theory of comparative advantage suggests that there are potential gains from trade for both parties, so that the extent to which both (or one country only) gains depends upon the circumstances. For instance the terms of trade may move against a country in a dynamic trading environment such that it need not necessarily gain from trade. Thus 'dynamic theories of comparative advantage' – consequent upon policy manipulation – are more well established in the literature than Zysman and Tyson tend to make out.
27. The MFA's operation in the UK context has recently been analysed in Silbertson (1984).
28. As did the President's own Council of Economic Advisors. See Government Printing Office, 1985b in particular, but also the 1986 edition.
29. Lawrence along with Litan of the Brookings Institute are authors of a recent study of American protectionism (Lawrence and Litman 1986 which argues against quotas in particular, since these serve to increase producer profits. Tariffs on the other hand increase government revenues, and are thus thought less harmful under conditions of budget deficits.
30. In a sense this Brookings Institution approach is paralleled by that argued for in Norton's survey, where he suggests the industrial policy debate has been undermined by an 'automatic' regional re-adjustment in manufacturing and employment creating activity (Norton, 1986).
31. In May 1986 a Bill was pushed through the House of Representatives which was described as a 'get tough' measure to penalize those countries that had an excessive balance of payments surplus with the US but which failed to open up

their home markets to American companies. It would require the president to impose quotas on the imports from such countries and create a $300 million 'war chest' to help exporters counter foreign subsidies, amongst other legislative measures.

32. In addition it should be noted that the dominant current formulation of the idea of reciprocity is characterized by a US insistence on 'free trade in services' in return for 'free imports of commodities'. But 'services' and 'commodities' are not necessarily comparable. For instance financial services – a strong point in the US's favour – can have powerful determining effects on manufacturing, and hence secondarily on commodity circulation itself.

33. The Gramm-Rudman-Hollings Act (passed in 1985) prescribes that federal budget deficits cannot exceed targets that are gradually reduced until the budget is balanced in 1991 (target for 1987, $144 billion). It may be declared unconstitutional by the Supreme Court.

34. See also the collection of papers in Barfield and Schambra (1986) for further discussion of industrial policy definitions, particularly Part One.

35. One instance of this would be the demands that have arisen, say, from the growth of smaller households (e.g. one-parent families) and indeed from smaller urban homes themselves (e.g. the miniaturization of many consumer durables). Another, likely to have a growing impact in the future, is the increasing cultural and regional diversity of many advanced industrialized countries and the consequences this is likely to have for patterns of consumption.

36. This critique of traditional economies of scale and DCF arguments has been taken up by Williams et al. (Chapter 4 of this book) in the context of UK nationalized industries' investment strategies. Here it is suggested that the American writers referred to above argue that DCF is not applicable to strategic investment decisions, whereas Williams et al. argue it is – if only used to justify an already agreed strategy. In fact the American authors are always more cautious than this, making the point that DCF can be legitimately employed in any investment situation if it is handled carefully and sensitively (e.g. Malpas, 1983, p. 124; Myers, 1984; Kaplan, 1986, p. 87).

37. The nature of the American political and administrative system which inhibits the installation of a national industrial strategy is well argued in Heclo (1986). See also Badaracco and Yoffie (1983).

38. The Labour Party's experience with the DEA and the NEB should bear witness to this point.

39. Here a more general issue arises which has been the subject of intensive debate in the US but which is not reviewed in this paper. This concerns the experience of the New Deal era of the 1930s in terms of the capacity of the American political system to generate genuine structural reforms in a time of national economic crisis. It also involves issues of so-called 'strong' and 'weak' state forms and the character of various 'national corporatisms' in organizing a response to economic change. There is an extensive American literature dealing with this, but good representative examples are Skocpol and Finegold (1982) and Weir and Skocpol (1985) on the first aspect, and Katzenstein (1985) on the second.

40. However in the British case this may be better than no car industry at all, which could be the alternative.

References

A. Alfred Taubman Center for Public Policy and American Institutions (1985) *Thinking about Economic Development,* Discussion Paper, Brown University, Providence, Rhode Island.

Abernathy, W.J., Clark, K.B. and **Kantrow, A.M.** (1983) *Industrial Renaissance: Producing a Competitive Edge for America,* Basic Books, New York.

AFL-CIO (1983) *Rebuilding America: A National Industrial Policy,* Industrial Union Department Washington DC.

Allen, C.S. and **Rishikof, H.** (1985) 'Tale thrice told: a review of industrial policy proposals', *Journal of Policy Analysis and Management,* vol. 4, no. 2, pp. 234–249.

AFL-CIO (1984) *Deindustrialization and the Two Tier Society: A Challenge for an Industrial Policy,* Industrial Union Department, Washington DC.

Anton, T.J. and **Reynolds, R.** (nd) *Old Federalism and New Politics for State Economic Development,* A. Alfred Taubman Center for Public Policy and American Institutions, Brown University, Rhode Island.

Anton, J.J. and **West, D.M.** (nd) *Nothing for Something: Popular Reactions to New Industrial Policy,* A. Alfred Taubman Center for Public Policy and American Institutions, Discussion Paper, Brown University, Providence, Rhode Island.

Badaracco, J.L. and **Yoffie, D.B.** (1983) 'Industrial policy: it can't happen here', *Harvard Business Review,* November–December, pp. 97–105.

Barfield, C.E. and **Schambra, W.A.** (1986) *The Politics of Industrial Policy,* American Enterprise Institute for Public Policy Research, Washington DC.

Bluestone, B. and **Harrison, B.** (1982) *The Deindustrialization of America,* Basic Books, New York.

Blume, M.E., Crockett, J.A. and **Friend, I.** (1981) 'Stimulation of capital formation: ends and means', in Watcher, M.L. and Watcher, S.M. (eds) *Towards a New US Industrial Policy,* University of Pennsylvania Press, Philadelphia.

Blumenthal, M. and **Dray, J.** (1985) 'The automated factory: vision and reality', *Technology Review,* January.

Borrus, M., Millstein, J.E. and **Zysman, J.** (1983) 'Trade and development in the semi-conductor industry: Japanese challenge and American response' Chapter 4 of Zysman and Tyson (1983).

Bosworth, B.P. (1984) *Tax Incentives and Economic Growth,* The Brookings Institution, Washington DC.

Bower, J.L. and **Rhenman, E.A.** (1985) 'Benevolent cartels', *Harvard Business Review,* July–August, pp. 124–32.

Bowles, S., Gordon, D.M. and **Weisskopf, T.E.** (1983) *Beyond the Wasteland,* Anchor Press/Doubleday, New York.

Bradford, D.F. (1984) *Blueprints for Basic Tax Reform* (2nd ed.), Tax Analysis, Arlington.

Bradford, D.F. (1986) *Unravelling the Income Tax,* Harvard University Press, Cambridge, Mass.

Carroll, J. *et al.* (1985) 'Economic development policy: why Rhode Islanders rejected the greenhouse compact', *State Government,* vol. 58, no. 3, Fall, pp. 110–112.

Clark, K.B., Hayes, R.H. and **Lorenz, C.** (eds) (1985) *The Uneasy Alliance: Managing the Productivity-Technology Dilemma,* Harvard Business School Press, Boston, Mass.

Disman, A.M. (1983) 'State capital formation and small business needs', *Governmental Finance,* December, pp. 13–21.

Ellsworth, R.R. (1985) 'Capital markets and competitive decline', *Harvard Business Review,* September–October, pp. 171–83.

Ferguson, C.H. (1983) 'The microelectronics industry in distress' *Technology Review,* August–September.

Ferguson, T. and **Rogers, J.** (1986) 'The myth of America's turn to the right', *The Atlantic Monthly,* May, pp. 43–53.

Gordon, D.M. (1986) 'Do we need to be No. 1?' *Atlantic Review,* vol. 257, no. 4, April, pp. 100–8.

Government Printing Office (1985a) *The President's Tax Proposals to the Congress for Fairness, Growth and Simplicity,* Washington DC.

Government Printing Office (1985b) *Economic Report of the President,* Washington DC.

Government Printing Office (1986) *Economic Report of the President,* Washington DC.

Hayes, R.H. (1985) 'Strategic planning – forward in reverse', *Harvard Business Review,* November–December, pp. 111–19.

Hayes, R.H. and **Garvin, D.A.** (1982) *The Discounting Concept and Industrial Disinvestment*', Harvard Business School Case Services, 9-682-077, p. 20.

Hayes, R.H. and **Wheelright, S.C.** (1984) *Restoring our Competitive Edge: Competing through Manufacturing*, Wiley, New York.

Heclo, H. (1986) 'Industrial policy and the executive capacities of government', in Barfield and Schambra (1986), pp. 292–317.

Hodgman, J.F. (1985) in *Seminar on State Initiated Technology Development Programs*, A. Alfred Taubman Center for Public Policy and American Institutions, Brown University, March 1, pp. 15–17.

Johnson, C. (1984) 'The industrial policy debate re-examined', *Californian Management Review*, vol. XXVII, no. 1, Fall, pp. 71–89.

Joint Economic Committee, US Congress (1986) *The American Economy in Transition: From the Second World War to the 21st Century*, Government Printing Office, Washington DC.

Kantrow, A.M. (1983) 'The political realities of industrial policy', *Harvard Business Review*; September–October, pp. 76–86.

Kaplan, R.S. (1986) 'Must CIM be justified by faith alone?' *Harvard Business Review*, March–April, pp. 87–95.

Katzenstein, P.J. (1985) *Small States in World Markets*, Cornell University Press, Ithaca, New York.

King, M.A. and **Fullerton, D.** (eds) (1984) *The Taxation of Income from Capital*, The University of Chicago Press, Chicago.

Krieger, J. (1986) *Reagan, Thatcher and the Politics of Decline*, Polity Press, Cambridge.

Kuttner, R. (1984) *The Economic Illusion*, Houghton Mifflin, Boston.

Labor-Industry Coalition for International Trade (1983) *International Trade, Industrial Policies and the Future of American Industry*, Washington DC.

Lang, M.S. (1985) *Seminar on State Initiated Technology Development Programs*, A. Alfred Taubman Center for Public Policy and American Institutions, Brown University, March 1, pp. 11–14.

Lawrence, P.R. and **Dyer, D.** (1983) *Renewing American Industry*, The Free Press/Collier Macmillan Publishers, New York.

Lawrence, R.Z. (1984) *Can America Compete?*, The Brookings Institution, Washington DC.

Lawrence, R.Z. and **Litan, R.E.** (1986) *Saving Free Trade: A Pragmatic Approach*, Washington DC, Brookings Institution.

Lodge, G.C. (1984) *The American Disease*, Alfred A. Knopf, New York.

Lodge, G.C. and **Crum, W.C.** (1985) 'US competitiveness: the policy tangle', *Harvard Business Review*, January–February, pp. 34–52.

Mckenna, R., **Borrus, M.** and **Cohen, S.** (1984) 'Industrial policy and international competition in high technology', *California Management Review*, vol. XXVI, no. 2, Winter, pp. 15–25.

Magaziner, I.C. and **Reich, R.B.** (1982) *Minding America's Business*, Harcourt Brace Jovanovich, New York.

Malpas, R. (1983) 'The plant after next', *Harvard Business Review*, July–August, pp. 122–30.

Mansfield, E. (1985) 'Public policy toward industrial innovation: an international study of direct tax incentives for research and development' in Clark, Hayes, and Lorenz (1985).

Melman, S. (1983) *Profits Without Production*, Alfred A. Knopf, New York.

Myers, S.C. (1984) 'Finance theory and financial strategy', *Interfaces*, vol. 14, no. 1, January–February, pp. 126–37.

Nehmer, S. and **Love, M.W.** (1985) Textile and apparel: a negotiated approach to international competition in Scott and Lodge (1985), pp. 230–59.

Norton, R.D. (1986) 'Industrial policy and American renewal', *Journal of Economic Literature*, vol. XXIV, March, pp. 1–40.

Phillips, K.P. (1984) *Staying on Top: the Business Case for a National Industrial Policy*, Random House, New York.

Piore, M.J. and **Sabel, C.F.** (1984) *The Second Industrial Divide*, Basic Books, New York.

President's Commission on Industrial Competitiveness (1985) *Global Competition: The New Reality*, US Government Printing Office, Washington DC.

Reich, R.B. (1982a) 'Why the US needs an industrial policy', *Harvard Business Review*, January–February, pp. 74–81.

Reich, R.B. (1982b) 'Making industrial policy', *Foreign Affairs*, Spring, pp. 852–81.

Reich, R.B. (1983) *The Next American Frontier*, Times Books, New York.

Reich, R.B. and **Donahue, J.D.** (1985) *New Deals: the Chrysler Revival and the American System*, Times Books, New York.

Reich, R.B. and **Mankin, E.D.** (1986) 'Joint ventures with Japan give away our future', *Harvard Business Review*; March–April, pp. 78–86.

Revzan, L. (1983) 'Enterprise zones: present status and potential impacts', *Governmental Finance*, December, pp. 31–7.

Rivlin, A. (ed.) (1984) *Economic Choices: 1984*, The Brookings Institution, Washington DC.

Rohatyn, F. (1983) *The Twenty-Year Century*, Random House, New York.

Russell, R.W. (1986) 'Congress and the proposed industrial policy structures', in Barfield and Schambra (1986), pp. 318–32.

Scherer, F.M. (1986) 'Takeovers: present and future dangers', *The Brookings Review*, Winter/Spring, pp. 15–20.

Schultze, C.L. (1983) 'Industrial policy: a dissent', *The Brookings Review*, Fall, pp. 3–12.

Scott, B.R. and **Lodge, G.C.** (eds) (1985) *US Competitiveness in the World Economy*, Harvard Business School Press, Boston, Mass.

Silbertson, A. (1984) *The Multi-fibre Arrangement and the UK Economy*, HMSO, London.

Skocpol, T. and **Finegold, K.** (1982) State capacity and economic intervention in the early new deal', *Political Science Quarterly*, vol. 27, no. 2, Summer, pp. 255–78.

Sub-Committee on Economic Stabilization of the Committee on Banking, Finance and Urban Affairs, House of Representatives (1984) *The Corporate Tax Code as Industrial Policy*, Government Printing Office, Washington DC.

The Business Week Team (1982) *The Reindustrialization of America*, McGraw Hill, New York.

Thompson, G.F. (1986a) *The Conservatives' Economic Policy*, Croom Helm, London.

Thompson, G.F. (1986b) *Economic Calculation and Policy Formation*, Routledge & Kegan Paul, London.

Thompson, G.F. (1987) 'The supply side and industrial policy', Chapter 9 of Thompson, G.F., Brown, V. and Levacič, R. (eds) *Managing the UK Economy: Current Controversies*, Polity Press, Cambridge.

Thurow, L.C. (1982) *What Kind of Industrial Policy?* Democracy Project Reports No. 2, Washington DC

Thurow, L.C. (1983) *The Zero Sum Society*, Basic Books, New York.

Thurow, L.C. (1985) *The Zero Sum Solution*, Simon & Schuster, New York.

UAW (United Auto Workers) (1983), *Solidarity: Blueprint for a Working America*, May 16–31, Detroit, Michigan.

UN Economic Bulletin For Europe (1985) *Flexible Manufacturing: A Step Towards Computerized Industrial Automation*, vol. 37, no. 3, September.

Vogel, E. (1985) 'North Carolina's research triangle: state modernization', in *Comeback*, Simon & Schuster, New York, Chapter 10.

Walton, R.E. (1985) 'From control to commitment: transforming work force management in the United States' in Clark, Hayes and Lorenz (1985).

Watkins, A.J. (1981) 'Felix Rohatyn's biggest deal', *Working Papers Magazine*, September–October, pp. 44–52.

Weil, F.A. (1983) 'US industrial policy: a process in need of a Federal Industrial Co-ordination Board', *Law and Policy in International Business*, vol. 14, no. 4, pp. 981–1039.

Weir, M. and **Skocpol, T.** (1985) 'State structures and the possibilities for "Keynesian" responses to the great depression in Sweden, Britain, and the United States', in Skocpol, T. (ed.) *Bringing the State Back In*, Cambridge University Press, Cambridge.

Weiss, L. (1984) 'The Italian State and small businesses', *Archive of European Sociology*, vol. XXV, pp. 214–41.

Weitzman, M. (1984) *The Share Economy*, Harvard University Press, Cambridge, Mass.

Westney, D.E. and **Sakakibara, K.** (1986) 'Designing the designers', *Technology Review*, April.

Wheelwright, S.C. (1985) 'Restoring the competitive edge in US manufacturing', *California Management Review*, vol. XXVII, no. 3, Spring, pp. 26–41.

Williams, K. (1984) 'Made in USA', *Economy and Society*, vol. 13, no. 4, pp. 484–509 (Chapter 3 of this book).

Williams, K. *et al.* (1986) 'Accounting for failure in the nationalized enterprises: coal, steel and cars since 1970', *Economy and Society*, vol. 15, no. 2, pp. 167–219 (Chapter 4 of this book).

Wolff, A.W. (1985) 'International competitiveness of American industry: the role of US trade policy' in Scott and Lodge (1985), pp. 301–27.

Working Papers (1980) 'Re-industrialization and jobs', *Working Papers*, vol. VII, November–December, pp. 47–59.

Working Papers (1983) 'An interview with Bennett Harrison and Barry Bluestone', vol. 10, no. 1, January, pp. 43–51.

Zanetti, G. (1983) 'The industrial structure and efficiency of the Italian economy: trends and planning aspects', *Review of Economic Conditions in Italy*, no. 2, June, pp. 249–99.

Zorn, C.K. (1986) 'Financing infrastructure to promote economic development in the North Central Region', *Government Finance Review*, April, pp. 29–34.

Zysman, J. and **Cohen, S.** (1983) 'Double or nothing: open trade and competitive industry', *Foreign Affairs*, Summer, pp. 1,113–39.

Zysman, J. and **Tyson, L.** (eds) (1983) *American Industry in International Competition*, Cornell University Press, Ithaca, New York.

3
Made in USA

Karel Williams

Text reviewed

Ira Magaziner and Robert Reich (1982) *Minding America's Business* Harcourt, Brace, New York.

As the world economy developed through the long secular boom from the early 1950s to the early 1970s, international trade in manufactures increased massively; manufactured exports increased in all the advanced countries, and import penetration simultaneously increased in all of them except Japan. With the ending of the long boom, rates of growth of manufacturing value added generally slowed down; in the advanced market economies manufacturing value added grew at a rate of 6.2 per cent in the period 1960–71, while in the period 1970–81 the growth rate fell to 3.3 per cent (Ballance and Sinclair, 1983). The result was an intensification of competition in the international trade in manufactures and this intensification of competition in the 1970s painfully exposed the inadequacies of the manufacturing sector in some national economies. There was cause for concern in America, as in Britain, because productivity growth was mediocre and the national share of world trade in manufactures was declining; the American share of world exports of manufactures slipped from 25 per cent in the late 1950s to 15 per cent in the late 1970s.

In recent years, as the British have continued their inquest into general manufacturing failure, the Americans have begun to investigate the causes of sectoral industrial uncompetitiveness and the remedies for manufacturing decline. Some of the best American work on these issues is being done by management consultants and business school professors. If the devil has the best tunes, so the *Harvard Business Review* has the most cogent articles on the causes of manufacturing uncompetitiveness. Magaziner and Reich's book represents a systematization and extended statement of this approach. To be more exact, their book represents one variant of this approach, in so far as Magaziner and Reich emphasize the necessity for a constructive government industrial policy. Abernathy *et al.*'s (1983) book *Industrial Renaissance* represents the mainstream Harvard orthodoxy which puts the main emphasis on the reorganization of productive capability in threatened industries like motor cars. This new American work deserves more attention than it has received in this country since it is pertinent to the whole question of why the British are bad at manufacturing and what should be done. We cannot uncritically endorse the problem definitions and solutions of the American writers, but if we critically reflect on their work, we can focus and refine our own analysis of the nature, causes of, and remedies for, poor manufacturing performance in Britain and elsewhere. This is the justification for an extended review of Magaziner and Reich which begins with an exposition of their argument and then proceeds to a critical analysis of their argument.

Magaziner and Reich's argument

In explaining poor manufacturing performances Magaziner and Reich are preoccupied with 'hard' questions of economic organiz-ation rather than 'soft' questions of national character. In this case, the issue is how are deficiencies of economic performance and organization to be conceptualized? Magaziner and Reich answer this question in two ways. Negatively, they develop a thorough-going attack on existing economic frameworks for thinking about the gains in welfare which result from international trade. They also criticize the accounting frameworks which claim to provide guides to enterprise decision-making in a competitive environment. More positively, Magaziner and Reich present their own alternative schema for thinking about the sources of competitive advantage in business. On this basis, they demonstrate how competitive advantage can be pursued by enterprises that make the right strategy choices which should be reinforced and supported by appro-priate government policies. In the paragraphs below, we will concentrate on a brief outline of Magaziner and Reich's arguments on these issues.

We can begin by examining Magaziner and Reich's negative critique of economics. They doubt whether the orthodox economic analysis of the gains from trade applies in the special case of an open national economy whose manufacturing sector is relatively uncom-petitive. Here, the national economy will capture few of the gains from trade because the benefits of cheap imports will be outweighed by other losses; low export volumes and high import penetration translate into lost production which depresses output and employ-ment in that national economy. Alternatively, if output is main-tained in a situation where it is relatively unsaleable, there are the debit items of lost profits and low wages. More fundamentally,

Magaziner and Reich doubt whether it is possible to construct an index of gains in welfare from trade because orthodox productivity measures are uninformative and unreliable. Such measures do not properly take into account the quality improvements and cost reductions achieved by manufacturers in many products lines. For Magaziner and Reich, economics is a discourse which provides a misleading and unconvincing apology for free trade.

At this stage, it may be useful to distinguish Magaziner and Reich's position from that of heretical economists, like Godley at Cambridge, who would also argue that free trade creates problems because it harms the relatively weak and inefficient. Godley (1979) concludes that the solution is a macro policy of protection for the uncompetitive national manufacturing sector; national prosperity will come from the control of international trade. Magaziner and Reich conclude that the solution is to be found at the micro level in business strategies and government industrial policies which help enterprises become more competitive; national prosperity will come from effective participation in international trade. Ultimately, therefore, Magaziner and Reich imply that economics is not so much wrong as irrelevant because the discourse provides no practical guide for enterprises which want to become more competitive. Thus, they have no difficulty in showing that the objective of 'improving productivity' is vacuous at the enterprise level. The key consideration for the enterprise is always productivity improvements relative to international competitors in specific businesses. When threatened by imports, the American producers of colour televisions managed exemplary improvements in labour productivity, only to be outflanked and forced out of the business by Japanese competitors who did even better in reducing the number of assembly hours required per set.

Magaziner and Reich are even more scathing about the management professors and their quantitative techniques which pretend to provide guides for enterprise decision-making. They make a substantial and sustained criticism of the return on investment (ROI) techniques which were taught in 1960s and 1970s management schools and are now used by most large American enterprises. Their criticism of ROI is not original (see Hayes and Abernathy, 1980; Ellsworth, 1983) but it is still sufficiently unfamiliar to require a brief summary and Magaziner and Reich do introduce some new arguments against ROI. Magaziner and Reich would agree with Hayes and other critics that ROI techniques bias enterprise calculation against large-scale strategic investment where returns are distant and uncertain; the logic of ROI is a patching defence of existing process technology and product lines. They also develop the argument that ROI is a static approach which neglects the key dynamics whereby the return on one enterprise's investment project will depend on the investments made by competing enterprises which are defending their position. They cite the example of a paper company whose projected returns from new and more efficient machinery never materialized because its competitors also invested, with the net result being over-capacity and price-cutting. More fundamentally, Magaziner and Reich raise the question of whether conventional investment appraisal techniques not only miscalculate return but also misdefine investment. They criticize the conventional Anglo–American concept of investment which includes fixed and working capital but excludes 'expense investment' such as the costs of the distribution network or the aggressive pricing that is required to enter a new export market. Such costs should be considered as investment expenditures because, just like new plant, they are non-day-to-day expenditures which create the opportunity for future production and sales.

If problems of manufacturing uncompetitiveness can be created or reinforced by ROI calculations, Magaziner and Reich do not suppose that the solution is a more sophisticated calculation of the appropriate quantum of investment, since they doubt whether investment in itself necessarily solves problems of manufacturing uncompetitiveness. Recent American analysis (Gale, 1980) and British experience with nationalized steel and cars suggests that, where businesses are uncompetitive and failing, putting in more investment mechanically depresses the rate of return because investment increases the burden of interest charges and/or heavy depreciation payments. More generally, Magaziner and Reich argue that, where enterprises can succeed, the crucial consideration is not the level of investment inputs but whether the investment is strategically committed to secure competitive advantage. This again fits with recent American analysis. In their different ways both Hayes and Garvin (1982) and Abernathy et al., (1983) have emphasized that in many product lines Japanese enterprises do not invest in more capital equipment than their American competitors; the Japanese advantage is better production planning and process control, which allows Japanese enterprises to use their capital equipment more effectively. Magaziner and Reich take this argument outside the factory and develop a much broader positive analysis of the conditions of successful investment.

The positive and constructive part of Magaziner and Reich's analysis is a 'how to do it' guide in the classic American tradition; what Masters and Johnson did for sex, Magaziner and Reich do for enterprise calculation. Inevitably, there is not one universal prescription for what management should do. Successful enterprise strategy depends on a series of calculations, and failure is the reward for managements which miscalculate or fail to make the appropriate calculations. Management must first identify the 'business' in which it competes; a business is defined as a space distinguished by similarity of production methods, cost structures, barriers to entry, methods of distribution, and so forth. The important point is that a business is not necessarily the same as an industry; Boeing and Cessna, for example, are in the same industry but airliners and light planes are different businesses. Having identified the business, management must then analyse the key competitive cost elements in that business. Do lower costs depend on access to raw materials or low wages or on productivity advantages which depend on an effective strategy and organization within the firm? Most of Magaziner and Reich's discussion is then devoted to this last kind of 'complex-factor-cost' business which is usually dominated by enterprises located in the advanced industrial countries. In any complex-factor-cost business there are sources of competitive cost leverage; purchasing, manufacturing, marketing and distribution, applications engineering, and research and development are all potential sources of cost leverage. There will also be investment barriers to entry which can include not only manufacturing scale but also skilled labour, proprietory techniques, sophisticated selling, and marketing and distribution.

Successful enterprise strategies locate the sources of competitive cost leverage in a particular business and exploit the barriers to entry which make competitive advantage sustainable over time. In each business the levers and barriers will be different, and strategy should be varied according to these particular circumstances. For example, in bulk steel, advantage could be obtained by production scale combined with careful process engineering; in speciality chemicals, applications engineering which tailors products to specific user requirements might be crucial; while, in some kinds of consumer goods production, the right kind of service or distribution network might be a prerequisite. Some recent American work discounts the importance of orthodox economies of scale as an advantage; Goldhar and Jellinek (1983) argue that computer-assisted design and manufacturing (CADCAM) inaugurates a new flexibility so that scale no longer more or less automatically confers advantage. Magaziner and Reich more cautiously suppose that scale may provide an opportunity for attaining a low cost position through moving along and down an experience curve. As the case of US Steel shows, this opportunity is not necessarily exploited and in many cases there will be other more potent sources of competitive cost advantage.

Magaziner and Reich do not presume that success is equally possible in all businesses. Enterprise strategy can achieve much but it cannot always prevail against certain 'natural' disadvantages imposed by resource limitations and relatively high wage levels. Thus cheap clothing and footwear must be ceded to Taiwan and Korea because developed countries cannot compete successfully in these businesses where low wages are a decisive advantage. Nevertheless, given a sophisticated manufacturing capability in complex-factor-cost business, the advanced countries can still develop existing and new businesses which will provide a base for expanding manufacturing output and employment. In Magaziner and Reich's schema of industrial development, the progress of the advanced countries will culminate in a movement towards new knowledge-intensive industries.

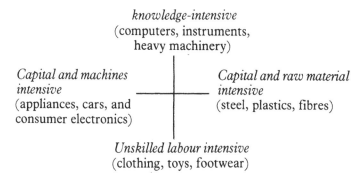

Figure 3.1 The four poles of industrial development.

If the four poles of industrial development are represented as, in Figure 3.1, the leading advanced countries like Germany and Japan are moving towards a disposition of manufacturing resources which looks like a top-heavy diamond.

Even where business success is possible in the advanced countries, the reformulation of enterprise strategy may be a necessary but not a sufficient condition for the enterprise's competitive success. Magaziner and Reich argue that the problems of an uncompetitive manufacturing sector cannot be entirely solved at the enterprise level because business strategy must be supported by an appropriate national industrial policy.

When all advanced countries do have industrial policies, the choice is not between industrial policy and no industrial policy. It is the kind of industrial policy which is crucial. Magaziner and Reich oppose traditional non-discriminatory and general industrial policies of the British type; general investment allowances or tax rebates for exporters are expensive and ineffective. As for those interventions which deal in a more specific way with particular industrial problems, Magaziner and Reich argue that, outside Japan, the objectives of such interventions are misconceived. The US government has retarded adjustment in declining and uncompetitive businesses by offering them various forms of protection at the expense of taxpayers and consumers. The UK government has again retarded adjustment by unconstructively subsidizing nationalized manufacturing. With high-technology growing businesses, US and UK policy has been equally inept; defence requirements and prestige projects have warped and displaced sensible priorities in research and development and high technology.

Positively, Magaziner and Reich argue for a targeted industrial policy with a constructive double aim. First, a targeted industrial policy should aim to ease the social costs of business decline by facilitating the necessary adjustments; labour movement out of declining industries should, for example, be actively promoted by appropriate re-training and relocation allowances. Second, a targeted industrial policy should aim to obtain competitive advantage in growing businesses with high value added. Growing businesses could be helped by such means as funding research and development where public and private returns diverge, subsidizing high risk investments, supporting key linkage industries which are strategic for others, sharing the costs of developing foreign markets, and subsidizing the cost of education and training. If forms of assistance are to be geared to the specific needs of particular businesses, Magaziner and Reich argue that it is necessary to create one relatively small central government department to oversee national industrial policy; they favour a MITI-type department where a couple of thousand civil servants work out specific, coherent and attainable industrial goals.

Questions arising from the argument

In this section we will begin to explore the limits of Magaziner and Reich's analysis by asking and answering two questions which arise fairly directly out of their argument: first, can enterprises choose different strategies; and, second, can governments pick industrial winners and losers? We will begin by discussing the first question about whether enterprises can choose.

Magaziner and Reich see 'business strategy' as the primary force which is responsible for enterprise success or failure; 'the few strategic decisions that a business makes each year set the basic course for the long run'. In the final analysis, business strategy is determined by senior management's understanding of the bases from which cost advantage may be derived. Magaziner and Reich's prescription for American enterprise is straightforward: clear away obstructive management systems and promote a clearer understanding of the sources of competitive advantage. When clear perception is the only precondition for correct business strategy, Schumpeter's heroic entrepreneur and Chandler's creative manager live on in Magaziner and Reich's book. The problem is that this concept of management promotes a voluntaristic and idealist concept of business strategy which abstracts from the institutional conditions and constraints on enterprise calculation. For example, Magaziner and Reich do not analyse how financial institutions and markets differently condition the capability of the manufacturing sectors in various advanced countries. They fail to examine the extent to which German and Japanese manufacturing success has been helped by their national arrangements for financing business. More seriously, they do not examine the extent to which American manufacturing has been handicapped by national banking practices which are preoccupied with short-term financial ratios, and by a peculiar American diversion into conglomerate merger. An institutional analysis of these issues would at the very least help explain why different national manufacturing sectors have such variable ability to find and exploit the strategic sources of competitive advantage.

The absence of this kind of institutional analysis weakens Magaziner and Reich's argument and reduces their analysis to romance. Magaziner and Reich must ultimately endorse an American dream; because success never has any material preconditions, success is always possible for enterprises which strive and deserve to succeed. The myth of social mobility for the humble individual is only reinscribed in another register as a myth of opportunity for small business; from log cabin to White House is transposed as silicon valley garage to international corporate head office. This kind of thing makes good copy when *Newsweek* writes about Steven Jobs and Apple computers, but the economic story is rather different from the journalistic romance. As I have argued elsewhere (Williams *et al.*, 1983), enterprises can choose their strategies, but only within limits established by external conditions such as market limitations, organized labour, financial institutions, and government policies.

Magaziner and Reich recognize only the industrial policy conditions set by government and they suppose that, in principle, these conditions are not a problem because government can smoothly adjust industrial policy. As we have seen, for Magaziner and Reich, a targeted industrial policy has a secondary role in reinforcing correct enterprise strategy in declining and growing businesses. Government should act as the disinterested promoter of the dynamics of competition, as analysed by Magaziner and Reich. But if we ask whether and how government can pick winners and losers, we encounter problems which Magaziner and Reich do not manage to pose, leave alone resolve. Politically, Magaziner and Reich appear to be proposing to take the politics out of politics. They argue that existing American industrial policy has been distorted by sectional 'interests' and special pleading. But, in this case, would not the priorities of any new industrial policy be upset by the same interests which could cynically use the rhetoric of industrial renewal? Magaziner and Reich's insistence on a MITI-type industry department is clearly designed to get round the political problem. But, even if such an institution were created in America or Britain, that would not solve the crucial practical problem; according to what criteria, or after what process of calculation, does a government agency pick winners and losers? This practical issue cannot be avoided when the record of American (or British) government agencies in the industrial policy field is discouraging.

To begin with, we can register a series of absences and omissions in Magaziner and Reich's arguments about doctoring losers and picking winners. They provide no clear guide to identifying losers and do not explain what should be done for traditional basic industries, like steel or motor cars, which are in serious trouble all over Europe and North America. For example, is steel a declining industry whose migration to Korea or Brazil should be hastened? Or, is steel a key 'linkage industry' which should be maintained because of its backward and forward linkages to the rest of the economy? If steel is a linkage industry, how does a European or American government define an appropriate strategy and determine acceptable losses in an industry which everywhere requires substantial new investment in balanced modern plant with a flexible product mix. If steel is a loser which should be run down, government policy becomes a self-fulfilling prophecy because, according to Magaziner and Reich, losers should be denied the resources to remain competitive. In such cases we would never know whether government made the right policy decision. Magaziner and Reich are no more explicit about picking winners. They provide a list of high-tech businesses of the future (biotechnology, fibre optics, lasers, computers, etc.), but that list is not an operational guide to sponsoring particular enterprises and projects in specific ways. In the same way, Magaziner and Reich make much of the Japanese government's success in picking winners, but they never explain exactly how this is done in Japan. They also neglect the obvious point that it is relatively easy to define the industrial goals of a 'follower' country like Japan in the 1950s and 1960s, or Korea in the 1970s and 1980s; this only requires a national plan which targets businesses like steel, cars, or shipbuilding where a follower country can attain and sustain advantage if national producers master the available techniques of production

(Yamauchi, 1983). It is much more difficult to choose high-tech priorities in leading industrial countries.

The omissions and silences in Magaziner and Reich's argument are so obvious that we must ask whether right-wing critics are correct when they argue that industrial policy will never work. We will do this by examining John Burton's (1983) polemic against industrial policy in an Institute of Economic Affairs pamphlet. Burton argues that civil servants generally make poor entrepreneurs because they lack a direct financial stake in enterprises which are being promoted or reorganized and because they lack a detailed, specific knowledge about the fine structure of production or market opportunities in particular businesses. Successful private entrepreneurship depends on a kind of intuitive understanding of these opportunities; there is no systematic body of knowledge which can provide a substitute basis for government action in the industrial policy field. On reflection, these arguments are neither convincing nor intellectually creditable. Direct financial incentive and detailed knowledge of the business are not sufficient conditions for the development of effective business strategy. If extravagant management incentive schemes had positive results, American manufacturing would lead the world. As for detailed knowledge of business, such knowledge may be necessary but, in itself, often produces a market trader mentality rather than strategic understanding. Furthermore, there is a strong flavour of irrationalism in Burton's general disparagement of the possibility of state action; ultimately, government industrial policy cannot come good because entrepreneurship is a mystery whose secret can only be understood intuitively.

In most of the right-wing literature on industrial policy, the category of entrepreneurship has an important obfuscating role. If we clear that obstruction away, we can see that there are definite conditions which, for example, determine the productive and financial outcome of business strategy when state money is invested in manufacturing activity.

1   A market for the final product must be available or has to be created by enterprise strategy or government policy. Without sales revenue and value-added, nothing will come right for the enterprise.

2   Balanced, state-of-the-art production facilities are necessary if the enterprise is to produce a high-quality and/or low-cost product. Without investment of the right kind in process technology and product development, the market will be lost.

3   Profit levels will depend on the extent of competition from foreign producers who have low-cost bases, or effective subsidies, or aggressive pricing policies. The strategies of

      foreign competitors will influence outcomes as powerfully as
      the strategy of the domestic producer.
4   Financial solutions through accounting manoeuvres are
      palliative expedients unless productive problems are solved in
      the factory and the market place. Without such solutions,
      asset write-downs, debt write-offs, launch aid, and so forth,
      offer only temporary relief.

The whole history of British state investment in manufacturing
could be written around these themes. By way of illustration, we can
cite the case of British Steel Corporation where more than £2,000
million of public money was wasted because all the pre-conditions
for success were neglected or ignored. The BSC invested in basic
oxygen steel production and created unbalanced production facilities
where capital utilization was poor and costs of production were
high. Government never safeguarded the market for steel, which
grew very weakly, while the BSC's market share at home and
abroad declined as the Corporation lost out to strategically smarter
competitors.

This kind of analysis not only undermines Burton's unreasoning
prejudice against industrial policy, it also illuminates the weakness
of Magaziner and Reich's reasoned support for industrial policy.
Ultimately, their position is weak because, just like Burton, they do
not see the necessity for examining the sectoral conditions which
determine whether government industrial policy can succeed and
why it does so often fail. Instead of tackling this primary intellectual
task, Magaziner and Reich get diverted on to the secondary task of
elaborating policy instruments and objectives. If this secondary task
is undertaken before analysis has established the conditions under
which policy can work, then industrial policy becomes wishful thinking which is bound to end in naive disillusion about inadequate
policy instruments and unattained objectives. This disillusion is all
the more certain when advocates of industrial policy, like Magaziner
and Reich, pretend that we have adequate policy instruments and
clear objectives in this field. No western government has solved the
problem of creating mechanisms of implementation which ensure
that semi-autonomous private enterprises conform to publicly
agreed plans. In a country like Britain, this would probably require
reform of the institutional constraints on enterprise calculation; for
example, financial institutions would have to be reformed so that
they provided capital in ways which were geared to long-run productive advantage rather than short-run financial return.

This possibility raises interesting issues because in this case
government would be intervening against financial institutions even
though they were profitable and viable enterprises by any criteria.

Magaziner and Reich refuse to recognize the need for this kind of intervention against financial or productive enterprises. This is because they assume that the pursuit of private advantage by corporate enterprises in manufacturing is socially beneficial, or even that private and social advantage substantially coincide. On this assumption, the proper role of government is only to adjust the institutional framework so that the pursuit of private advantage becomes more effective. In taking this position on industrial policy, Magaziner and Reich are restating a traditional American view of the government/business relation which is manifested in mid-nineteenth century American attitudes towards government policy on banking, railways, and public land. We would argue that in its historic or current form this view involves almost as much wishful thinking as the romantic mythology of social mobility for the individual and opportunity for the enterprise. There are important discrepancies between enterprise calculation and government calculation and the rest of this review will analyse the nature and significance of these discrepancies.

Discrepancies between enterprise calculation and government calculation

The issues discussed in this section have traditionally been posed in terms of 'interest'. The classic question here would be: Do the interests of central government and manufacturing enterprises coincide? But this is a mis-posed question because interests do not exist outside the calculations of advantage within which they are identified. Thus we would re-pose the classic question in a rather different way. Our question is: What is the nature and form of the discrepancy between enterprise calculation and government calculation?

In making their calculations, enterprises and governments are not obliged to take into account the same considerations and attach the same value to each consideration. The resulting discrepancies are much more radical than are admitted in orthodox economic cost-benefit analysis which counterposes the narrow private and the broad public variants on one felicific calculus. The calculations of enterprises and governments are discretionary, in that no logic of 'objective interest' requires them to be made in a particular form. There is no set list of objectives and instruments and consequences which must be considered, leave alone valued in the same way. The discretionary calculations of agents and institutions deal in 'subjective' identifications, which are made through the medium of a variety of knowledges, from political ideologies to management practices. None of these knowledges has the quasi-permanence of (natural) science and within one generation the most fixed and cherished of them will be identified as misinterpretation and misinformation. These rather abstract points can be illustrated by briefly considering the role of the objective of cost competitiveness, which Magaziner and Reich argue should be privileged by management and government because it is the key to achieving competitive advantage.

The control of costs in the production process is often an important objective in enterprise calculation; careful planning of process technology, tight stock control, or strict labour discipline can improve productivity, output levels, or profit margins at low (or no) investment cost. On the other hand, much evidence indicates that it is the non-price characteristics of manufactured goods which determine their success or failure in the market place. This point is indirectly conceded by Magaziner and Reich when they admit that competitive advantage can be based on elaborate distribution or service networks, product technology leadership, or a well-established brand image. An enterprise which achieves competitive advantage through these means usually gains the freedom to tolerate the cost penalties which arise from poor operational controls on production. And there is at least a possibility that any remaining cost problem can be palliated if market success allows larger-scale production. Matters are further complicated if we consider the calculations of government. The analysis of Fetherston *et al.* (1977) shows that cost competitiveness is not crucial to the success of a national manufacturing sector; Germany and Japan have gained share of world trade despite a deterioration in their cost competitiveness. A government which read such articles from Cambridge would not privilege the pursuit of manufacturing cost competitiveness. On the other hand, as long as our present government prefers Mr Sam Brittan's column in the *Financial Times*, national cost competitiveness will appear to be an important issue. Generally, the grip of neoclassical presuppositions is so strong that governments are much concerned with cost competitiveness despite all the evidence that it does not matter.

If enterprises and governments have latitude and discretion about the pursuit of an objective like cost competitiveness, there must be innumerable possible sources of discrepancy between the calculations of enterprises and governments. Having made this point, we can now focus the argument on one important general discrepancy between enterprise and government calculation. This general discrepancy arises over labour displacement when in various circumstances enterprises want to shed labour. Enterprises in declining industries, like European steel or shipbuilding, will adjust by closing capacity and sacking workers. Enterprises in expanding businesses, like motor cars outside Europe and North America, may seek advantage through the purchase of smart, programmable automation which allows more output with fewer workers. In static markets, some enterprises must cope with changes in the technological base; for example, the advent of electronics in traditional telecommunications products like telex machines displaces existing electromechanical skills and many of the process workers previously required. Technical change and market forces do not, of course, have an inherent and invariable propensity to displace labour. The point is rather that they often do and when labour is displaced, the enterprise and national government are generally affected in very different ways.

In most forms of enterprise calculation, the employment of labour is a variable which is adjusted in the light of other productive and financial objectives. Ultimately, this is so because accounting frameworks for financial calculation are always geared to the stewardship of capital rather than human resources; profit is, of course, the surplus remaining after the value of the firm's capital has been maintained. Enterprises which are in profit have latitude about the employment of labour and may tolerate overmanning. But enterprises which incur operating losses, or have problems about cash flow, usually find that sacking labour is an attractive option. Redundancy takes wages costs out and, under the western rules of the game , the enterprise is in no way responsible for its workforce after it has been made redundant. The enterprise's responsibility ends when it has paid the last week's wages and made whatever *ex gratia* or statutory lump sum payments to which redundant workers are entitled. The history of nationalized manufacturing since the early 1970s shows this dismal logic at work; it explains, for example, why the British Steel Corporation, which once employed 200,000 workers, now plans to reduce its workforce to just 55,000 workers.

What happens next is no concern of the enterprise, but is of concern to workers threatened with displacement who suspect redundancy will be followed by prolonged unemployment. Regrettably, these sentiments are of little practical significance because workers cannot (or will not) fight redundancy and with more or less good grace go straight into the dole queue. The struggle of the British mine workers is the exception which proves the rule in an era of slump and factory closure. At the point where workers go into the dole queue, labour displacement does create intractable and ineluctable problems for government because, under the western rules of the game, the state must bear a variety of costs which begin when the worker is made redundant. If there are insufficient new jobs of the right kind there are the direct costs of income maintenance as long as workers remain unemployed and there are also the indirect costs which arise when the unemployed are more prone to ill health and so forth. In so far as new jobs are created for displaced workers, the state must bear a significant part of the costs of job creation which include, for example, the expense of retraining, grants, and subsidies paid to employers who create new jobs.

If income maintenance for the unemployed is the main social cost, we should note that state income maintenance for displaced workers is not an invariant and necessary feature of advanced capitalism. From 1850 to 1914, Britain managed with virtually no state assistance for the unemployed (Williams, 1981) and Japan currently shows that, in specific circumstances, the state can still abdicate its responsibilities. It is also true that government does not directly have to meet the costs of supporting the unemployed entirely, or mainly, out of its own revenues. This is the real significance of social insurance techniques, whereby wage earners and consumers pay most of the cost of maintaining unemployed labour through higher social insurance contributions and higher final product prices. Even before the invention of social insurance, government did not have to pay; the burden of maintaining the unemployed in nineteenth century Britain was effectively placed on private charity, the family, and the trade union. But the detail about who pays does not alter the general argument. The maintenance of displaced labour is not a cost to the enterprise but is a cost to society and, currently, in all advanced western countries (except Japan) government is heavily involved in meeting these costs. As long as the social account includes the cost of maintaining displaced labour and as long as the private accounting framework is geared to the preservation of capital, there is always a potentially serious discrepancy between enterprise calculation and government calculation.

Significance of the discrepancy about labour displacement

Magaziner and Reich do not identify the discrepancy between enterprise calculation and government calculation which arises at the point of labour displacement. But, if the discrepancy is of limited practical significance, their omission does not matter. The significance of the discrepancy depends on whether the economic process creates enough jobs of the right kind inside the national economy. We must now ask whether this is so in America and, more generally, in the other advanced countries. This question can be answered in two ways by examining, first, the patterns of job creation which are likely in the future and, second, the record on job creation in the recent past. We will begin by considering medium- and long-term prospects for manufacturing employment.

Magaziner and Reich emphasize the notion of a ladder of

industrial development which all nations can ascend; in their scheme of things, the advanced countries will move towards new knowledge-intensive industrial bases and cede low wage and unsophisticated businesses to less developed countries. This optimistically over-simplifies the long-run employment prospects of the less developed countries and the advanced industrial economies. To begin with, there has only been a limited migration of manufacturing to the less developed countries; from 1960 to 1981, the less developed countries increased their share of world manufacturing value added from 8.0 per cent to just 10.3 per cent (Ballance and Sinclair, 1983). The so-called new industrializing countries (NICs) like Taiwan, Korea, Hong Kong, or Singapore are all special cases; with limited domestic markets and natural resources, these countries have developed export-oriented manufacturing economies on the basis of low wages. All this suggests that the future movement of manufac-turing employment to less developed countries is likely to be much less dramatic than Magaziner and Reich suppose. But, as we shall now see, that does not ensure rosy employment prospects for the advanced industrial countries further up the ladder of development.

If the long-run future of manufacturing in advanced countries depends on the high-technology businesses of the late twentieth century, these businesses may become increasingly congested as all the advanced countries converge into microelectronics and bio-technology. The prophets of techno-serendipity, like Freeman (1983) and Peretz (1983), envisage a rather different future. They argue that microelectronics provides a new technological base which can, in principle, sustain a secular economic upswing in all the industrial countries; governments can hasten the upswing by invest-ing in a new infrastructure and training the workforce. If the 'great depression' of the late nineteenth century was what happened after the railways had been built, on this view our present troubles in the late twentieth century are what is happening before the micro-electronics and information technologies come on line. Even if this view is generally correct, the new knowledge-intensive industrial base will hardly generate enough jobs of the right kind in the advanced countries. There is certain to be a qualitative mismatch between the labour requirement of the new knowledge-intensive industries and those of declining smoke-stack industries where the labour force is usually male, middle-aged, and low-skill or industry-specific skilled. The American evidence (Bluestone and Harrison, 1982) already shows that workers displaced from traditional manu-facturing industries, like steel or textiles, must often accept lower wages and inferior jobs which do not use their existing skills when they are reabsorbed into the labour force. The reasons for this downward mobility are straightforward; even after re-training, middle-aged manual labourers in Pittsburgh will never become systems analysts in the sun belt. The journey from Consett to Newbury in the UK is likely to be equally difficult.

Much must therefore depend on the short-run employment prospects in existing manufacturing industries, many of which are long established. Here, Magaziner and Reich effectively recommend enthusiastic participation in the competitive international trade in manufactures as a means of stabilizing, or even increasing, employment in manufacturing. But it is doubtful whether the trade in manufactures can now create anything like the right quantity of employment.

In the recent past, output lost *via* manufacturing uncompetitiveness did feed through into job loss; this effect explains why Britain uniquely suffered absolute job losses in manufacturing from the early 1960s. But, in the near future, it is doubtful whether moderate output gains from manufacturing competitiveness will feed through into new jobs; the CBI estimates that British output would have to increase by 10 to 20 per cent before there was any impact on employment. The position is similar in the other advanced countries for two reasons: first, there is over-capacity and under-utilization of existing capacity in many businesses, partly because output levels are still often below 1979 pre-slump level; second, new capacity using CADCAM technology can offer remarkable productivity increases, partly through the substitution of capital for labour. Everywhere, the end result is that the relation between manufacturing capacity utilization or capacity growth and employment has taken a secular turn for the worse. Given this worsening relation, one nation's competitive success in manufacturing may not stabilize the employment base in that country and it certainly will not mop up the 10 per cent plus unemployment which now exists in most of the advanced countries. Anyone who doubts this should consider the experience of West Germany, which has the strongest national manufacturing sector in Europe and access to a free trade area of 300 million people in the EEC/EFTA area; even after sending the *gastarbeiter* home, West Germany has 10 per cent unemployment.

To get very much effect on employment in the advanced economies, it would be necessary to resurrect the long trade-led boom of the 1950s and 1960s and also to ensure that the rapid secular expansion of trade benefited all the advanced countries significantly. It is very unlikely that either condition can be met.

To begin with, there are structural constraints on, and policy inhibitions about, any collective expansion of the advanced economies. It is hardly likely that trade-induced multiplier processes can transcend the structural imbalances in the world payments system which have persisted in a low-growth world since the 1973 oil crisis;

through the later 1970s and early 1980s, most advanced industrial countries were balance of payments constrained and to that extent Keynesian transmission mechanisms could not operate as they had in earlier decades. Even if the structural constraints on the advanced countries have eased with the collapse of the OPEC cartel, policy inhibitions about collective expansion will remain an obstacle. At present, it is not very encouraging to find that the Americans are doing the right things for the wrongs reasons; world recovery is being assisted by the huge American deficit which is caused by arms expenditure. Nor is it reassuring to find other western governments complaining that the resulting high interest rates are a burden on their own recovery.

Even if a virtuous circle of trade-led growth could be started, there remain awkward issues about whether all the advanced national economies would benefit. Consumers in all the advanced countries will benefit from the trade in manufactures in so far as they obtain higher quality and cheaper manufactured goods. But consumers can have strong preferences for consumer goods which are based on trivial packaging differences; is the welfare of Italian consumers so much lower because imports of Japanese cars are banned? In any case the availability of manufactures is only one determinant of the overall welfare of consumers; the quality of health care is surely more important than cheap radio-cassettes or cameras. The benefits to consumers from trade in manufactures have probably been overrated. Furthermore, if we consider the issues from the point of view of job loss and job creation, we can register more fundamental doubts. There is often an asymmetry in the international distribution of trade benefits between consumers and producers. In a free trade area, like the Common Market, the benefits of manufacturing trade for consumers will certainly be diffuse and spread over the whole area. On the other hand, if there are differences in the competitiveness of various countries, benefits to producers are likely to be concentrated in one or a few countries; for industrial producers the Common Market is a benefit club for West German enterprises. At the periphery, in an uncompetitive country like Britain, producers' capital will be rendered worthless and labour will be made redundant as uncompetitive enterprises are forced to contract or go out of business. From the producer welfare point of view, the European trade in manufactures does look like a zero sum game.

Our conclusion must be that, in the short run and medium term, the expansion of international trade in manufactures is constrained and the benefits of such trade will probably be distributed unequally. In this situation the Magaziner and Reich type of national industrial policy would probably be damaging rather than beneficial. Japanese manufacturing success has been based on enterprise strategies of a stereotyped kind. The enterprise aims for process quality and scale production which together ensure a high-quality, relatively cheap product which is then aggressively marketed according to plans which target particular market segments in specific national economies. In the North American market for motor cycles or third world markets for steel the strategies worked brilliantly because the Japanese were the only ones playing this game. It is clear that the results for the Japanese and everybody else will be very different if other national players join the same game when their governments adopt industrial policies which reinforce the pursuit of competitive advantage. Economists have traditionally worried about the wasteful irrationality of oligopolistic competition between enterprises on the domestic market. How much more frightening is the prospect of international competition for export markets between national majors whose aggressive pricing and market strategies are funded by national governments. Perhaps the *de facto* tendency within the EEC towards cartellization and output limitation in industries like steel is much more rational than Magaziner and Reich admit. And, if the results of competition are potentially damaging and wasteful, maybe we should find national policy goals other than 'competitiveness'?

The discussion so far has concentrated on future prospects of job creation and job loss in the advanced countries and it is inevitably rather speculative. But, if we turn to examine the recent economic history of the advanced countries, the record on job loss and creation in the past is hardly encouraging and confirms our apprehensions about the future. We will begin to demonstrate this point by considering the development of the American economy before we broaden out the discussion to consider the other advanced capitalist economies.

Magaziner and Reich fail to register the basic point that, over the postwar period since 1945, American manufacturers have competed through the development of overseas manufacture as a substitute for direct exports from America. By the early 1970s, American enterprises produced abroad four times as much as they directly exported from the USA (United Nations, 1978); in no other major industrial country is the ratio of overseas production to exports anywhere near as high. At the enterprise level, there were always good productive and financial reasons for this development. The Americans started off with the advantage of a huge internal market which was largely supplied by domestic manufactures. In the 1950s and 1960s the development of quasi-independent manufacturing operations in Europe allowed American enterprises to get round tariff barriers and to develop products tailored specifically to European demands. By the 1970s and 1980s overseas production in Europe and the less developed countries was being integrated into a global division of production which was organized from America; intermediate products and finished goods from low-cost production areas were now brought back as 'captive imports' on to the European and American markets.

Furthermore, contrary to Magaziner and Reich's allegations, American enterprises have made a reasonable success of their foreign manufacturing operations; as Dunning's classic work (1976) shows, American firms in Europe consistently outperformed their indigenous competitors in the late 1960s. American manufacturing has had its troubles since, but there can be no doubt that the profitability of the major American multinationals is substantially improved by their global trade in 'captive imports'. Given American cost structures, General Motors cannot make money by building small cars in the USA, but GM could take a handsome dealing profit if the politicians would allow it to import Suzuki cars from Japan.

If American enterprises calculated that overseas manufacture was advantageous and if this decision has been vindicated by financial and productive results, it can hardly be said that American manufacturing failed. The point is rather that enterprise calculations of private advantage created social problems back in the USA. The remitted profits from overseas manufacture of the dealing profits from 'captive imports' are necessarily smaller than the value added from domestic manufacturing. More importantly, from our point of view, the domestic employment base will necessarily be smaller to the extent that overseas manufacture is developed as a substitute for direct export. Under the western rules of the game, the enterprise is in no way responsible for these wider social consequences and these problems therefore represent another instance of the discrepancy between enterprise calculation and government calculation. In fact it represents a special case of the labour displacement discrepancy which arises where multinational enterprises develop overseas manufacture and export jobs rather than goods from the advanced countries.

The social costs of multinational manufacturing strategies have been palliated by the creation of non-manufacturing jobs in the service sector of the American economy. Demographic trends and rising female participation rates may have kept the American economy away from full employment but, through the whole postwar period, the job-creating capability of the American economy has been quite awesome. In the years of the long boom, 20 million new jobs were created in the 1950s and 1960s. More surprisingly, the American economy created 13 million new jobs in the years 1973–9 between the oil crisis and the onset of the slump; and in

1983, as the American economy moved out of the slump, it created 3 million new jobs (Martin, 1984). Latterly, most of these jobs have been in the service sector; 70 per cent of all new private jobs created from 1973 to 1980 were in services (Rothschild, 1981). Employment grew fastest in eating and drinking places, health care, and 'business services'; Rothschild has claimed that the *increase* in employment in American eating and drinking places from 1973 to 1980 was greater than *total* employment in the car and steel industries combined.

Generally, the other advanced countries show a similar pattern of expansion in the quantity of service employment which more or less compensates for a decline in the quantity of manufacturing employment. Consider, for example, the case of Britain where since 1961 manufacturing employment has declined by approximately 3 million to a total of 5.3 million employees; in the same period, service employment has increased by approximately 3 million to 13.1 million. There are of course substantial differences in the trend rates of change and in the causal mechanics at work in the different advanced countries. In Britain, for example, the decline of manufacturing employment was hastened by uncompetitiveness rather than a positive strategy of developing overseas manufacture. And the expansion of service employment in Britain before the oil crisis was powerfully influenced by the growth of public sector employment; while private sector employment grew by only 3 per cent between 1959 and 1974, public sector employment increased by 15 per cent, largely because local government employed increasing numbers of service workers (Gough, 1979). The details may be different in various advanced countries, but the end result is strikingly similar. We can sum up this result in one proposition: service jobs always expand proportionately as manufacturing employment contracts. When American fast food chains have done so much to turn this abstraction into a reality, the basic proposition might be called McDonald's law. In the context of this general shift towards service employment, the peculiarity of the American experience is straightforward. The relative expansion of service employment started earlier and has progressed further in the United States (and Canada) than in the other advanced industrial countries; by the early 1970s service employment accounted for 62 per cent of United States employment, while it accounted for 40–50 per cent of employment in the major west European countries (Robertson *et al.*, 1982).

If America shows us future patterns of job creation, in quantitative terms that future works. With the benefit of fiscal expansion, the American unemployment rate has currently (March 1984) fallen below 8 per cent and longer term prospects for the creation of more service jobs remain good. Demand for services grows with affluence because the income elasticity of demand for them is high. Many services will remain labour intensive because productivity levels are necessarily low and static in personal service and care activities. Furthermore many services are untradeable because, like haircuts or meals out, they have to be supplied locally at the point of consumption. For all these reasons, mundane service employment, rather than glamorous high-tech businesses, will provide the employment base of the future.

In all the advanced countries there is, however, one problem. The expansion of service employment does not compensate for the relative decline of manufacturing employment in qualitative terms because the private service sector everywhere recruits marginal workers and offers them inferior pay and conditions. Consider, for example, the American eating and drinking places which employed 2 million in 1959 and 5 million in 1983 (Martin, 1984). In this sector, there was much part-time employment at low pay; eating and drinking places have the shortest working hours and the lowest average earnings (excluding tips) of any employment. Partly this is because the eating and drinking places recruit disproportionate numbers of women, blacks, and 'ethnics' for dead-end unskilled jobs; women account for more than half of all workers employed in American eating and drinking places, while they account for less than one-third of all workers in manufacturing (Rothschild, 1981).

At this point, we can return to the discrepancy between enterprise calculation and government calculation, which we originally conceptualized as a matter of direct labour displacement from employment into unemployment. We have now shown that there are also a variety of other indirect labour displacements between different kinds of employment; some workers are made redundant from high-quality manufacturing jobs while other workers are recruited into low-quality service jobs. Both the direct and indirect displacements are significant in all the advanced economies. In Britain, the direct displacement accounts for a standing army of 3 million unemployed workers and, over the past twenty years, the indirect displacement has shifted 3 million of the workforce into mainly low-grade service jobs. Our original emphasis on direct displacement reflects the conventional way in which we all see our social problem as the one which is dominated by unemployment. It is time we recognized that the second kind of indirect displacement is, or threatens to be, as much of a problem as unemployment; and it is a problem for exactly the same reasons as unemployment.

The ethical virtue of work has surely been overrated; it is not accidental that most recommend the therapy of work for other people. Direct displacement of workers into unemployment is an evil primarily because of its effects on the distribution of income. This is certainly so in Britain since the abolition of the earnings related supplement at the beginning of 1982. The dole now offers a maintenance which is well below the worst full-time wage; in 1982–3 the average payment per unemployed claimant of insurance or social assistance was just £32.50 per week (Trinder, 1983). Indirect displacement of the labour force into low-paid employment is also likely to increase inequality. The effects of the indirect displacement on income distribution are complicated mainly because in Britain, as in the USA, we now have so many two-income families. In Britain now nearly one-half of all married women work and 70 per cent of all women workers are employed in the service sector; many of the ill-paid female service workers are second-wage earners in affluent working-class households. More research is needed on this issue. But, with the marriage failure-rate rising towards one in three, service employment cannot function smoothly as a supplementary source of income for working-class couples. For the moment, we should assume that the expansion of low-paid employment increases inequality. The two forces for inequality are even symbiotically related in so far as unemployment is disproportionately concentrated on the unskilled whose ill-paid employments are punctuated with bouts of unemployment. This symbiosis would be institutionalized if and when a large 'secondary labour market' offering poor pay and conditions develops in this country (Atkinson, 1984); in this case many of our service workers would become the modern equivalents of late-nineteenth-century casual workers.

Because the distributional effect is the same, both direct and indirect labour displacement are instances of the same discrepancy between government and enterprise calculation; both require an expensive social response to the private actions and calculations which create the unacceptable conditions of unemployment and low pay. As a matter of course, unemployment is met with social income maintenance. To a lesser extent, so is low pay; low-paid workers with families can claim family income supplement and a variety of means tested benefits as well as the universal child benefit. It is true that the unemployed draw full maintenance, while the low paid draw only partial maintenance from the government. But, if the numbers of low paid workers are large, the cost of their partial maintenance will also be a very large item in the social account. At least this will be so if the government recognizes that the low paid have a right to income maintenance.

Here we encounter what is, or should be, the key political line of division between left and right in contemporary British politics. The right-wing solution for unemployment is 'pricing people back into jobs' and keeping quiet about the problem of low wages. This is simply a matter of elevating the current tendency of our national economy into a conscious economic strategy. The right's strategy will never work to absorb all the unemployed because it requires a frontal assault on trade union power and on income maintenance guarantees. Even in Mrs Thatcher's Britain, these measures are likely to remain politically inexpedient. It is nevertheless important to recognize that 'pricing people back into jobs' can work to absorb some of the unemployed at the expense of arbitrary sacrifice, social injustice, and greater inequality as low-paid employment expands. The intellectual task of the left is to insist that this kind of pricing people back into jobs is not a solution but part of the problem. The implication is that we must re-think the laudable objective of full employment. Keynes and Beveridge assumed that full employment would be associated with relatively decent pay and conditions for all; a residual problem of poverty in large families would be solved by the simple corollary of child allowances which could adjust wages to family size. We can no longer assume that all of this could be true. Practically, this means that we need economic and social policies which not only aim to increase employment but also aim to modify pay and conditions of work.

Our conclusion must be that the discrepancy between enterprise calculation and government calculation does matter because labour is being displaced into unemployment and ill-paid work. These direct and indirect displacements define our current social predicament in all the advanced countries. It is against this redefinition of the economic and social problem that we should finally judge Magaziner and Reich's proposal for a new industrial policy which would effectively encourage the enterprises's pursuit of competitive advantage. In the earlier sections of this chapter we argued that their proposal was inadequate because Magaziner and Reich never specified how their industrial policy ends could be achieved. This inexplicitness was traced back to certain oversights; Magaziner and Reich never analyse the conditions which determine industrial policy outcomes or the institutional constraints on enterprise calculation. Our argument in the last two sections of this chapter raises more fundamental questions about their policy ends. If our analysis of job creation and job loss is correct, an industrial policy geared towards competitiveness can only have a limited role to play; such a policy could only safeguard some high-quality manufacturing jobs and it might achieve this at the expense of intensified labour displacement. The relative decline of manufacturing in the advanced countries is not an isolated technical problem which is amenable to a specialist policy fix. Manufacturing decline is fundamentally rooted in the financial calculations of capitalist enterprises and has very broad social repercussions. To deal with all that, we will have to re-invent most of our existing economic and social policies.

References

Abernathy, W.J., Clark, K.B. and **Kantrow, A.M.** (1983) *Industrial Renaissance*, New York, Basic Books.

Atkinson, J. (1984) *Manning for Uncertainty*, Brighton, Institute of Manpower Studies, University of Sussex.

Ballance, R.H. and **Sinclair, S.W.** (1983) *Collapse and Survival*, London, Allen & Unwin.

Bluestone, B. and **Harrison, B.** (1982) *The De-industrialization of America*, New York, Basic Books.

Burton, J. (1983) *Picking Losers*, London, Institute of Economic Affairs.

Dunning, J.H. (1976) *US Industry in the UK*, London, Wilton House.

Ellsworth, R. (1983) 'Subordinate financial policy to corporate strategy', *Harvard Business Review*, November–December, pp. 170–82.

Fetherston, M. *et al.*, (1977) 'Manufacturing export shares and cost competitiveness of advanced industrial countries', *Economic Policy Review*, no. 3, pp. 62–70.

Freeman, C. (1983) 'Keynes or Kondratiev', *British Association for the Advancement of Science*, Section X8, August.

Gale, B.T. (1980) 'Can more capital buy higher productivity', *Harvard Business Review*, July–August, pp. 78–86.

Godley, W. (1979) 'Britain's chronic recession – can anything be done?', in Beckerman, W. (ed.), *Slow Growth in Britain*, Oxford, Clarendon Press.

Goldhar, J.D. and **Jellinek, M.** (1983) 'Plan for economies of scope', *Harvard Business Review*, November–December, pp. 141–8.

Gough, I. (1979) *The Political Economy of the Welfare State*, London, Macmillan.

Hayes, R.H. and **Abernathy, W.J.** (1980) 'Managing our way to economic decline', *Harvard Business Review*, July–August, pp. 67–77.

Hayes, R.H. and **Garvin, D.A.** (1982) 'Managing as if tomorrow mattered', *Harvard Business Review*, May–June, pp. 70–9.

Huxley, J. (1984) 'Tomorrow's workers', *Sunday Times*, 15 April.

Martin, P. (1984) 'The great American job-burger', *Sunday Times*, 22 April.

Peretz, C. (1983) 'Structural change and assimilation of new technologies', *Futures*, October, pp. 357–75.

Robertson, J.A.S. *et al.* (1982) *Structure and Employment Prospects of the Service Industries*, London, Department of Employment Research Paper.

Rothschild, E. (1981) 'Reagan and the real America', *New York Review of Books*, 5 Feb.

Trinder, C. (1983) 'Income in work and when unemployed', *National Institute Economic Review*, February, pp. 56–83.

United Nations (1978) *Transnational Corporations in World Development*, New York, UN Department of Economic and Social Affairs.

Williams, K. (1981) *From Pauperism to Poverty*, London, Routledge & Kegan Paul.

Williams, K. *et al.* (1983) *Why are the British Bad at Manufacturing?*, London, Routledge & Kegan Paul.

Yamauchi, I. (1983) 'Long range strategic planning in Japanese R and D', *Futures*, pp. 328–41.

4
Accounting for failure in the nationalized enterprises – coal, steel, and cars since 1970

Karel Williams, Colin Haslam, Andrew Wardlow and
John Williams

Abstract

This chapter analyses the nature of the strategic miscalculations in nationalized British coal, steel, and cars since the early 1970s. Specifically, it examines the extent to which the initial strategic miscalculations were causes by an uncritical use of return on investment (ROI) techniques and the extent to which subsequent operational retreat was determined by profit and loss considerations. The general conclusion is that financial (mis)calculation was a secondary problem in enterprises which did not identify their productive problems and could not solve their market difficulties. In our three cases, large-scale investment was futile when the state did not safeguard the market for the final product.

Defining the problem

In this chapter we are immediately concerned with two forms of accounting calculation – net present value (NPV) and profit and loss. We do not want to tackle directly the large questions of why these forms of calculation exist and what is their relation to organizations and society. Our aim is to pose and answer a more modest question about whether and how these kinds of accounting calculation have determinate consequences in particular contexts; what are the implications of using NPV to guide strategic investment, and profit and loss to guide disinvestment?

By posing this question we are led to examine the implication of accounting rules. After all, NPV claims to provide rules for wealth-maximizing strategic investment, just as profit and loss provides rules for operational profit maximization. Our position is that NPV and profit forms of calculation are not simply instruments but are themselves conditions facilitating certain kinds of outcome. We therefore examine the possibility that these forms of calculation directed to wealth and profit maximization may (in some contexts) have paradoxical tendencies or implications. Social actors, like politicians, managers, and academics, are enmeshed in self-justifying calculations whose paradoxical implications are often not understood.

To anticipate our conclusion, we would argue that the uncritical use of wealth-maximizing appraisal techniques and profit-maximizing performance measures does not always produce sensible results. This proposition could be demonstrated in a variety of ways by examining different cases. It could, for example, be approached through an examination of managerialism and the universities; the mechanical application of cost and staff–student ratios in the universities has absurd consequences which we all know about. We, however, have decided to examine the case of three nationalized enterprises – the National Coal Board (NCB), the British Steel Corporation (BSC), and British Leyland (BL) in Britain from 1970 to the time of writing (mid-1980s). These cases were immediately interesting because NPV and profit forms of calculation have been extensively and influentially applied in these enterprises and, it will be argued, the results in terms of wealth and profit creation have been disastrous.

We chose to examine the three cases together because we were intrigued by certain similarities between them. To begin with, key strategy documents in the 1972–4 period all recommended massive strategic investment as a solution to the problems of the enterprises; these recommendations can be traced in steel's 1972 development strategy (British Steel Corporation, 1973), just as in the 1974 Ryder Report on BL (Ryder, 1975) or the 1974 Plan for Coal (National Coal Board, 1974). Furthermore, very large sums of money were invested in the three enterprises. Some idea of the scale of investment can be obtained by adding up the totals for capital expenditure (in nominal end-of-year values) for the three enterprises. By our calculation approximately £9,500 million was invested in nationalized coal, steel, and cars after 1974; the nominal value sub-totals for the individual enterprises are £4,315 million for coal, £3,202 million for steel, and £1,918 million for cars. The state's largesse released steel and cars from the constraints on investment established by low profitability before nationalization. For coal, the ready availability of state funds for investment represented a reversal of the pre-oil crisis policy of running the industry down.

The results of massive strategic investment were equally disastrous in all three enterprises. Strategic investment was undertaken in the expectation of profit but the net result was massive operating losses and disorderly retreat from about 1979 onwards. After 1979 our three nationalized enterprises accumulated pre-tax losses of almost exactly £4,250 million; the sub-totals for the individual enterprises are £1,785 million lost at BSC up to the end of 1984, £1,196 million lost at BL over the same period, and £1,275 million lost at the NCB up to the end of 1983. The financial pressures of huge operating losses resulted in large-scale plant closure in steel and cars, and provoked a bitter strike about closure in coal. The decline in the size of the workforce provides a rough indication of the extent of contraction and retreat. Nationalized coal, steel, and cars employed 643,000 workers in 1973 but by 1983 the number employed was down to 364,000; half the 200,000 workers in BL have gone and more than half the similar number in BSC. Finally, we should note that in all three cases, the financial crisis after 1979 was monitored by market failure. Cars and steel lost home and export market shares, while coal was more peculiarly the victim of recession. In all three cases there is a painful contrast between planned high levels of production and actual low levels of output; by 1982 and 1983 steel and cars were making roughly half the output they had planned.

Our three nationalized enterprises thus provide us with similar *prima facie* cases of strategic investment which failed and led to agonized operational adjustment. How was the original strategic miscalculation related to the NPV form of accounting calculation? How has more recent operational adjustment related to profit and loss calculations? In the next two sections of this chapter we take up these issues.

What are the implications of using net present value calculations for strategic investment choice?

It may be useful to begin by recalling the origins of this calculation which is now universally used by British and American enterprises in investment choices. Bayne and Shaw originally promoted the calculation as 'the investor's method'. Net present value was intended as a form of financial calculation for an individual investor managing a portfolio, and there is no doubt that the calculation is satisfactory for this purpose because it adequately deals with the time preference of a coupon-clipping rentier. But American critics of the calculation (Hayes and Abernathy, 1980; Hayes and Garvin, 1982) have questioned whether NPV is appropriate for the manufacturing enterprise's decisions about productive investment. They allege that NPV appraisal techniques may lock the enterprise into technological backwardness and uncompetitiveness which ensures failure in the market place so that disinvestment appears to be the only way out.

The Americans provide a coherent explanation of why the NPV calculation can produce these perverse results.

1   NPV calculations bias enterprise calculation against large-scale strategic investment. This bias is a matter of simple arithmetic when the method applies a compound depreciation factor which reduces the value of cash-flow earned in future years. Large-scale strategic investment in, for example, new process technology should capture earnings in the long run but these distant and uncertain returns are worth less in terms of present value. For this reason, Hayes argues that the logical outcome of NPV is a patching investment strategy which defends existing process technology and product lines. This strategy is attractive in NPV terms since it offers short-run returns which are substantial in relation to the modest investment expenditures required. Because it encourages such a preoccupation with short-run returns, the NPV calculations may inhibit the innovative exploitation of new process technology and product lines necessary to long-run market success; the calculation will bias the enterprise towards developing products for existing markets and towards product designs of an imitative rather than an innovative nature.

2   NPV calculations encourage a single enterprise static approach to investment and neglect the dynamics whereby the returns on one enterprise's investment project will depend on the investments which are made by competing enterprises. To take a simple example of this effect, the projected returns from one enterprise's purchase of new and more efficient productive techniques may never materialize if competing enterprises also invest in the same technology, with the net results being over-capacity and price cutting. The recent history of European steel and cars provides a dismal illustration of this kind of effect. Furthermore, the NPV calculation in itself provides no guidance on the crucial question of whether and how competing enterprises will invest strategically in process and product renewal. If most firms use the NPV calculation, they will still come to different conclusions about similar projects, if only because they are likely to use different discount rates. Rogue enterprises may decide not to use NPV or to ignore the results of NPV calculations.

3   NPV calculations are associated with a misdefinition or an overly restrictive definition of investment expenditure. The conventional Anglo-American concept of investment includes

fixed and working capital but excludes 'expense investment' such as the costs of the distribution network or the aggressive pricing that is required to enter a new export market. Magaziner and Reich (1982) would argue that such costs should be considered as investment expenditure because, just like new plant, they are day-to-day expenses which create the opportunity for future production and sales. Investment appraisal calculations which are preoccupied with the return on fixed capital investment may be associated with a bias against the 'expense investment' which is necessary to sustain the enterprise's competitive position.

The American critics make a number of sensible points about the limits of this form of financial calculation. But they are wrong to suppose that NPV calculations have an inherently powerful logic which results in a general bias against large-scale strategic investment. NPV's bias is mutable and this point is very clearly demonstrated by the way in which our three nationalized enterprises were able to justify massive strategic investment within an NPV framework. It is instructive to ask why and how the enterprises were able to do this. If we are to answer this question, we must begin by emphasizing that any NPV calculation deals in projected financial results in the form of cash-flows. But the relevant financial magnitudes can only be estimated after the enterprise has made assumptions about productive and market possibilities. At this level of the preliminary non-financial assumption the enterprise can introduce assumptions about, for example, the benefits of new process technology or larger-scale production. These assumptions will feed back into the arithmetic of NPV and cancel any bias against the strategic.

On the issues of the benefits from new process technology and larger-scale production, our three nationalized enterprises accepted the then orthodox assumptions about the economics of western mass production. It was presumed that the enterprise had the productive opportunity to move down a long-run average cost curve by embracing large-scale capital-intensive techniques of production. If the enterprise did this, the market would not be a problem because unit costs would come steadily down and sales and profits would look after themselves. This was the western production engineer's version of the American dream; the original model of such success was, of course, provided by Ford with the Model T. None of the key strategy documents was explicit about these assumptions. But it is significant that they all placed great emphasis on the handicap arising from a legacy of under-investment in coal, steel, and cars; in the western mass production model, shortage of investment funds figures as the only real obstacle to success.

It was always doubtful whether the assumptions of western mass production were relevant to coal, steel, and cars. Belief in the relevance of these assumptions was based on a very partial and superficial reading of the relevant academic literatures on the economies of scale. This was clearest in the cases of cars and steel, where the academics suggested that economies of scale would continue to be achieved up to very high levels of output; scale economies continued up to 500,000 units per annum of one car model and up to 10 million tonnes per annum of steel (on steel see Pratten, *et al.* (1965), Benson Committee (1966), Cockerill and Silbertson (1974); and on cars see Pratten (1971), Rhys (1972), White (1971)). But the academic literatures also showed that most of the economies of scale were exhausted at much lower levels of output; in steel, for example, more than 90 per cent of the scale economies from a 10 million ton plant could be obtained from a 2 million ton plant.

These academic subtleties were lost on strategic planners whose dogmatic adherence to the assumptions of mass production emerges very clearly in their commitment to giantism. In coal and steel this was manifested in the commitment to giant plants. In steel, under the 1972 Plan, average size of steel plant was expected to more than double from 2.2 million tonnes in 1972 to 6 million tonnes in 1983 and one giant complex at Teeside was to be built up to a capacity of 11 million tonnes. In coal, the 1974 Plan provided a charter for super-pits. The NCB embarked on the construction of Selby which would produce 10 million tonnes of coal per annum or nearly 1 ton in 10 of all deep-mined coal. To put this into perspective, it should be remembered that the small Welsh pits produce less than 250,000 tonnes per annum. In cars, BL already had large assembly plants at Longbridge and Cowley, and the giantism emerged in the slightly different form of an organizational prescription. Ryder proposed one monster car division which would include all volume and specialist car production so as 'to achieve the maximum possible integration of engineering, production and marketing' (Ryder, 1975).

The simple arithmetic of NPV calculation was never a serious obstacle in the way of justifying a massive investment in giantism which offered a distant prospect of return. As the NCB's mine appraisal procedure shows, the arithmetic of a NPV calculation can be rigged so as to justify this massive investment. This illustration shifts the focus from investment strategy to individual project. But that hardly matters when these new mines are very large projects which dominate the NCB's investment strategy; nearly half the NCB's new investment goes into new mines and the one super-pit at Selby has already cost £1,400 million at the time of writing. In the new mine appraisals, the NCB concentrated on pushing up present value by four expedients on the cash inflow side of the equation.

1 Cash-flows from new mines were calculated over a long period. In new mines 'life of the seam' was the relevant time period and in the case of the Thorne appraisal this life was estimated at forty-seven years. By way of contrast, cash inflows from investment in existing mines were calculated over a maximum period of just fifteen years.
2 Low discount rates were used so that the distant receipts were more valuable. The NCB favoured an 8 per cent discount rate which made £1 ten years away worth 46p. By way of comparison, the BSC in its 1972 strategic evaluation exercise favoured a 16 per cent discount rate which makes £1 ten years away worth just 23p in present value.
3 It was assumed that target rates of output would be achieved. The NCB assumed that its Selby super-pit would achieve its target output rate of 10 million tonnes. This was flatly contrary to past experience; the Monopolies and Mergers Commission's sample of NCB major projects showed their output was on average 10 per cent below 'stage two estimates'.
4 Incremental output was valued on a highly favourable basis. One of the two price projections made for new mines apparently allowed the NCB to assume the coal prices would increase in real terms at 2 per cent per annum. This is remarkable when, at the beginning of the slump, the NCB agreed with the CEGB to limit rises in coal price in line with retail prices. It is also worth noting that incremental output from existing mines is valued only at distress stock or export prices.

This kind of arithmetic will not convince sceptics who can easily demonstrate its fragility. The NCB can find £322 million of NPV in the Selby project. But, as the *Aberystwyth Report* (Cutler *et al.* 1985) showed, the NPV goes negative if the discount rate is increased from 8 to 10 per cent and Selby's output is quoted down from 10 to 9 million tons. If the financial representations are so malleable, the NPV form of calculation cannot have a powerful inherent bias against the strategic. The malleability is so striking that we can ask a more fundamental question. Does NPV calculation usually function as a way of appraising genuinely different strategy options or does the calculation function as a way of justifying one pre-existing strategic choice? Certainly in the case of steel and cars the calculation had the latter role.

In steel the 1972 strategic evaluation exercise looked at the NPV arising from twelve different 'options'. But all the options were differentiated versions of management's preferred strategy of concentrating production in large coastal works which used imported ore. The options differed only about the extent, timing, and form of a further shift to the coast. All presupposed a large market of 23–36 million tonnes. All presupposed a rundown of inland steel-making at Corby, Consett, and Shotton. All presupposed there would be no large-scale development of mini-mills. In cars the procedures of justification were even more blatant because there never was any formal examination of alternatives. The Ryder team did undertake a cash-flow analysis, but this was only so that the team could endorse a pre-existing management investment plan; this plan existed in the form of an internal 'management concept study' of investment projects which would be desirable given relatively free availability of funds. In steel and cars, NPV played a priestly role.

In this way, NPV functioned as a weak form of calculation which in our three cases facilitated the massive strategic miscalculations whose nature we will analyse in later sections of this chapter. The American critics of NPV are therefore wrong about the role of the calculation in strategy choice. We would argue they also fail to see that NPV can create problems of a quite different sort. These problems which concern us arise from the relation between the strategic and the operational. The NPV representation of enterprise choice in strategic financial terms abstracts from a number of operational problems which the enterprise will encounter as the strategy is being implemented. Enterprises which plan to prosper strategically in the long run must still survive operationally in the short run. The paradox is that the long-run financial plan can make it more difficult to get by in the short run.

Strategic investment can create operational problems of a productive and financial kind. Productively, where NPV is supplemented with western mass-production assumptions, the strategy aims to move the enterprise down the long-run average cost curve which is represented in idealized form as a smooth and continuous function. But, unless the slate is wiped clean and production begins anew on one greenfield site, the enterprise must in the short run operate a collection of old and new plants and processes. This can create operational problems about capacity utilization, process imbalance, and technological mix. On the financial side, strategic planning can create other problems. Strategic planning in NPV terms deals in *ex-ante* cash inflow and outflow over periods of up to a decade. But that does not suspend the constraint of twelve-monthly accounting calculation which deals in *ex-post* accruals and the balance between revenue and expenditure. This can create operational problems about the finance of operating losses in the early years of the strategy when expenditure is incurred on investment projects which are not yet completed and earning revenue.

The conflict between the strategic and the operational can be palliated by careful planning which makes short-run productive, market, and financial decisions contribute to strategic outcomes. But the conflict may be unmanageable if the productive discontinuities and imbalances are severe or if large-scale investment is contemplated when the current financial position of the enterprise is unfavourable. This latter point is worth developing because it demonstrates again that NPV does not have invariant effects; when it comes to the conflict between the strategic and the operational, it all depends on the context in which NPV is applied. NPV will not create operational problems if it is used for investment project appraisal in an enterprise whose existing assets do earn decent accounting rates of return. NPV will create severe operational problems if it is used for investment strategy choice in an enterprise which suffers from chronically low rates of return. The operational problem here is that the old investments cannot carry the new investments in profit terms in the early years of the strategy.

Coal, steel, and cars were all in this position. As our graphs (Statistical appendix, Figures 4.A4, 4.A5, and 4.A6, pp. 159–61) show, their rates of return were always low and declining or fluctuating towards zero. The investment strategies promised to redress the low rate of return problem in the long run. Thus, as the House of Commons Expenditure Committee (1975) pointed out, Ryder promised to make BL, by the mid-1980s, more profitable than any European car firm had ever been. But these benefits were a long way away and in the early years of the strategy our three enterprises had to finance a negative cash-flow. In the 1974 Ryder Report it was envisaged that it would be seven years before the investment strategy made a positive contribution to cash-flow. In the BSC's 1972 plan it was envisaged that this interval of negative cash-flow would be no less than eleven years. Thus NPV justified strategic investment but created operational problems. In our next section we will examine how these operational problems manifested themselves and were resolved in a profit and loss framework.

What are the implications of using profit and loss to guide operational adjustments?

We will begin by establishing the basic point that, in our three enterprises, operational problems were caused and aggravated by the financial effects of massive strategic investment in an unprofitable enterprise. Most obviously, in the profit and loss account, larger

Table 4.1 Depreciation and profit and loss per tonne/vehicle

	Year	Depreciation per tonne/vehicle (£)	Profit/loss per tonne/vehicle (£)
BSC	1973	3.58	0.35
	1982	8.94	(25.39)
BL	1973	37.9	44.2
	1982	285.16	(429.1)
NCB	1973	0.52	(0.28)
	1982	2.13	(0.69)

Note: Figures in brackets denote losses.
Source: Statistical appendix, Tables 4.A7, 4.A8 and 4.A9, pp. 148–9.

depreciation charges arising from new investment automatically depressed rates of return whch were low or negative to begin with. This point emerges clearly from Table 4.1 which compares depreciation per tonne or vehicle and profit/loss per tonne or vehicle.

In the cyclically good year of 1973, before the large-scale investment had started, the prevailing low depreciation charges were sufficient to more or less wipe out any profit in BSC and NCB. The position was different in BL only because the enterprise was not making any depreciation provision for a large amount of elderly, fully depreciated capital equipment. In the depressed year of 1982, when the strategic commitments had been made, the burden of larger depreciation charges accounted for just over one-third of BSC's losses and exactly two-thirds of BL's losses; and, without the burden of depreciation, the NCB would have shown a healthy profit in 1982.

The investment strategy also multiplied financial pressures on the enterprises through the burden of interest charges. Substantial interest charges were inevitable when strategic investment could not be financed out of retained profits and when it was financed by government and private loans. As Table 4.2 shows, at their peak levels, interest charges have been a substantial burden on our three enterprises.

When the enterprises found it difficult to make any profit on sales, an amount equivalent to between 3.5 and 10 per cent of sales revenue was being diverted to meet the obligation of interest payments. Technically, interest payments did not reduce operating profits which were of course calculated before interest charges were levied. But that was small consolation because interest charges increased the revenue deficit of the enterprise and larger interest

Table 4.2 Interest *versus* sales revenue

	Year	Interest charge per tonne/vehicle	Sales revenue per tonne/vehicle
BSC	1981	15	248.2
BL	1982	187	5.464
NCB	1984	4.50	41.44

Source: Statistical appendix, Tables 4.A7, 4.A8 and 4.A9, pp. 148–9.

charges required a larger government revenue deficit grant. This raised the level of apparent public subsidy and promoted the impression that these enterprises had major problems which required urgent attention. The revenue deficit is also increased by the burden of 'extraordinary items' which show the cost of asset write-offs and redundancy payments caused by plant closure. The strategic plans of coal and steel always envisaged such closures; and, as we will argue later in this section, closure plans were accelerated in coal, steel, and cars when strategy had failed. Asset write-offs on closure account for a larger part of the 'extraordinary items' charge in our three enterprises; in steel they account for 72 per cent of the extraordinary item charge between 1972 and 1982. These write-offs are, in effect, an accelerated depreciation charge on assets which are being scrapped.

It is the total size of the enterprise's revenue deficit which is the operational problem. The extent to which the strategic investment plan contributes to this problem is best measured by adding together three sub-totals (depreciation plus interest plus extraordinary items) which represent the operational cost of the strategy (Table 4.3). This table gives the cumulative results for our three enterprises over the decade ending in 1982 or 1983. It shows that the relative importance of the three sub-totals does vary; the extraordinary items charge in coal, for example, is low because the value of the old assets had already been written down just before our calculation begins. But the overall result is the same in all three enterprises; if we add up the sub-totals then we obtain an 'operational burden' which is, in each case, significantly larger that the accumulated revenue deficit. The results are most remarkable in the case of coal which is not a chronic loss-maker because it earned profits up to 1978; the operational burden is here two and a half times as large as the government deficit grants which have been paid to cover subsequent deficits.

If investment strategy created operational problems in this way,

Table 4.3: Operational costs and revenue deficits

Charges	£ million
BSC 1972–83	
Accumulated depreciation charges	1,159.7
Accumulated interest charges	1,357.5
Accumulated extraordinary items	1,925.9
Accumulated 'operational burden'	£4,443.1
Accumulated revenue deficit	£3,804
BL 1975–82	
Accumulated depreciation charges	719.5
Accumulated interest charges	501.6
Accumulated extraordinary items	445.0
Accumulated 'operational burden'	£1,666.1
Accumulated revenue deficit	£1,514.7
NCB 1974–83	
Accumulated depreciation charges	1,456.1
Accumulated interest charges	1,572.5
Accumulated extraordinary items	51.5
Accumulated 'operational burden'	£3,080.1
Accumulated government deficit grant	£1,241

Source: Statistical appendix, Tables 4.A10, 4.A11, 4.A12, pp. 150–2.

what was to be done? In the remaining part of this section of the chapter, we will examine the logic of operational retreat. And we can begin by observing that when operational problems present themselves in financial form, enterprises will usually seek a financial solution in two ways – through book-keeping adjustments and plant closure. The book-keeping adjustments include capital write-offs and debt write-downs which remove the burden of depreciation and interest charges from the accounts. Thus, after the formal abandonment of the BSC development strategy in 1978, BSC obtained a deal whereby assets in the balance sheet were written down by £1,300 million, capital employed was written down by £4,000 million, and £650 million of loans owed to the government were written off. A loss-making nationalized enterprise cannot always negotiate such a deal with the government. Coal has not had a

Table 4.4 Reductions in numbers employed

	Year	Numbers employed (thousands)
BSC	1973	175
	1979	142
	1983	69
BL	1973	204
	1979	177
	1983	103
NCB	1973	264
	1979	232
	1984	192

Source: Statistical appendix, Tables 4.A4, 4.A5, and 4.A6, pp. 146–7.

capital write-off or debt write-down since 1973, when the decks were being cleared financially for the new investment strategy to begin. If book-keeping adjustments cannot be made, or cannot be made on a sufficiently grand scale, then plant closure is the remaining option.

At this point in the argument it should be emphasized that over-capacity has been and, at the time of writing, is a problem in all three enterprises because the market demand which the strategic planners envisaged never materialized. Since 1980, the BSC has had 26 million tonnes of steel-making capacity in its five major plants. Some 14.3 million tonnes of this capacity is, at the time of writing, manned and output since 1983 has been running at a level of about 11 million tonnes. In BL the over-capacity problem is most obvious in the volume car Austin Rover business. Here the Cowley and Longbridge facilities have a capacity of 750,000 cars per annum. But in 1983 Austin Rover sold just 458,000 cars and in 1984 sales declined to 423,000. The problem of over-capacity presents itself in a different form in coal. Investments in new mines have long lead times and the NCB's problem relates to large amounts of new capacity which is under construction. Since the onset of the present recession, the demand for deep-mined coal has been stuck at around 100 million tonnes, when the NCB has nearly 25 million tonnes of new capacity hanging over the market.

Plant closure is attractive in such situations of over-capacity. It helps trim operating costs by taking out the excess capacity while simultaneously reducing avoidable costs because it lowers the wage bill. The dramatic contraction in numbers employed in our three enterprises provides some indication of the extent to which the closure option has been pursued (Table 4.4).

As Table 4.4 shows, both steel and cars have lost 100,000 workers since 1973 and coal has lost 75,000 workers; the reductions account for 60 per cent of the 1973 workforce in steel, 50 per cent in BL, and over 25 per cent in coal. The table also shows that most of the reduction has been achieved in the period of retreat and operating loss after 1978. The workforce reductions reflect influences other than plant closure. All the enterprises have sought lower manning levels; in the year before the coal strike, the NCB took the equivalent of one man off each coal-face in the UK (Burns *et al.*, 1984). At the same time, plants which remain open have often been slimmed down in a major way; by mid-1982 Longbridge employed 9,500 workers, or less than half the 19,400 of 1977 (*Financial Times*, 17 June 1982). But plant closure remains the dominant influence on workforce reduction.

Financially motivated closures have knock-on consequences for plant configuration, product mix, and market penetration; closure is a discontinuous process, with production and market consequences which are particular to the individual enterprise. If we ignore these complications and look simply at which plants close, we can see that there is a common pattern in the closure decisions of our three nationalized enterprises. In steel, the small inland works at Corby, Consett, and Shotton were closed so that bulk steel production could be concentrated in the five large coastal works. In cars, branch assembly operations at Canley, Speke, and Solihull were closed, while the two major assembly plants at Longbridge and Cowley survived. In coal, three of the twelve coalfields bore the brunt of closure. From the beginning of 1974 to the end of the first quarter of 1982–3, small pits in the geographically peripheral coalfields of Wales, Scotland, and Durham accounted for nearly 60 per cent of all closures (Monopolies and Mergers Commission, 1983, vol. 1, p. 175).

There are anomalies in this process. Retreat is usually disorderly and leads to the abandonment of recent defensive investments in the peripheral plants. All three enterprises provide examples of such anomalies. The billet mill at Consett was modernized in 1977–8 just before the closure of the works in 1980 (Cottrell, 1981). At Polmaise pit in Scotland the NCB spent £15.8 million on development before deciding not to re-open the pit (Kerevan and Saville, 1985). In Solihull BL abandoned a newly-built assembly plant which reputedly had some of the most modern paint facilities in Europe. But the basic pattern of closure is always the same. The large central facilities of the enterprise are defended and maintained, while closure is concentrated on the smaller, peripheral facilities.

This pattern of closure has a double rationale because it simultaneously controls fixed costs and takes out avoidable costs. The large capital-intensive central plants have proportionately higher fixed costs than the smaller peripheral plants and the central plants have to be fully utilized if their unit costs are to be kept low. In a situation of over-capacity, closure at the periphery loads the central plants with throughput and contains their operating costs. 'Senior company sources' at BL have provided some information on the throughput requirements of Austin Rover's two central assembly plants which have a maximum capacity of 750,000 cars per annum (*Financial Times*, 12 January 1985). Even after major cost-cutting exercises, operating costs were such that the Longbridge and Cowley plants could not break even at a trading level (without covering depreciation) if throughput fell below 435,000 cars per annum. A volume of around 650,000 cars per annum was required if the company was to earn sufficient profit to cover depreciation and finance new investment. If the central plants have economics of this sort, it is hardly surprising that enterprises choose to concentrate production in them.

The other advantage of closure is that it takes out avoidable costs; the labour force in the closed plants is sacked and that reduces wage costs. In coal and steel there have been redundancy and retirement schemes which buy out old workers at some cost to the enterprise and the government, while some wage-related costs, like pensions, will continue after closure. Nevertheless, from the enterprise's point of view, after once-and-for-all redundancy expenses and continuing costs have been taken into account, closure does save avoidable wage costs. This sets up a second mechanism which puts peripheral plants at risk because such plants are often more labour intensive. After selective investment in modernization, this was certainly the case in our three nationalized enterprises. The results are clearest in coal, where output per man-shift provides a direct measure of labour intensity per ton of coal produced. Low OMS (output per man shift) pits are concentrated on the geographic periphery: in 1981–2 South Wales, Scotland, and Durham accounted for forty-five of the seventy pits with an OMS below two tonnes (Monopolies and Mergers Commission, 1983, vol. 2, appendix 3.7). It is hardly surprising that the NCB chooses to close low OMS pits because, other things being equal, closing these pits takes out avoidable wage costs faster.

Our argument so far focuses on the composition rather than the level of costs. The high fixed-cost central plans must be protected and labour-intensive peripheral plants will be sacrificed. From this point of view, an 'uneconomic' works is not a high-cost works but a works which is peripheral to the management's investment strategy because it has the wrong cost composition. At the same time we would argue that the bias in favour of central plants is often reinforced when issues about level of costs, profit, and loss are taken into account. These issues often figure prominently in debates and struggles about plant closure. No one will need to be reminded that, through the long and bitter coal strike, the NCB and government insisted that the issue was management's right to close high-cost and unprofitable pits. More generally, the issue of high costs and no profits cannot be avoided because, from a right or centrist point of view, closure on these grounds is legitimate.

We have a good deal of sympathy for the position of those accountants who argue that profit and loss calculations should *not* be used as basis for closure decisions. Many accountants would argue with good reason that backward-looking profit and loss calculations are irrelevant to closure; in the nature of things such calculations can only provide a look in the rear view mirror on capital maintenance. As the Manchester team (Berry, *et al.*, 1985b) pointed out, the decision to abandon assets should ideally be based on the prospective return from using them in the future. The same team also points out that accounts developed for operating purposes necessarily do not make most of the distinctions between categories of cost which are required where closure is contemplated.

Partly no doubt for this reason, when closure is contemplated, profit and loss calculations are often used opportunistically and cynically to justify what management wants to do and has already decided. In this way, profit and loss can play the same justificatory role in closure as NPV does in strategic investment. This is possible because in profit and loss calculations, as in NPV, it is possible to rig the arithmetic without breaking the relevant accounting conventions. There are a variety of ways in which this can be done so that the results favour the maintenance of central plants by creating an appearance of lower costs and superior profitability in those plants. A careful allocation of throughput and output quotas is one of the simplest ways of doing this. Consider, for example, the cost figures produced when BSC wanted to close Shotton. These showed that Port Talbot apparently had lower costs than Shotton. But, as Bryer and Brignall (1982, p. 199) noted, the BSC compared Shotton's costs when open with those of Port Talbot after it had been loaded with extra throughput from the closure of Shotton. This allocation consideration is also relevant to all those NCB justifications of super pits as a low cost option; pits like Selby will never be low-cost pits unless they are given the necessary output quotas.

So far we have emphasized the malleability of profit and loss calculations, but we would also argue that, in some contexts, the logic of profit and loss calculation does powerfully reinforce management's centralizing preferences. Profit and loss may produce acceptable incremental adjustments to the size of the industry in a perfect competition type of situation where there is a multiplicity of small enterprises. But profit and loss is a poor guide to massive adjustments in a giant enterprise after its investment strategy has failed. In the latter case the profit and loss calculation has an inherent bias which protects the capital-intensive central plants and sacrifices the labour-intensive periphery.

The bias arises because profit and loss accounts are prepared after levying an historic cost depreciation charge but without levying current replacement cost depreciation or any interest charge on capital employed. There is nothing sacrosanct about this procedure of admitting one capital charge and excluding two capital charges which can individually be quite as large. The procedure is a convention and nothing more. Nevertheless, the convention has definite effects because it introduces a low capital charge at the plant level. As we showed in the *Aberystwyth Report on Coal* (Cutler *et al.,* 1985), adding on the two extra capital charges would decisively change the rank order of NCB pits in terms of costs and profitability. The existing convention makes the capital intensive plants look good. Enterprises can invest strategically in cost reductions in the central plants at a relatively modest price in terms of reduced operating profit; in this account, investment's only cost is historic cost depreciation.

What do losses or high costs in individual plants under this convention signify in a giant enterprise which is in retreat after its investment strategy has failed? Losses do not represent an objective signal from the outside economy about the closures which are necessary on grounds of economic efficiency. Losses may only provide a signal about which plants have been denied effective strategic investment in cost reduction. In this case, disinvestment in a second period of retreat on the basis of profit and loss calculation reflects only the enterprise's disposition of investment funds in the first period of strategic investment. This more or less describes the situation of the NCB, where investment has been concentrated on new mines and on the more profitable of the existing mines; under the historic cost depreciation system, the profits of the central pits are a self-fulfilling prophecy just like the losses of the peripheral pits. The miners of South Wales were therefore crucified on the cross of historic cost depreciation. At an enterprise level the burden of historic cost depreciation (plus interest and extraordinary items) creates serious operating problems. At a plant level, historic cost depreciation (without an interest charge) does not allocate a large capital charge to the central high investment pits which are therefore never on the closure list.

As this example shows, the logic of profit and loss only becomes really vicious when the enterprise is burdened with hefty interest charges. This condition is satisfied in all three of our enterprises where the funds for investment are not financially free and have to be borrowed at rates of interest of up to 14 per cent. This is clearest in coal, where the NCB financed its strategy by borrowing from the government; this enterprise pays an average of 13.8 per cent on its post-1973 borrowings from the Secretary of State. In cars and steel the story is different but the end result is much the same. BL obtained some £2,300 million after 1974 in the form of equity (public dividend capital) but that has not been enough and the enterprise has made ends meet by borrowing from private sources. BSC obtained debt write-offs but these were not on a sufficient scale to solve the problem of indebtedness.

Our conclusion must be that when debt-encumbered nationalized enterprises retreat strategically, the logic of profit and loss powerfully reinforces management's natural tendency to safeguard the central high investment plants which embody the physical remains of the original strategy. At the same time we do not think that these problems can be solved by proposing a change of accounting convention which would somehow make the closure process more 'fair'. Academics would be better employed in trying to understand, and helping to avoid, situations of over-capacity which require massive closure on the basis of profit and loss. In the next section of this chapter, therefore, we will try to be more analytic about what exactly went wrong in our three nationalized enterprises.

What went wrong with the initial strategic plans and why do operational adjustments fail to deliver profitability?

Successful strategy has one general precondition; the enterprise must find a harmonious relation between three sets of considerations by balancing productive, market, and financial calculations. The strategies of our three nationalized enterprises were misconceived and doomed to failure because they established no basis for this harmony in the three dimensions of enterprise calculation. The underlying problem was the assumptions of western mass production which ensured that the productive and market calculations of the enterprises were naive. Our analysis in previous sections has shown the enterprises grappling with the financial implications of this naivete. In this section we will argue that the different cases illustrate different combinations of productive and market miscalculation, and we will begin by analysing the productive miscalculation.

In steel, coal, and cars, the investment strategies were all obsessed with the productive potential of large-scale investment in new greenfield or brownfield development. This was a productive miscalculation because such investment was inherently a high-risk option. The super-pits in coal provide a classic illustration of this point. The geological risks are obvious when a super-pit like Selby will try to win 10 million tonnes of coal per annum from one set of coal measures. Quite apart from the problem of having all the enterprise's (productive) eggs in one (geological) basket, there are other risks. Super-pits tie the enterprise to one local customer. All Selby's coal, for example, goes on merry-go-round trains to local power stations. Super-pits also use an unproven capital-intensive technology which is vulnerable to disruption. This is certainly the case at Selby where, when the pit is fully operational, continuous conveyors 30 kilometres long will be required to take the coal from the furthest of the five collieries to the railhead.

At the same time the strategic emphasis on new green- and brownfield development ensured that our enterprises retained some pieces of older process technology which desperately needed to be replaced. Again steel provides a documented example. Because the investment funds had been spent on steelmaking, the BSC could not make improvements in downstream finishing processes. These improvements were necessary to retain customers who increasingly demanded the differentiated quality products which they could easily obtain from BSC's European competitors. BSC's share of Ford's steel purchases fell from 80–85 per cent in 1975 to 55 per cent thereafter because BSC could not supply a sheet product which met Ford's quality requirement (Bryer and Brignall, 1982, pp. 158–9). The BSC was in this position because it had not replaced the antiquated strip mill at Port Talbot which had been designed in 1938 and continuously used since 1950. Aggravated market failure was the result of this kind of persistence with inadequate process technology.

More culpably, our three enterprises did not make the most of what they had. None of the strategies emphasized 'fine tuning' of existing process technology which could have increased productive efficiency in general and machine utilization in particular at a very low cost. Many commentators on Japanese manufacturing techniques have emphasized that the Japanese pursue manufacturing efficiency not only through expensive investment in new process technology but also through low-cost modification of existing process technology. Shonberger (1982) explains this approach to constant modification of process equipment, plant layout, and working practices. The approach is epitomized by the way in which Kawasaki (Lincoln) improved machine utilization and reduced the set-up costs of changing dies on its punch presses; each press was fitted with a carousel arrangement so that the new die could be swung into place and clamped up as the old die was swung aside.

In contrast, our three nationalized enterprises had accepted a stereotype of western mass production and were not much interested in this kind of eastern production engineering. Where the British did tackle the problem of machine utilization, for example, they did not do so in the modest cost-effective Japanese way. The NCB's MINOS is a British high-tech approach to the problem; this monitoring and control system promises higher machine utilization through the prevention of mechanical breakdown and tighter control over the labour process. Parts of the MINOS system will work, particularly at the face where machinery is working productively for approximately one-third of the available time. Here the MIDAS system for diagnosing maintenance condition and guiding shearer position can pay for itself in forty days (Burns, et al., 1984). But the MINOS system as a whole is an expensive attempt to recreate Bentham's panopticon underground in a coal mine equipped with the latest electronics. The results so far (Hopper et al., 1985) are not overly encouraging; complete visibility and perfect control over men and machines is likely to remain a management fantasy.

All the points made so far support one conclusion about productive miscalculation. The investment strategies of our three enterprises abstracted from the productive problems inherent in running a multi-plant, multi-process, multi-product enterprise; rather than addressing these mundane but real productive problems, the enterprises got diverted into buying glamorous bits of high technology. In this context the basic oxygen converters in steel, the robotized body shops in BL, and the super-pits with MINOS in coal, all represented a kind of ritual modernization. Such facilities could no more transform the productive process in an enterprise or industry than an international airport or a teaching hospital can make a less developed country more developed. Indeed, in a precise sense, the new facilities were counter-productive. Our three enterprises would have benefited from useful modernized and efficient facilities for manufacturing steel and cars or extracting coal. Instead, they chose to make expensive rhetorical public statements about modern manufacturing and bought in processes and plants which could not increase efficiency because they represented a risky investment in unbalanced and inflexible production.

This conclusion will be confirmed by any systematic analysis of the physical consequences of new investment in terms of productivity measures which relate inputs to outputs. Influenced by the assumptions of western mass production, the key strategy documents of the early 1970s had argued that our three enterprises were handicapped by problems of under-investment; production was physically inefficient, as well as financially unprofitable, because the enterprises had too few assets per man or per unit of output in the production process. The commitment of investment resources ensured that this 'deficiency' was rectified. This is clearest in NCB and BL, where the real value of gross assets has increased by approximately 50 per cent over the decade from 1973 to 1983 (Statistical appendix, Tables 4.A13 and 4.A14, pp. 152–3). As Tables 4.5 and 4.6 show, with static or sharply declining output and

Table 4.5: Real capital stock per man (constant 1975 money values)

	Year	£
NCB	1976	4,403
	1983	10,900
		+ 148 per cent
BL	1976	3,338
	1983	8,815
		+ 160 per cent
BSC	1976	16,000
	1981	21,100
		+ 32 per cent (on manned capacity)

Source: Statistical appendix, Tables 4.A13–4.A16, pp. 152–5.

Table 4.6 Real capital stock per unit of output (constant 1975 money values)

	Year	£ per tonne/vehicle
NCB	1977	8.60
	1983	19.10
		+ 122 per cent
BL	1977	632
	1983	1,609
		+ 155 per cent
BSC	1977	143
	1981	186
		+ 30 per cent (after asset write-offs)

Source: Statistical appendix, Tables 4.A13–4.A16, pp. 152–5.

manpower trends, the increase in assets at NCB and BL is such that real capital assets per man or per unit of output have increased by between 100 and 150 per cent since the mid-1970s. The position is different in BSC, which shows a 40 per cent decline in the real value of gross assets since 1972 (Statistical appendix, Table 4.A15, p. 154). As Tables 4.5 and 4.6 show, the decline in output and employment at BSC in the long run keeps pace with the decline in real assets, so that real capital assets per unit of output and per man show only modest increases. But this anomalous result at BSC simply reflects accounting adjustments in a retreating enterprise which has accepted that many of its assets are not and will not be productive in the revenue earning sense; the asset base has been reduced by large-scale write-offs and capital stock per man is calculated on a manned-capacity basis (14.3 million tonnes out of a 26 million tonne total). If BSC's real assets per man or per tonne were calculated on the same basis as at BL and NCB, the result would be an equally marked increase in capital intensity. Consequently, it could now be argued that all three enterprises suffer from pathological over-investment because the capital intensity of production has increased without any of the benefits materializing.

The figures on capital stock per unit of output imply that capital productivity is poor; that is, of course, just what we would expect from poor capacity utilization. More remarkable is the trend of labour productivity in the three enterprises, which confirms the thesis of productive miscalculation. In all three enterprises, produc-

Table 4.7 Labour productivity

	Year	Tonnes/vehicles per man-year
BSC	1973	143.6
	1979	121.6
	1983	169.0
BL	1973	5.69
	1979	3.91
	1983	5.47
NCB	1973	2.13
	1979	2.24
	1982	2.40

Source: Statistical appendix, Tables 4.A4–4.A6, pp. 146–7.

tion engineers played a major part in the formulation of strategy; indeed, the NCB, in particular, appears to have been a highly 'productionist' organization which was planned in physical output terms rather than controlled by financial ratios (Berry, *et al.,* 1985a). In all three enterprises strategic investment was initially justified partly on the productionist grounds that it would raise labour productivity. Thus, in steel's strategic plan it was envisaged that output per man would more or less double to 225 tonnes per man-year by 1982.

Table 4.7 summarized the labour productivity record of the three enterprises and shows that the ambitious productivity aims were never achieved. A more detailed examination of the series will confirm our first glance conclusion: none of our enterprises has achieved significant and lasting gains in labour productivity and in all three enterprises the long-run trend of labour productivity is flat.

The NCB has the excuse that, in labour productivity terms, the best is yet to come; at the time of writing, a substantial *tranche* of high-output-per-man super-pit capacity has yet to be brought into production and the Board has also now gained the freedom to close low-labour-productivity pits. But the flat trend of labour productivity in steel and cars is really quite remarkable given the extent of the retreat on to central plants and the wholesale sackings which were described in earlier sections of this paper. BL has disclosed little about its disposition of productive investment and claimed the credit for a 'productivity miracle' at Longbridge. It is, therefore, particularly worth emphasizing that the productivity record of the Austin Rover volume car division is awful. The volume car business employs just over 40,000 and sales totalled 458,000 in 1983 and

423,000 in 1984, so the current robotically-aided performance is about 10 cars per man-year. This is mediocre by the standard currently achieved by the more successful European producers like VW. And it is just about the same productivity level as the Austin-Morris volume car division of BLMC achieved in the bad old days of under-investment in the early 1970s; in 1972 Austin-Morris achieved 8.9 cars per man year (Williams *et al.*, 1983).

Our interpretation of flat and mediocre labour productivity is straightforward. Restrictive labour practices and over-manning can hardly be an important problem when management has gained the freedom to change working practices and workers can be sacked *en masse* in steel and cars. Flat labour productivity in these enterprises must reflect the combined influence of a productively inept investment strategy plus the influence of market failure which leaves giant plants short of throughput. It might be argued that if the central plants could be loaded then everything would come good. This would help, but it is doubtful whether better loading would solve the labour productivity problem. The productive imbalances established by strategic investment are probably so acute that the central plants in steel and cars are inherently low productivity plants; individual processes may have theoretically high levels of labour and capital productivity but these performance levels cannot be sustained steadily because of physical imbalances between different processes. We would like to be proved wrong. But that crucial test would require an expansion of demand to full capacity levels and that is unlikely because the market is simply not there.

This brings us to the market miscalculations and the way in which the available market was grossly over-estimated by two of our three enterprises. The exception here is coal. The NCB did project a large coal market of 125 million tonnes in the early 1980s. But that estimate was hardly unrealistic when it was made in the immediate aftermath of the first oil crisis. No one could reasonably have foreseen the combined effects of conservation and recession which dampened demand after 1979. Steel and cars, on the other hand, based their strategic plans on naively optimistic market forecasts. In steel the 1972 strategic evaluation exercise projected output levels of between 28 and 36 million tonnes by 1982. In cars, the Ryder report projected car sales of 843,000 by 1980 and 961,000 by 1985 (Bhaskar, 1979, p. 175). These scenarios envisaged substantial expansion of steel and volume car output. In steel, for example, the actual 1972 output was just 21.5 million tonnes and the BSC never produced much over 25 million tonnes in the halcyon years of the early 1970s.

Optimistic sales projections were rendered plausible by defining market objectives in percentage terms and by making a highly aggregative market analysis. Both BSC and BL assumed that their enterprises could maintain a constant share of the home market and make some gain in their share of export markets. Thus Ryder assumed, in a very anodyne way, that BL could maintain its home market share at 33 per cent and increase its European market share from 1.7 to 4.0 per cent. In absolute terms the task looked much harder; Ryder supposed that by the mid-1980s, BL could find an extra 200,000 sales on the home market and an extra 200,000–300,000 sales on European export markets. Optimism was reinforced by the highly aggregative form of the market forecasts which allowed BSC and BL's planners to avoid the issue of which products would be sold in what segments of particular national markets. Thus Ryder was able to ignore the constraints on BL sales imposed by the existing distribution network; BLMC and BL were never able to sell volume cars in France and Germany because the enterprise never had a proper retail distribution network in these national markets.

When the forecasts were made in the early and mid-1970s, it was obvious that they were unrealistic. After McKinsey was brought in to appraise BSC's strategy, the consulting firm concluded that the steel market would 'at best' take just 23 million tonnes of BSC steel by 1983. If BL and BSC had wanted to be realistic, they would have undertaken disaggregated, product by product, market by market analysis. If such an analysis could not be made, then an extrapolation of the early 1970s trend of market share losses provided a simple and realistic base for guessing the future. Our graphs (Statistical appendix, Figures 4.A1 and 4.A2, pp. 156–7) show that this kind of straight-line extrapolation provides a reasonably accurate predictor of market demand in the early 1980s. As a result of continuing loss of home and export market share, by 1982 and 1983 BSC and BL were selling roughly half the output which their strategic plans had predicted; steel output was falling away from the 1982 level of 14 million tonnes and volume car output was stuck significantly below the half million level.

Market miscalculation on this massive scale has a major feedback effect on production. In the planning stage, under the orthodox assumptions of western mass production, BSC and BL had assumed that they would benefit from a virtuous circle where productive achievement led via lower unit costs to market success. In practice, when the strategies had failed, the enterprises were caught in a vicious circle whereby market failure created productive problems. As we noted in the case of the car assembly plants, contraction of the market leaves the capital-intensive facilities with their high break-even points under-utilized. In this situation high unit costs and trading losses are the problem; this is the underlying cause of

Austin Rover's operating loss of £26 million in 1984 (*Financial Times*, 20 March 1985). When losses persist in this way, further closures are the easiest defensive response.

When management makes workers redundant and closes factories, it always promises that the end result will be a profitable low unit-cost enterprise. If the NCB's management is making this promise as we write, it is clear that BSC and BL's managers have broken theirs. Cars and steel continue to make operating losses even though the last round of major closures in both enterprises ended in 1981. If the experience of these two enterprises is any guide, the NCB will not solve its problems by closure. We must now analyse how and why such operational adjustments fail to deliver profit in a low unit-cost enterprise. The reasons follow fairly obviously from our earlier argument. At a financial level, closure takes out avoidable wage costs and lowers operating losses. But it does not remove the fixed costs of depreciation and interest charges which must then be spread over the smaller remaining output. Capital write-offs and debt write-downs can deal with this financial problem. But such financial adjustments are only a cosmetic palliative in enterprises that have the productive and market problems of the sort which we have analysed in this section.

At the productive level, financially motivated operational adjustments do not tackle, and may indeed exacerbate, problems about productive inflexibility. The closure of peripheral plants which produce a specialist output will aggravate inflexibility. Imbalance problems in a multi-plant, multi-process enterprise can usually only be solved by massive investment and such investment is usually impossible in retreating, loss-making enterprises. This is certainly so in steel and cars; our series on real capital expenditure levels shows that, *in real terms*, from 1981 onwards, capital expenditure in BL and BSC has slumped and at the time of writing was running *below* the very low levels of the years of under-investment in the mid-1960s in steel and early 1970s in cars (Statistical appendix, Tables 4.A2 and 4.A4, pp. 145–6). The same real capital expenditure series shows that the NCB survives as the last of the big spenders, with investment running around £750 million per annum in recent years (Statistical appendix, Table 4.A3, p. 146). But when nearly half the investment goes on new pits, this will not solve the enterprise's problems because it will exacerbate market problems. As we have argued, market contraction is a more threatening problem when the enterprise retreats into central capital-intensive plants with high break-even points. It should also be noted that, even if cost-cutting exercises succeed, they will produce disappointing results in the market place where, as in cars and steel, market failure is caused by the non-price characteristics of the product.

To sum up, therefore, operational adjustment (even with financial concessions on depreciation and interest charges) must fail in so far as it does not address the productive and market constraints which guarantee losses at ever lower levels of output and employment. This point is illustrated by the plight of BSC. At the time of writing the Corporation wants to close one of its five major plants; the 1983 MacGregor corporate plan called for the closure of Ravenscraig which would take out 2.7 million tonnes of the enterprise's 14.3 million tonnes of manned capacity. Closure of one or more of the major plants would reduce capacity and save avoidable costs. But it would not solve the BSC's problems. As a result of productively inept investment in unbalanced and inflexible facilities, the BSC does not have *any* low unit-cost plants to retreat on to. In this situation, profit-and-loss-based surgery is simply an irrelevance because it does not tackle the problems which cause the losses.

As we write, the situation at BL is more complex but prospects are equally dismal. BL will avoid plant closure by retreating from car manufacture into the assembly of Honda cars. It has already been announced that BL will manufacture Honda gearboxes under licence and engines will almost certainly be bought in from Honda's new Swindon assembly plant. The new big Rover saloon (Model XX) shows how body shells can be 'jointly developed' with Honda. The decisions on engine and gearbox sourcing immediately save £250 million in development costs and most of the remaining productive problems can be solved by retreating into assembly. But this solution means that the direct and indirect labour requirement at Austin Rover will be modest. This is all the more true because prospects for volume sales in the market place are not encouraging; the existing British-assembled Honda (Triumph Acclaim, Rover 213/216) has sold in small volume at around 50,000 cars per year. The Honda–Austin collaboration may be just the latest in a series of Anglo–Japanese co-op ventures which have failed; GEC–Hitachi and Rank–Toshiba are the two obvious examples in consumer electronics. When the joint venture collapses, the Japanese graciously take over and maintain a token assembly operation.

At the NCB we academics are like playgoers in the interval waiting for the last act of the drama. Now that management has won the right to impose closure unilaterally for financial reasons, it is difficult to be sanguine about the prospects. All we can say is that the productive misinvestment in new pits continues unabated and the mechanisms which promote a financially futile policy of closures will operate here as strongly as they did in cars or steel. These dramas never have a happy ending.

Constructive alternatives and new directions

Rather than wait for the unhappy ending we should work for a constructive outcome. Our analysis of what has gone wrong in coal, steel, and cars is helpful because it has definite policy implications. The lesson of strategic failure is that we must start again from basics and plan to establish a harmonious relation between the productive, market, and financial domains of calculation in the three enterprises. From this point of view, the first prerequisite is to get the productive and market problems sorted out. If these primary aims are achieved, then it should be possible to establish a harmonious relation between the financial and the two other domains. In this section of the paper we examine how the productive and market problems can be solved and why it is essential, for all our futures, that these problems should be solved. We will begin by sketching an alternative production strategy before turning to the more difficult issue of safeguarding the market.

The trend against productive giantism in modern manufacturing is now obvious. Academics are revising their positions on the benefits of the economies of scale and volume production of one standard product. In the 1970s the literature on the future of the world car industry predicted the emergence of six mega-corporations, each producing world cars to standard designs. In Altshuler et al.'s (1984) book, which summarizes the findings of a large MIT project on the car industry, all that has vanished; new production technologies and the persistence of differentiated national demands will apparently ensure the survival of many smaller car producers. The trend against giantism is equally marked if we examine corporate behaviour in the leading industrial countries. The Japanese steel industry, which provided a model of giantism for the BSC, is retreating from its largest works of 16–20 million tonnes per annum capacity. Nippon Kokkan's recent investment has apparently been concentrated on the renovation of the 6 million tonne Keihin works because the company is now trying to exploit what it calls 'qualitative improvements' rather than 'the earlier so-called economies of scale or quantitative expansion' (Ide, 1984).

In the mid-1980s, what Goldhar and Jellinek (1983) call the 'economies of scope' have acquired a new importance. The productive aim of investment in new facilities, or the 'fine tuning' of existing facilities, becomes a balanced production system which offers the most flexible high-quality product mix available. The economies of scale are still important in many areas of manufacturing and should not be under-estimated; new CADCAM technology rarely offers minimum economic quantities of one. But the future lies with 'smart' automation, not inflexible giantism of the old kind. The potential benefits of the new technology are considerable. The new technology maximizes operational scope so that the enterprises can vary product mix and output levels without suffering low volume diseconomies. The knock-on effects should be an easing of financial pressures; with new technology, smooth operational adjustments are possible and this eases the accounting conflict between the short and the long run.

British enterprises have been slow in adapting to the requirements of the new technological paradigm and in exploiting its potential; any text on British manufacturing techniques would consist mainly of examples of 'how not to do it'. Part of the problem is that Britain is now in so many areas a follower country and follower countries often buy in production engineering concepts which are one generation behind. Fiat's Lingotto car plant provides the classic example; this was a huge multi-storey, concrete-framed building built in imitation of Ford's Highland Park plant and, when it was completed in 1926, Ford was already moving into the long single-storey sheds of the Rouge complex (Banham, 1985). British coal and steel with their super-pits and big basic oxygen steel converters provide further examples of the Lingotto syndrome. BL's Metro lines at Longbridge have been presented as a model modern manufacturing facility but, in fact, they are a monument to an obsolete technological paradigm of inflexible automation. The West Works bodyshop is 'dedicated' and can produce only Metros because just 10 per cent of body welds are made by robots and 70 per cent are made by inflexible multi-welders.

The immediate problem is that the necessary investment in new technology requires large expenditures, especially in our three cases where large sums of money have been sunk in the wrong kind of plant. But the investment can hardly be justified if the market is not there, and, as we have seen, the market is a problem for all three of our enterprises. We would explicitly reject the 1970s assumptions that market difficulties will be more or less automatically solved by investment in productive efficiency which secures an increase in market share for low-cost producers. On the contrary, we would argue that, under present conditions, the problems of the market cannot be solved by any decisions or actions of the enterprise. Our argument is that the market for our three nationalized industries will have to be secured and safeguarded by the actions of the British government. Perhaps we had better begin by explaining why we have come to such a conclusion.

In competitive manufacturing activities like cars, and to a lesser extent steel, foreign producers, and the multinationals producing in Britain, do not play fair according to one set of competitive rules. In different ways it is attractive for Thyssen and General Motors to use their productive and financial strength to buy market share from weak enterprises like BSC and BL. This is exactly what GM's British subsidiary Vauxhall is doing. As the Japanese know so well, long-run market share is inherited by the enterprise which has the productive and financial strength to survive the short-run sales war which knocks out weaker enterprises. In such contests, the British can be relied upon to be last into the market with investment in new technology and new capacity; the BSC and NCB provide perfect illustrations of this point. If the British cling to outmoded notions of competitive fair play against strong and ruthless foreign competitors then the British will also be first out; this is already happening in steel, where a DTI committee estimates that 45 per cent of the steel jobs lost in the EEC have been lost in Britain (ASTMS, 1984).

In coal, the government can hardly leave the enterprise to get on with its competitive job because there is an administered market for the product and outcomes, in terms of sales and revenue, entirely depend on government decisions. As we argued in the *Aberystwyth Report* (Cutler *et al.*, 1985), the size of the future market for coal depends on a political decision about the relative importance of coal and nuclear power in electricity generation. Whatever the NCB does or does not do, if the government decides to go 70 per cent nuclear by 2010, then the overall demand for coal will be 70 million tonnes or less. Kerevan and Saville (1985) would add the point that the government also sets the transfer price at which coal is sold from the NCB to the CEGB for power stations; a low transfer price has ensured losses for the NCB while the CEGB makes large profits and pays the Treasury nearly £750 million per annum. Of course, coal is a special case because nearly three-quarters of British coal goes to the power stations for electricity generation. But it is also worth pointing out that coal is less of a special case than it used to be; under ECSC rules, steel is already being sold in a market which is partly administered.

If a retreat towards the market in a world of unfair international competition will damage weak British enterprises, why not enlarge the existing role of the state in regulating product markets? Formulated in these terms, our proposal sounds socialist, but there is nothing necessarily socialist or anti-capitalist about it. On the contrary, we are realistically responding to the capitalist international order as it is. The utopians who reject or deny this world are the marketeers and free-traders who will not recognize the consequences of international competition for the backward and unsuccessful. Furthermore, the alternative which we are proposing is not intervention of the state against the market but integration of the state in the market. All the more successful advanced capitalist national economies practise such integration and the Japanese provide us with a particularly pertinent example of how to do it well.

The success of the Japanese strategies for coal, steel, and cars makes an interesting contrast with the failure of British strategies for these industries. The Japanese success shows how national government and financial institutions can sponsor success. The aim was to develop the national manufacturing base; good cheap steel was required for that purpose and the domestic coal industry was deliberately run down because it could not provide cheap inputs for the steel industry. Large coastal steelworks were developed in the knowledge that they would at best make small profits. These profits were guaranteed by developing user industries like cars and shipbuilding whose volume base was built up on the protected home market before they moved into exports. The British failure shows how national government can blunder into failure. The British government inadvertently took the profit out of bulk steel-making in the 1960s by letting coal prices rise from hitherto unrealistic levels. The major steel companies responded by proposing a move to large coastal works which was too risky for any private financial institution. When the government, after nationalization in 1967, funded the industry's plan, it never took any responsibility for safeguarding the market.

This contrast between Japanese success and British failure allows us to develop some ideas about how safeguarding the market could work in Britain. The difference of outcome is based on a difference in national forms of calculation. The Japanese achieved their strategic aims because they developed a linkage policy which, in the context of a protected home market, guaranteed demand. Clearly, at least in our sheltered industries, there is scope for a constructive linkage policy in Britain.

The potential is most obvious in the case of coal which sells nearly three-quarters of its output to the CEGB. Because of a balance of payments constraint on the import of fossil fuels when the oil runs out, we will have to develop either domestic coal or nuclear when the oil runs out. If the linkage from coal is intelligently developed there should be gains in terms of cost and efficiency. As we argued in the *Aberystwyth Report* (Cutler, *et al.*, 1985), electricity from coal should be cheaper than electricity from nuclear. An energy base in domestic coal would also allow the development of combined heat and power on a district basis; this is an attractive conservation option when 70 per cent of coal's thermal value is lost through the cooling towers of a conventional power station. Nuclear locks us into central electricity generation.

Other linkages could be developed, particularly in the heavy utility sectors of our industrial infrastructure. Coal is again pertinent here when British Steel is the NCB's most important industrial customer and coal movement is British Rail's most important freight business. But there are limits to the extent to which a linkage policy can be pursued in an unprotected home market, and the political nettle of protectionism will have to be grasped if a linkage policy is to succeed. At this point, much would depend on how the national market was safeguarded. We are critical of the existing proposals for protection made by Godley and the Cambridge Department of Applied Economics. When it is non-price characteristics which make imported manufactures attractive, Cambridge's tariff would be a high one and it would featherbed the inefficiency of existing producers. Instead, we would favour safeguarding the market by value-added content regulation combined with a positive policy of encouraging foreign manufacturers to locate in Britain.

The potential is most obvious here in the case of cars. It was a strategic mistake to pour investment funds into BL as a kind of national champion and then hope it would succeed in the market place. Value-added content regulation applied to Ford and GM (Vauxhall), as well as BL, would have been more appropriate. Ford and GM sell nearly half the cars sold in Britain while BL sells less than one in five. Because of the rise of tied imports and the growth of kit car assembly, the UK content of the cars which Ford and GM sell in Britain has slumped; according to Daniel Jones (*Financial Times*, 18 January 1985) the UK content of the cars GM sold in Britain fell from 89 per cent to 26 per cent between 1973 and 1983, while the UK content of the cars which Ford sold in Britain fell from 85 to 43 per cent over the same period. In so far as Austin Rover becomes an assembler of Honda cars, its UK content will also fall dramatically. As a result of the past decade's trends, the market open to UK component companies in 1983 was only 40 per cent of the size of the 1973 market.

Linkage plus value-added regulation is the only policy which can address these problems; it is a prerequisite in our three enterprises if a productive investment in flexibility is to stand a chance of earning a profit. But why do we need such a solution which would obviously create major problems with our trading partners in the EEC? This question cannot be avoided when the present government has a do-nothing alternative. It is benignly presiding over the decline of British manufacturing under the free trade system as the same time as it is financially pressuring our three nationalized enterprises into retreat. At the time of writing Austin Rover is retreating into the assembly of Honda cars because the government is taking a tough line on financing BL under its next five-year plan; no more state funds will be made available to finance unprofitable production or cover investment requirements (*Financial Times*, 6 April 1985). The NCB was offered a final £2,600 million grant to cover losses; in future it will only be able to invest around £750 million per annum if it presses ahead with the closure of uneconomic pits (*Financial Times*, 26 April 1985).

From the point of view of short-run enterprise profit or cash flow the government's policy is an immediately sensible one. Since the onset of the present recession, coal, steel, and cars have all been chronic loss makers in the advanced western countries. The situation is most dramatic in the European car industry where there is aggressive international trade in volume cars which are usually sold at a loss. Renault announced a £1,000 million loss for 1984 and the six largest European car companies lost £3,200 million over the five years to 1984. Furthermore, according to Bhaskar (1979), the European industry as a whole is not earning the cash flow necessary to finance its capital expenditure requirement of £80 to £100 billion over the decade between 1981 and 1990. In this situation, BL's retreat into assembling Hondas offers the most certain prospect of moderate profit. For that matter, profit could also be secured if the company were to retreat one stage further from assembly into distribution, as GEC has done with televisions and video-recorders.

Although screwdriver and sticker operations can earn profit, there are good macroeconomic arguments for safeguarding coal, steel, and cars and for extending the policy to cover areas of private manufacturing. We have already made the point that when the oil runs out, we will not be able to afford imported fossil fuels. At this stage we should add the argument that when the oil runs out we will not be able to afford a high level of manufactured imports either; the balance of trade in manufactures has deteriorated continuously since the early 1950s and we now run a large and growing deficit on manufactured trade. Exchange rate adjustments will not solve this problem because it is non-price characteristics which determine international trade in manufactures. Furthermore, as the foreign content of British manufactures increases, the balance of payment constraint worsens; any increase in demand will only draw in the components and kits necessary for 'British manufacture'. As Smith (1984) points out, looming payments problems threaten all our futures.

Apart from easing macro constraints, a policy of safeguarding has other benefits which arise at, or from, the enterprise level. Profits are the least important of these benefits. Of course we need profits to sustain expansion. But, as the Japanese case shows, if the national institutional structure is right, then high rates of expansion can be financed with modest levels of profit. Apart from this, we should remember that profit is a conventionally measured surplus on capital and it is a small residual. If we ask who has the major interest in any modern manufacturing enterprise, the answer is the wage-earners rather than the shareholders; as Patrick Hall (1985) emphasized, on average labour accounts for 70 per cent of the value added in a manufacturing enterprise. If there are three accounting desiderata – profits, cash flow, and value added – then the greatest of these is value added.

At the enterprise level we need coal, steel, and cars for the same fundamental reason as we need a broad manufacturing base; we need them for the value added and the employment which these enterprises generate. Value added measures real wealth production and a high value added economy is the basis for our future prosperity. We need employment because it is the primary way in which wealth is distributed; as the dismal literature on replacement ratios shows, we have yet to invent a social security system which adequately looks after those who are out of work. We need manufacturing employment because it is the only way in which we can preserve high-quality well-paid male jobs; services will only expand slowly in a low-income industrialized economy and the service sector creates ill-paid female part-time jobs.

From this point of view, the underlying problem is that our present forms of enterprise calculation in the nationalized industries and elsewhere diminish value added and employment. That is the conclusion of an analysis which will have struck many of our readers as eccentrically rationalistic. How is it possible to analyse strategic investment and operational retreat in a chapter of this length without paying any attention to the 'political' determinants of calculation and miscalculation within each enterprise and the broader society? We expect our audience to protest at the bareness of our analysis. Indeed, we are not unsympathetic to those who favour the different approaches of political science or organization theory which are both more realistically descriptive and more theoretically informed. Though we are tolerant of other discourses we would also defend our own. What we have tried to do is simply to analyse the logic of the situation as it operates at a particular level of enterprise calculation in three major British enterprises. In a sense, the accounting *a priori* is the object of analysis in this chapter and in other papers which we have produced. The distinctive result is a kind of academic archaeology of enterprise calculation that paradoxically finds its own justification at the political level which it apparently neglects. The political virtue of our analysis is that, more clearly than most of the discursive alternatives, our analysis highlights the way in which present forms of enterprise calculation threaten all our futures.

Note

This chapter on the three nationalized industries was part of a programme of team research on the British crisis and its historical background. The first major result of this was the book *Why are the British Bad at Manufacturing?* (Routledge & Kegan Paul, 1983). In 1985 the department produced *The Aberystwyth Report on Coal.* Tony Cutler of Middlesex Polytechnic collaborated on that report and on *Keynes, Beveridge and Beyond,* a book on postwar economic and social policy published by RKP in 1986.

Statistical appendix

Table 4.A1 UK steel (BSC post-1967), nominal and real capital expenditure

Year	Nominal capital expenditure (£ million)	Steel plant[3] index	Real capital expenditure 1972 money values (£ million)
1960	146	70	208
1961	199	70	284
1962	170	70.5	241
1963	77	70.5	109
1964	55	71	78
1965	50	71	70
1966	42	71	59
1967	42	71	59
1968	72	71	101
1969	74	71	104
1970[1]	39	76	51
1971	143	83.8	171
1972	204	94.4	216
1973	197	100	197
1974	186	107.3	173
1975	311	135.8	229
1976	530	170.9	310
1977	579	198.7	291
1978	476	230.6	206
1979	318	260	122
1980	282	289.7	97
1981[2]	185	327.1[4]	56.6
1982[2]	197	355.2[4]	55.5
1983[2]	138	390.0[4]	35.3

Source: 1960–7 *UK Steel Industry Statistics,* Iron and Steel Statistics Bureau; 1967–83 *BSC Iron and Steel Statistics,* British Steel Corporation.
Notes.
1 Results for six months only, where the Corporation was adjusting accounting period from year ending September to year ending March.
2 Estimates supplied by M. Upham of the ISTC.
3 Expenditure totals 1960–61 deflated using CSO retail price index. Post-1971 expenditure totals deflated using BSC's own capital plant index. See Bryer *et al.* (1982) p. 169.
4 Estimates using data supplied by M. Upham of the ISTC.

Table 4.A2 BL nominal and real capital expenditure 1968–83

Year	Nominal capital expenditure (£ million)	Real capital[1] expenditure 1975 money values (£ million)
1968	55.5	124.8
1969	51.3	110.8
1970	66.7	130.7
1971	50.4	89.7
1972	42.0	70.1
1973	62.7	97.8
1974	108.3	137.5
1975	92.4	92.4
1976	114.2	97.1
1977	148.8	108.8
1978	233.3	152.7
1979	258.9	151.2
1980	284.1	146.0
1981	200.8	88.0
1982	229.9	91.6
1983	247.7	91.4

Source: BL, *Annual Report and Accounts*, 1968–83.
Note: 1 Expenditure totals deflated using the index of wholesale prices for 'mechanical engineering' in *CSO Statistics* (Green Book) Table 18.10, various years.

Table 4.A3 NCB nominal and real capital expenditure 1970–81

Year	Nominal capital expenditure (£ million)	Real capital[1] expenditure 1975 money values (£ million)
1970	66.7	130.7
1971	51.0	90.8
1972	55.0	91.9
1973	76.0	118.6
1974	68.0	86.4
1975	112.0	112.0
1976	211.0	181.9
1977	266.0	201.5
1978	334.0	232.0
1979	454.0	285.5
1980	617.0	339.0
1981	736.0	381.3
1982	722.0	350.0
1983	826.0	385.9
1984	691.0	304.4

Source: NCB, *Report and Accounts*, 1970/1–1983/4.
Note: 1 Expenditure totals deflated using the index of wholesale prices for 'mechanical engineering' in *CSO Statistics* (Green Book) Table 18.10, various years.

Table 4.A4 BSC output, employment, and labour productivity 1970–83

Year	Manpower	Crude steel output (million tonnes)	Tonnage per man
1970	200,340	12.3	—
1971	201,790	26.1	129.3
1972	182,470	21.5	117.8
1973	174,830	25.1	143.6
1974	171,820	23.0	133.9
1975	166,470	20.8	125.0
1976	163,620	17.2	105.1
1977	155,970	19.7	126.3
1978	155,130	17.4	112.1
1979	142,250	17.3	121.6
1980	137,420	14.1	102.6
1981	104,920	11.9	113.5
1982	82,600	14.1	170.7
1983	69,200	11.7	169.0

Source: BSC, *Annual Report and Accounts*, 1969/70–1982/3.

Table 4.A5 BL output, employment, and productivity 1970–83

Year	Average weekly employment	Total vehicle sales	Vehicles per man
1970	200,000	984,000	4.92
1971	194,000	1,057,000	5.44
1972	191,000	1,127,000	5.90
1973	204,000	1,161,000	5.69
1974	208,000	1,020,000	4.90
1975	191,000	845,000	4.42
1976	183,000	981,000	5.36
1977	195,000	785,000	4.02
1978	192,000	797,000	4.15
1979	177,000	693,000	3.91
1980	157,000	587,000	3.74
1981	126,000	525,000	4.16
1982	108,000	519,000	4.80
1983	103,000	564,000	5.47

Source: BL, *Annual Report and Accounts,* 1969/70–1982/3.

Table 4.A6 NCB output, employment, and labour productivity 1970–84

Year	Manpower yearly average	Output per man shift (tonnes)
1970	283,100	2.20
1971	286,400	2.24
1972	274,000	2.13
1973	263,800	2.33
1974	242,500	2.15
1975	248,800	2.29
1976	243,700	2.28
1977	242,100	2.21
1978	239,300	2.19
1979	232,400	2.24
1980	233,200	2.31
1981	224,800	2.32
1982	212,800	2.40
1983	207,600	2.44
1984	191,500	2.43

Source: NCB, *Annual Report and Accounts,* 1969/70–1983/4.

Table 4.A7 BSC sales revenue, profit, depreciation, and interest per tonne

Year	Revenue per tonne (£)	Pre-tax profit (loss) per tonne (£)	Depreciation per tonne (£)	Interest per tonne (£)	Output (million tonnes)
1970	55.4	0.98	4.06	1.30	12.3
1971	55.8	(0.38)	3.56	1.30	26.1
1972	60.1	(3.25)	4.27	1.76	21.5
1973	58.9	0.35	3.58	1.59	25.1
1974	77.2	2.17	4.26	2.30	23.0
1975	108.6	4.00	5.57	3.22	20.8
1976	137.0	(14.83)	7.20	6.27	17.2
1977	155.2	(4.82)	6.19	8.53	19.7
1978	181.2	(25.46)	6.61	11.32	17.4
1979	190.0	(17.86)	7.68	12.00	17.3
1980	220.0	(38.65)	7.44	13.33	14.1
1981	248.2	(56.13)	9.58	15.37	11.9
1982	244.2	(25.39)	8.94	7.37	14.1
1983	276.1	(33.00)	8.03	9.23	11.7

Source: BSC, *Annual Report and Accounts,* 1969/70–1982/3.

Table 4.A8 BL sales revenue, profit, depreciation, and interest per vehicle

Year	Revenue per vehicle (£)	Pre-tax profit (loss) per vehicle (£)	Depreciation per vehicle (£)	Interest per vehicle (£)	Output (thousand vehicles)
1970	1,037	4.0	42.6	10.5	984
1971	1,113	30.8	44.5	13.5	1,057
1972	1,137	28.3	38.1	8.1	1,127
1973	1,347	44.2	37.9	5.9	1,161
1974	1,564	2.3	41.2	16.8	1,020
1975	2,211	(90.1)	59.2	45.0	845
1976	2,948	71.9	73.4	48.1	981
1977	3,314	4.0	78.9	68.3	785
1978	3,856	19.2	95.5	70.3	797
1979	4,314	(161.9)	121.2	95.3	693
1980	4,901	(660.1)	183.9	159.2	587
1981	5,464	(634.1)	255.3	168.2	525
1982	5,919	(429.1)	285.3	186.7	519
1983	6,066	(118.9)	315.5	126.2	564

Source: BL, *Annual Report and Accounts,* 1969/70–1982/3.

Table 4.A9 NCB sales revenue, profit, depreciation, and interest per tonne

Year	Revenue per tonne (£)	Pre-tax profit (loss) per tonne (£)	Depreciation per tonne (£)	Interest per tonne (£)	Output (million tonnes)
1971	55.8	0.25	0.44	0.25	141
1972	60.1	(0.99)	0.66	0.33	119
1973	58.9	(0.28)	0.52	0.31	139.9
1974	77.2	(0.92)	0.49	0.30	107.7
1975	108.6	0.32	0.47	0.29	126.0
1976	137.0	0.42	0.65	0.41	124.8
1977	155.2	0.92	0.77	0.67	119.8
1978	181.2	0.91	0.88	0.72	119.8
1979	190.0	0.99	0.99	1.13	121.5
1980	220.3	0.23	1.51	1.51	121.6
1981	248.2	0.55	1.68	2.05	124.9
1982	244.2	(0.69)	2.13	2.81	122.5
1983	276.1	(1.08)	2.59	3.05	119.0

Source: NCB, *Annual Report and Accounts*, 1970/1–1982/3.

Table 4.A10 BSC total depreciation charge, interest charge, and
extraordinary items *versus* revenue deficit 1972–82

Year	Depreciation charge (£ million)	Interest charge (£ million)	Extraordinary items (£ million)
1972	92.5	37.6	17.6
1973	90	44.2	5.4
1974	98.2	52.9	10.5
1975	116	67.2	3.3
1976	107	107.6	13.5
1977	102	168	21.5
1978	98	197	69.5
1979	111	208	47.6
1980	105	188	1,239
1982	114	183	352
1982	126	104	146

Accumulated revenue deficit at the start of 1982		3,804
Accumulated extraordinary items	1,925.9	
Accumulated depreciation charges	1,159.7	
Accumulated interest charges	1,357.5	
		4,443.1

Source: BSC, *Report and Accounts.*

Table 4.A11 BL total depreciation charge, interest charge, and
extraordinary items *versus* revenue deficit 1975–82

Year	Depreciation charge (£ million)	Interest charge (£ million)	Extraordinary items (£ million)
1975	36.7	38.0	59.6
1976	72.0	47.2	—
1977	62.2	53.6	43.9
1978	75.7	56.0	38.3
1979	83.6	66.0	23.0
1980	107.5	93.6	139.0
1981	134.0	88.3	152.0
1982	147.8	96.9	58.8
Accumulated revenue deficit at end 1982 (minus cumulative up to 1975 £29.0m)			1,514.7
Accumulated extraordinary items (minus cumulative up to 1975 (£83.4m)	455.0		
Accumulated depreciation charges	719.5		
Interest charges	501.6		
			1,666.1

Source: BL, *Annual Report and Accounts.*

Table 4.A12 NCB total depreciation charge, interest charge, and extraordinary items *versus* revenue deficit 1974–83

Year	Depreciation charge (£ million)	Interest charge (£ million)	Extraordinary items (£ million)
1974	53	32.2	15.1
1975	59	36.2	3.9
1976	80.9	51.8	6.3
1977	92.5	79.6	0.7
1978	105.6	87	0.2
1979	120	138	0.3
1980	164.7	184.7	—
1981	210.3	256.2	20
1982	261	341	2
1983	309	366	5
Accumulated government deficit grants			1,241

Accumulated extraordinary items	51.5	
Accumulated depreciation charge	1,456.1	
Accumulated interest charges	1,572.5	
		3,080.1

Source: NCB, *Annual Report and Accounts.*

Table 4.A13 BL real capital stock per vehicle

Year	Gross fixed assets (£ million)	Index	Real value of gross assets (£ million) (1)	Output (thousand vehicles) (2)	Capital/ output ratio i.e. 1÷2 (£)
1976	719.2	1.16	620	981	632
1977	816.1	1.32	618	785	787
1978	991.0	1.44	688	797	863
1979	1,172.6	1.59	737	693	1,063
1980	1,350.2	1.82	742	587	1,262
1981	1,418.4	1.93	734	525	1,398
1982	1,526.6	2.06	741	519	1,428
1983	1,944.8	2.14	908	564	1,609

Source: BL, *Annual Report and Accounts,* 1975/6–1982/3.

Table 4.A14 NCB real capital stock per tonne of coal

Year	Gross fixed assets (£ million)	Index	Real value of gross assets (£ million) (1)	Output (million tonnes) (2)	Capital/ output ratio i.e. 1÷2 (£)
1974	1,025.5	1.27	1,301	107.7	12.1
1975	1,133.4	1.00	1,133	126	9
1976	1,245.2	1.16	1,073	124.8	8.6
1977	1,485.7	1.32	1,125	119.8	9.4
1978	1,877.5	1.44	1,303	119.8	10.9
1979	2,285.3	1.59	1,437	121.5	11.8
1980	2,864.7	1.82	1,573	121.6	12.9
1981	3,555.7	1.93	1,842	124.9	14.7
1982	4,191.5	2.06	2,034	122.6	16.6
1983	4,859	2.14	2,270	119	19.1
1984	5,290	2.27	2,330	104	22.4

Source: NCB, *Annual Report and Accounts.*

Table 4.A15 BSC real capital stock per tonne of steel

Year	Gross fixed assets (£ million)	Index	Real value of gross assets (£ million) (1)	Output (million tonnes) (2)	Capital/ output ratio i.e. 1÷2 (£)
1972	2,098	1.67	3,503	21.5	163
1973	2,246	1.56	3,505	25.1	140
1974	2,387	1.27	3,031	23.0	132
1975	2,665	1.00	2,665	20.8	128
1976	3,172	1.16	2,734	17.2	159
1977	3,716	1.32	2,815	19.7	143
1978	4,151	1.44	2,883	17.5	166
1979	4,368	1.82	2,400	17.3	139
1980	4,452	1.92	2,307	14.1	164
1981	4,563	2.06	2,215	11.9	186

Source: BSC, *Annual Report and Accounts,* 1971/2–1980/1.

Note on methods employed in Tables 4.A13–4.A15

Capital stock is measured on a 'gross capital' basis; that is no allowance is made for depreciation of capital equipment. Use of the perpetual inventory method enables annual estimates of capital stock to be made by subtracting annual scrappings and adding annual additions to an initial estimate of order level capital. On this see R. Wragg and J. Robertson, *Post-war Trends in Employment* (Dept. of Employment Research Paper No. 3.)

In order to deflate our measure of capital stock, we have used in each case the 'mechanical engineering' index, taken from the CSO *Annual Abstract of Statistics.* This index ties in quite well with BSC and NCB capital cost increases reported by Bryer and Brignall and the Bradford Report on Coal (Burns *et al.* 1984).

Having deflated the level of gross capital stock employed each year we have then divided through by the level of output. The result gives the real amount of capital stock employed per tonne of output or vehicle produced. The series of results allows us to compare capital productivity over time.

Table 4.A16 BL, NCB, BSC real assets employed per man

Year	*British Leyland* Employment (1)	Real gross capital (£ million) (2)	Real assets per man (£) (2÷1)	*National Coal Board* Employment (1)	Real gross capital (£ million) (2)	Real assets per man (£) (2÷1)	*British Steel Corporation* Employment (1)	Real gross capital (£ million) (2)	Real assets per man (£) (2÷1)
1972							182,470	3,503	19,197
1973							174,830	3,504	20,000
1974				242,500	1,301	5,365	171,820	3,031	17,640
1975				248,800	1,133	4,553	166,470	2,665	16,000
1976	183,000	620	3,388	243,700	1,073	4,403	163,620	2,734	16,700
1977	195,000	618	3,169	242,100	1,125	4,646	155,970	2,815	18,000
1978	192,000	688	3,583	239,300	1,303	5,445	155,130	2,883	18,600
1979	177,000	737	4,164	232,400	1,437	6,183	142,250	2,400	16,900
1980	157,000	742	4,726	233,200	1,573	6,745	137,420	2,307	16,800
1981	126,000	734	5,825	224,800	1,842	8,194	140,920	2,215	21,100
1982	108,000	741	6,861	212,800	2,034	9,558			
1983	103,000	908	8,815	207,600	2,270	10,934			
Increase in gross capital stock per man			160%			104%			10%

Source: Calculated from accounts of BL, NCB and BSC.

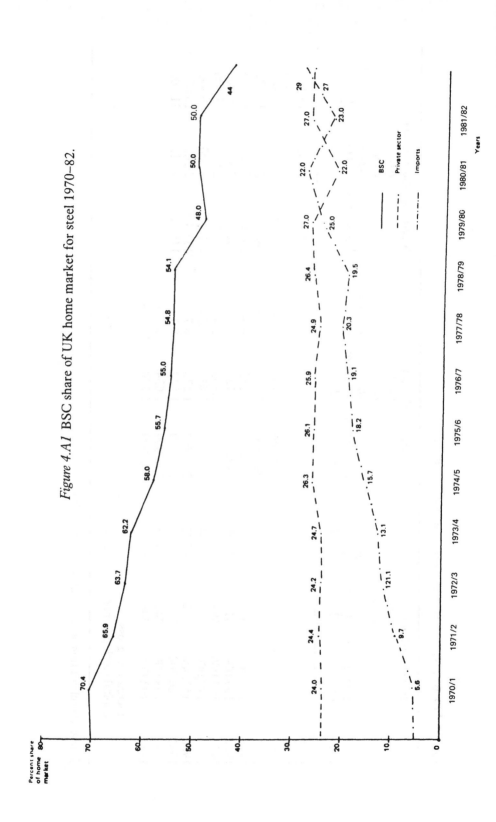

Figure 4.A1 BSC share of UK home market for steel 1970–82.

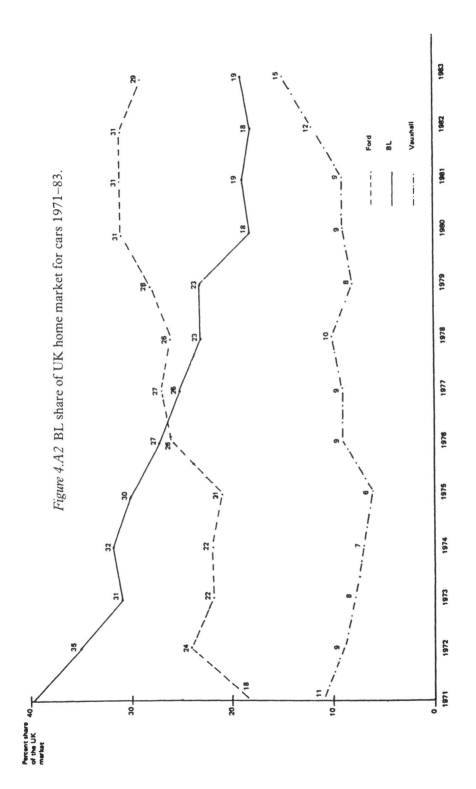

Figure 4.A2 BL share of UK home market for cars 1971–83.

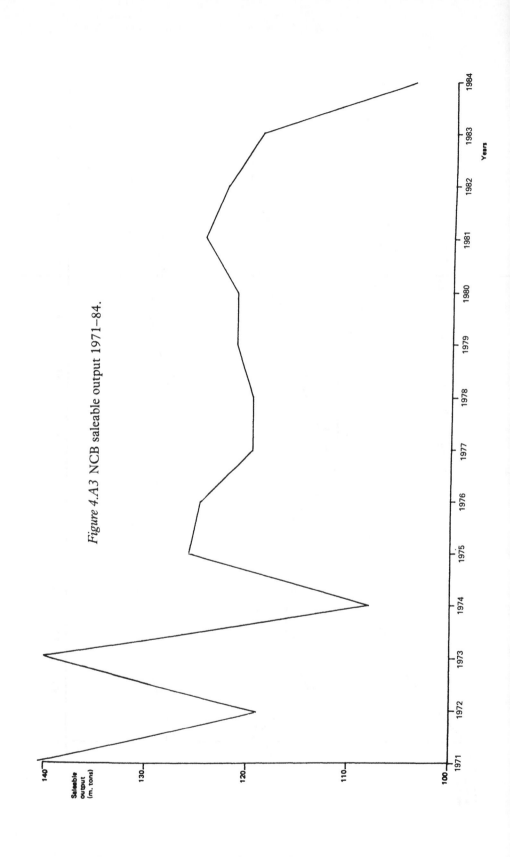

Figure 4.A3 NCB saleable output 1971–84.

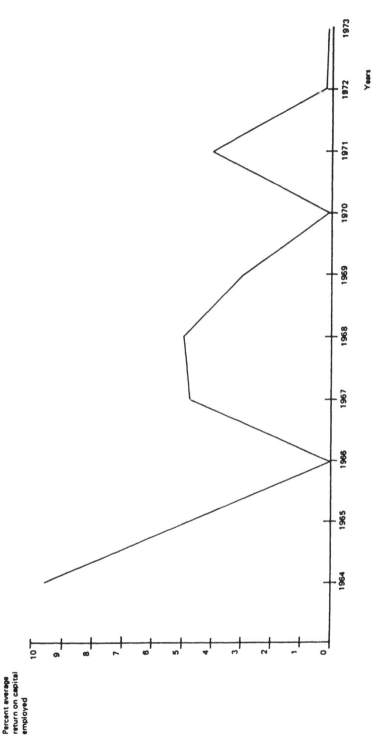

Figure 4.A4 NCB average return on capital employed 1964–73.

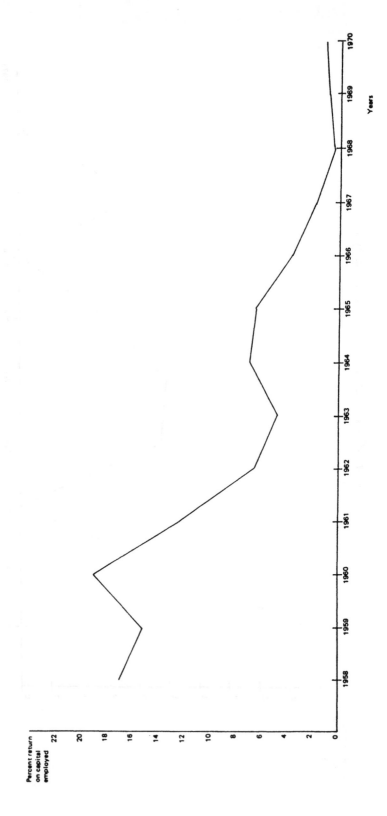

Figure 4.A5 UK steel industry return on capital employed 1958–70.

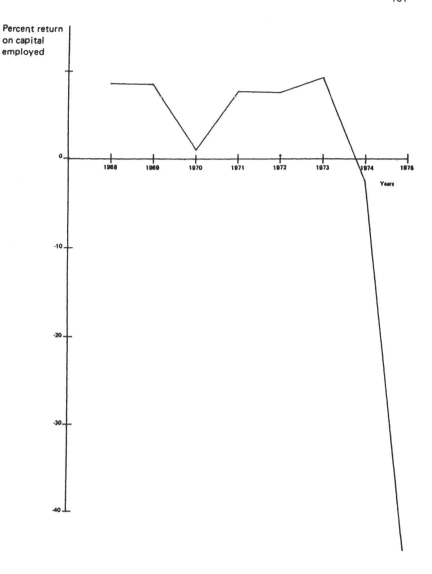

Figure 4.A6 BLMC/BL return on capital employed 1968–75.

References

Altshuler, A. *et al.* (1984) *The Future of the Automobile,* London, Allen & Unwin.

ASTMS (1984) Memorandum on 'The imbalance of trade in manufactured goods between the United Kingdom and existing and prospective members of the EEC', House of Commons Paper 461/329–4, Trade and Industry Sub-Committee, 2nd Report and Evidence, House of Commons 1983–4 session, HMSO, London.

Banham, R. (1985) 'FIAT: The phantom of order', *New Society,* vol. 72 no. 1164, 18 April.

Benson Committee (1966) *The Steel Industry* (Stage 1 report of the Development Co-ordinating Committee). British Iron and Steel Federation.

Berry, A.J. *et al.* (1985a) 'Management control in an area of the NCB', *Accounting, Organisations and Society,* vol. 10 no. 1, pp. 3–28.

Berry, A.J. *et al.* (1985b) 'NCB accounts – a mine of misinformation?', *Accountancy,* January, pp. 10–12.

Bhaskar, K.N. (1979) *The Future of the UK Motor Industry,* London, Kogan Page.

British Steel Corporation (1973) *10 year Development Strategy* Cmnd 5226, HMSO, London.

Bryer, R.A. and **Brignall, R.** (1982) *Accounting for British Steel,* Aldershot, Gower.

Burns, A. *et al.* (1984) *Second Report on MINOS,* Working Environment Research Group, Report No. 6, University of Bradford.

Cockerill, A. and **Silbertson. A.** (1974) *The UK Steel Industry,* Occasional Paper No. 42, Cambridge University Press.

Cottrell, E. (1981) *The Giant with Feet of Clay,* Centre for Policy Studies, London.

Cutler, A., Haslam, C., Williams, J. and **Williams, K.** (1985) *Aberystwyth Report on Coal,* Aberystwyth, mimeo.

Goldhar, J.D. and **Jellinek, M.** (1983) 'Plan for economies of scope', *Harvard Business Review,* November–December, pp. 141–8.

Hall, P. (1985) *The Decline and Resuscitation of the UK's Manufacturing Wealth Creation System,* mimeo.

Hayes, R.H. and **Abernathy, W.J.** (1980) 'Managing our way to economic decline', *Harvard Business Review,* July–August pp. 67–77.

Hayes, R.H. and **Garvin, D.A.** (1982) 'Managing as if tomorrow mattered', *Harvard Business Review,* May–June, pp. 70–9.

Hopper, T. *et al.* (1985) *Financial Control and the Labour Process in a Nationalized Industry,* mimeo.

House of Commons Expenditure Committee (1975) (14th Report), *The Motor Vehicle Industry,* London, HMSO.

Ide, S. (1984) 'Information systems in the Japanese steel industry', International Iron and Steel Institute 8th Annual Conference, Chicago, October.

Kerevan, J. and **Saville, R.** (1985) *The Economic Case for Deep-Mined Coal in Scotland,* mimeo.

Magaziner, I. and **Reich, R.** (1982) *Minding America's Business,* Harcourt, Brace, New York.

Monopolies and Mergers Commission (1983) *National Coal Board,* Volumes 1 and 2, London, HMSO (Cmnd 8920).

National Coal Board (1974) *Plan for Coal,* National Coal Board, London.

Pratten, C.F. (1971) *Economies of Scale in Manufacturing Industry,* Occasional Paper No. 28, Cambridge University Press.

Pratten, C.F. *et al.* (1965) *The Economies of Large Scale Production in British Industry,* Occasional Paper No. 3, Cambridge University Press.

Pryke, R. (1981) *The Nationalised Industries,* London, Martin Robertson.

Rhys, D.G. (1972), *The Motor Industry, an Economic Survey,* London, Butterworths.

Ryder, D. (1975) *British Leyland: The Next Decade,* London, HMSO.

Shonberger, R.J. (1982) *Japanese Manufacturing Techniques,* New York, Free Press.

Smith, K. (1984) *The British Economic Crisis,* Harmondsworth, Penguin.

White, L.J. (1971) *The Automobile Industry Since 1945.* Harvard University Press, Cambridge, Mass.

Williams, K. *et al.* (1983) *Why are the British Bad at Manufacturing?,* London, Routledge & Kegan Paul.

5
The end of mass production?

Karel Williams, Tony Cutler, John Williams and Colin Haslam

Text reviewed

Michael Piore and Charles Sabel (1984) *The Second Industrial Divide: Possibilities for Prosperity*, Basic Books, New York.

As the economic performance of the advanced western economies has deteriorated since the early 1970s, so there has been growing interest in the nature, origins, and outcome of the present difficulties. Piore and Sabel's book *The Second Industrial Divide* is a contribution to this debate. These two American academics present a distinctive account of what has been increasingly perceived as a 'general crisis of the industrial system' (Piore and Sabel, 1984, p. 165). Their book ranges widely over many themes but the basic thesis is a simple one; Piore and Sabel argue that 'the present deterioration in economic performance results from the limits of the model of industrial development that is founded on mass production (Piore and Sabel, 1984, p. 4). As for solutions, Piore and Sabel are agnostic about what will or must happen, but they present 'flexible specialization' as an alternative model of industrial development which offers us the possibility of a prosperous future.

In the United States, *The Second Industrial Divide* was well received and 'flexible specialization' has been taken up as an idea whose time has come. In Britain the reception has been more mixed. Hyman (1986) has produced a trenchant neo-Marxist critique of the 'myth' of flexible specialization. But others on the left have reacted quite differently. Murray (1985) has taken up the idea of the obsolescence of mass production with enthusiasm in an article which was provocatively titled 'Benetton Britain'. More significantly, Piore and Sabel's concepts are already being used to provide a framework for further research. A recent book on the car industry, edited by Tolliday and Zeitlin, is boldly sub-titled *Between Fordism and Flexibility*. This reception justifies a review article which summarizes and criticizes some of Piore and Sabel's main arguments.

Given this objective, our review article is organized in a fairly straightforward way. It begins by presenting an analytic summary of the *Second Industrial Divide*'s main arguments and then moves on to raise a series of critical questions about these arguments. Is it possible to distinguish between mass production and flexible specialization? Is there a unitary system of mass production which triumphed for reasons which Piore and Sabel identify? Is mass production breaking up? And, finally, how do we regenerate manufacturing and what benefits can be obtained from this regeneration?

Piore and Sabel's argument

The *Second Industrial Divide* is based on a conceptual distinction between two types of industrial production, mass production and flexible specialization. On the one hand we have 'mass production', which is characterized by 'the use of special purpose (product specific) machines and of semi-skilled workers to produce standardized goods' (Piore and Sabel, 1984, p. 4). The more general the goods, the more specialized the machines, and the more finely divided the labour that goes into their production (Piore and Sabel, 1984, p. 27). On the other hand we have flexible specialization or craft production which stands in a neat polar opposition to mass production. This type of production is based on skilled workers who produce a variety of customized goods (Piore and Sabel, 1984, p. 17).

The text builds a large and ambitious superstructure on the basis of this one opposition. The superstructure has three interrelated elements: first, a theory of types of economy, their characteristic problems, and how these problems can and have been resolved; second, an interpretative meta-history of the development of modern manufacturing since 1800; third, and finally, an analysis of the current crisis of the advanced economies and its possible solutions. Seldom in the history of intellectual endeavour can so much have been built on the foundation of one opposition. Piore and Sabel's book is best approached by examining the three superstructural elements in turn, beginning with the theory of types of economy.

For Piore and Sabel, mass production and flexible specialization are not only paradigmatic types of production; they can also be historically realized as types of economy where one kind of production dominates over a given geographic area – regionally, nationally, or internationally. Thus the United States from the late nineteenth century created a mass production national economy which was successfully imitated by follower countries in the post-1945 period, thereby creating an international 'mass production economy'; the term itself is used in the title of chapter 7. On a regional basis, viable local economies based on flexible specialization were realized in nineteenth-century European industrial districts, from Lyon to Sheffield, which produced textiles and metal goods (Piore and Sabel, 1984, p. 28).

If they repeatedly assert and assume that one type of production can dominate a given area, Piore and Sabel never specify criteria which might be used in deciding whether or not one type of production is dominant in a particular case. When it comes to conceptualizing mass production, this issue is of some importance because there is no possibility of a real national economy where all production is undertaken on a mass production basis; as Piore and Sabel concede, 'some firms in all industries and almost all firms in some industries continued to apply craft principles of production' (Piore and Sabel, 1984, p. 20). The survival of something other than mass production is necessary when some end-user demands are too small or too irregular to justify mass production, and the special-purpose machinery required for mass production cannot itself be mass produced (Piore and Sabel, 1984, p. 27). In a very orthodox way, Piore and Sabel suppose that the industrial *locus classicus* of modern mass production is in the manufacture of consumer durables (especially cars) and in industries linked to consumer durables such as steel, rubber, and plate glass (Piore and Sabel, 1984, p. 77).

One further complication arises because Piore and Sabel argue that follower countries had, and used, discretionary choice about the organization of work and methods of labour control and therefore about the degree to which they substituted semi-skilled workers for craftsmen as they introduced mass-production (Piore and Sabel, 1984, p. 134). The American mass production system of 'shop floor control over the work process' (Piore and Sabel, 1984, p. 111) involved narrow job definitions and seniority rights (Piore and Sabel, 1984, p. 173) in an authoritarian system where management directed the semi-skilled. By way of contrast, countries like West Germany and Japan (Piore and Sabel, 1984, pp. 144, 161) retained important elements of an alternative 'craft system of shop floor control' (Piore and Sabel, 1984, p. 116) in their factories where management co-operated with multi-skilled workers. In such cases, a mass production national economy can include the labour control elements of its craft opposite, and the distinctiveness of mass production in these cases rests narrowly on part of the basic opposition, namely the use of specialized machines to make standardized goods.

Although the distinction between types of economy is thus blurred, the notion of differences is sustained partly through the argument that the two types of economy have characteristically different secular economic problems. In both mass production and flexible specialization, economic stagnation always threatens to interrupt economic development and often does so. But the causes of stagnation are different in the two types of economy, and the ways in which development can be, and has been, restored are very distinct.

Mass production is represented as not so much an economic state as a technologically dynamic trajectory. As mass production develops, the supplying enterprise can capture economies of scale and realize ever-lower production costs and selling price through investing in new generations of product-specific equipment which turns out even larger volumes of standardized goods (Piore and Sabel, 1984, pp. 52–4). But if the market will not absorb the output, then the mass producer suffers the high fixed costs of an inflexible mass production system. Piore and Sabel argue that we have learnt in the twentieth century 'that the product specific use of resources pays off only when market stability is ensured' (Piore and Sabel, 1984, p. 163). To resolve this problem, mass production economies require regulatory institutions that secure a 'workable match' between the production and consumption of goods (Piore and Sabel, 1984, p. 4).

Existing institutional arrangements often fail or are inadequate for the purpose of regulation. Where they do fail the result is a 'regulation crisis' as in America in the 1890s or 1930s (Piore and Sabel, 1984, p. 5). Such crises can only be solved through institutional reconstruction and innovation. Thus, the crisis of the 1890s was ended with the development of the large corporations which at a micro level stabilized their individual markets by such tactics as ensuring that the fluctuating component of demand was supplied by small marginal producers (Piore and Sabel, 1984, pp. 55–6). The crisis of the 1930s was resolved after the Second World War at a macro level through an assortment of Keynesian novelties: in the United States these included new state initiatives such as welfare expenditure; high levels of arms expenditure; and 'private' arrangements like wage bargaining on the 1946 UAW/GM pattern which ensured expansion of demand through tying wage rises simultaneously to productivity increases and the rate of inflation (Piore and Sabel, 1984, pp. 79–82).

If the problem of mass production *is* one of stabilizing the market, the problem of flexible specialization is one of ensuring that technical dynamism which Piore and Sabel term 'permanent innovation' (Piore and Sabel, 1984, p. 17). Under flexible specialization, adjustment to the market is not a major problem and macro regulation is not so crucial. This is because flexibly specialized producers employ general purpose equipment (like the Jacquard loom) which enables the enterprise to shift within and between families of products (Piore and Sabel, 1984, p. 30). But Piore and Sabel argue that systems of flexible production run a high risk of stagnating technologically because variation in product design and process technology can be limited while firms attempt to cut production costs by sweating labour and using inferior materials (Piore and Sabel, 1984, p. 263). On this reading of historical experience 'innovation is fostered by removing wages and labour conditions from competition and by establishing an ethos of interdependence among producers in the same market' (Piore and Sabel, 1984, p. 272). These objectives can be achieved in a variety of ways. In nineteenth-century industrial districts, municipalism, paternalism, and familialism all provided organizing principles for limiting and structuring competition (Piore and Sabel, 1984, p. 31). But, one way or another, it is presumed that resources can only be mobilized for permanent innovation if the community is involved and there is a fusion of economic activity, or production in the narrow sense, with the larger life of the community.

The theory of types of economy that we have discussed so far is distinct from the meta-theory of history which is the second major element in the superstructure that Piore and Sabel erect on the basis of the opposition between flexible specialization and mass production. It is logically separate because it would be possible to advance a theory of types of economy without developing a meta-history. The meta-history of manufacturing which Piore and Sabel present is a variant on the stages theories of economic growth and modernization which were popular in the 1960s. If this kind of meta-history is not being revived by Piore and Sabel, it is being revived in a variant form. The notion of unilinear progress to modernity is rejected, as is the notion of a single divide which separates the traditional 'before' from the modern 'after'. That much is signalled by Piore and Sabel's title 'the second industrial divide'.

The meta-history of Piore and Sabel is built on the assumption that mass production and flexible specialization are not only concepts but empirical forms which persist and recur throughout the modern period. Although technology changes and techniques of micro and macro regulations develop, the empirical forms retain the same identity in the 1800s or the 1980s. Thus Piore and Sabel can claim that 'throughout the nineteenth century two forms of technological development were in collision' (Piore and Sabel, 1984, p. 19). Equally, there is nothing new about the kinds of flexible specialization which are being developed in the 1980s. Piore and Sabel repeatedly claim that the spread of flexible specialization now amounts to a revival or 'return to craft methods of production regarded since the nineteenth century as marginal' (Piore and Sabel, 1984, p. 252; see also pp. 6, 17). On this view, history must be a process which permutates the two empirical forms which are always the same.

As Piore and Sabel set it up there are only rare moments of choice 'when the path of technological development is at issue' (Piore and Sabel, 1984, p. 5) and at which societies can choose between a future built on one or other of the two forms. These moments of technological choice are termed 'industrial divides' and Piore and Sabel identify two of them. The first occurred 'in the nineteenth century' when the emergence of mass-production technology – initially in Great Britain and then in the United States – limited the growth of less rigid manufacturing technologies which existed primarily in various regions of western Europe (Piore and Sabel, 1984, p. 5). The second industrial divide is contemporary and dates from the stagnation of the international economic system in the 1970s, which is still continuing in the 1980s. Although the two 'divides' are separated in time, the choice is necessarily the same in both cases; it can only be between mass production and flexible specialization.

This schematic meta-history is buttressed with arguments about how and why social choice of technological development occurs rarely and with an account of the determinants of that choice. Crises are not unusual in mass-production economies, but most of these crises are 'regulation crises' about the institutions which connect production and consumption rather than 'industrial divides' where the technological form of development is at issue (Piore and Sabel, 1984, p. 5). A kind of inertia holds manufacturing economies on to one 'trajectory' after the choice of technology has been made. As Piore and Sabel argue, 'technological choices, once made, entail large investments in equipment and know how, whose amortization discourages subsequent different choices' (Piore and Sabel, 1984, p. 38). After an industrial divide one of the contending forms of production wins out and 'the tendency towards uniformity is reversed only when some combination of developments in the market and in the capacity to control nature makes it economically feasible to strike out in new directions' (Piore and Sabel, 1984, p. 39).

When it comes to conceptualizing the determinants of choice at each divide, Piore and Sabel quite reasonably want to deny any iron law of historical necessity and, more specifically, to avoid the kind of technological or market determinism which the last quotation hints at. Thus, they reject what they call the classical view which attributes the triumph of mass production in the twentieth century to lower production and selling costs. No examples of cost differentials between craft and mass production are presented, but throughout the text it is assumed that at the first and second divides flexible specialization was, and now is, an economically viable and efficient alternative to mass production. On Piore and Sabel's account, the outcome at a divide is settled by the exercise of political power and the commitment of financial resources. 'The technical possibilities that are realized depend on the distribution of power and wealth: those who control the resources and returns from investment choose from among the available technologies the one most favourable to *their* interests' (Piore and Sabel, 1984, p. 38, emphasis in original). What follows is that mass production did not succeed because of its superior economic efficiency in prevailing conditions but rather due to the resources thrown behind those engaged in promoting and using mass production techniques.

Piore and Sabel's anti-classical theory of technological choice is garnished with a rhetorical contrast between the reality of openness at each divide and the ideological appearance of closure after the divide. Piore and Sabel imply that the choice could have gone the other way at the first divide and could now go either way at the second divide. We live in 'a world in which technology can develop in various ways; a world that might have turned out differently from the way it did, and thus a world with a history of abandoned but viable alternatives to what exists' (Piore and Sabel, 1984, p. 38). They thus offer a 'branching tree view of history' (Piore and Sabel, 1984, p. 67) and claim that the limbs of this tree 'thrive or wither according to the outcomes of social struggles, not some natural law of growth' (Piore and Sabel, 1984, p. 15). This openness is ideologically obscured after each industrial divide by the triumph of a 'technological paradigm' which presents the newly dominant form of production as the natural and inevitable victor. Piore and Sabel here borrow the concept of paradigm which Kuhn applied to scientific theory and apply it to a 'vision of efficient production'. They claim 'a new technological paradigm . . . creates the conditions for a new orthodoxy . . . at best half aware that their imagination has been circumscribed by convention, technologists push down the new path' (Piore and Sabel, 1984, p. 44). When the paradigm operates to confirm certain techniques and excludes others, the triumph of mass production in the twentieth century is a result both of material support and ideological effect.

The meta-history outlined above does not completely determine their position on the current 'general crisis of the industrial system' (Piore and Sabel, 1984, p. 165). Piore and Sabel's position on these issues can therefore be considered a third element in the superstructure which they build on top of the basic opposition between mass production and flexible specialization. But the identification of the crisis at a meta-historical 'second industrial divide' does influence their treatment of the crisis which is self-consciously 'open' about causes and outcomes. Thus Piore and Sabel present two supposedly 'alternative' accounts of the origins of the crisis which is caused either by external shocks or internal structural problems in the mass production economies. Equally, they maintain the crisis could be resolved with the victory of either flexible specialization or a revived Keynesianism. Our authors are avowedly neutral; either of the two causal accounts might be correct and both outcomes are possible (Piore and Sabel, 1984, pp. 166, 251. But on our reading, this neutrality is a decorous pretence. The two 'alternative' explanations are largely complementary in so far as the external shocks exacerbate the structural difficulties which advanced economies are beset by, while in terms of outcome there can be no real alternative to flexible specialization because their preconditions for a regeneration of Keynesianism cannot be met.

The first account of the causes of the present crisis presents it as an 'accident' caused by external shocks such as the oil price rises of 1973 and 1979 or the breakdown of postwar regime of fixed exchange rates (Piore and Sabel, 1984, pp. 66–82). These shocks generated uncertainty; the viability of products and processes depended, for example, on the unpredictable future level of oil prices. Such uncertainty inhibits investment and thus has a depressing effect. In the second account, what we have is a kind of internal structural crisis of mass production where the problem is the level and composition of demand nationally and internationally (Piore and Sabel, 1984, pp. 183–93). On this structural account the problem is 'the saturation of core markets' and 'the break up of mass markets for standardized products'. The structural explanation is complementary because the internal problems inhibit investment just like the external shocks. Thus confusion about the level and composition of demand had the effect of 'reducing the portion of demand that employers saw as sufficiently long term to justify the long-term fixed cost investments of mass production' (Piore and Sabel, 1984, p. 83).

The immediate market problem is 'saturation of industrial markets in the advanced economies' (Piore and Sabel, 1984, p. 187). The argument here is focused on the market for long-established consumer durables such as cars and washing machines; 'by the 1960s domestic consumption of the goods that had led the postwar expansion began to reach its limits' (Piore and Sabel, 1984, p. 184). This was a problem because 'no new products emerged to stimulate demand for mass produced goods' (Piore and Sabel, 1984, p. 189); specifically computers and home entertainment never became mass production industries. The other market problem for the mass producers was the 'break up of mass markets for standardized goods' (Piore and Sabel, 1984, p. 183) in a world of increasing product differentiation on the supply side and growing diversity of tastes on the demand side. The effect of mass-market saturation and break-up in the advanced countries was accelerated by the development strategies of many third world countries. The protectionist Latin American countries closed off their internal markets while the Asian NICs aggravated market congestion in the advanced countries by pursuing strategies of export-led growth. (Piore and Sabel, 1984, p. 189).

If these are the dominant market trends, they constitute a problem for mass production and an opportunity for flexible specialization which operates with multi-use low-cost capital equipment. Current trends in manufacturing technology, particularly the development of computer-controlled equipment, reinforce the advantage of flexible specialization in meeting such demand. Piore and Sabel maintain that flexible specialization is dynamic 'independent of any particular state of technology' and recognize that computers can be put to rigid use by mass-producing enterprises. But potentially computer control of equipment like machine tools offers major advantages to flexibly specialized firms producing the small batches and short runs which a differentiated market requires. It is not necessary to replace the machines as in mass production or to change tools and fixtures manually as in old-fashioned flexible specialization; with computer technology, the equipment can be put to new use without physical adjustment 'simply by re-programming' (Piore and Sabel, 1984, p. 260). Piore and Sabel's discussion of new technology concludes with a paean of praise for the computer as the contemporary equivalent of the nineteenth-century artisan's tool which now has the liberating potential to ease the tyranny of specialized machinery over semi- and unskilled workers; 'the advent of the computer restores human control over the production process, machinery is again subordinated to the operator' (Piore and Sabel, 1984, p. 261).

Despite all this, Piore and Sabel formally insist that Keynesianism might be revived and markets could be stabilized so that mass production might provide a basis for renewed prosperity on the other side of the present industrial divide. But a new form of 'international Keynesianism' would require large changes which, according to Piore and Sabel, can only be initiated by national governments acting together. If Keynesianism is to make the world safe for mass production, their prerequisite is new global regulatory mechanisms which raise purchasing power in at least some of the less developed countries. Positively, for example, there must be arrangements which ensure that demand expands at a rate equal to the expansion of productive capacity and mechanisms which apportion the expansion of productive capacity between advanced and developing countries (Piore and Sabel, 1984, pp. 252–7). No doubt the IMF could act more expansively and perhaps currency exchange rates could be managed. But when the European countries cannot agree on co-ordinated reflation, it is incredible that the United States, Europe, and some of the less developed countries could agree on the much more far-reaching changes which Piore and Sabel insist are necessary.

Against this background of a supposed internal blockage of mass production, Piore and Sabel are able to find regional islands of prosperity built on flexible specialization which have already 'challenged mass production as the paradigm' (Piore and Sabel, 1984, p. 207). Industrial districts like Prato or Emilia Romagna in central and north-western Italy provide a model for our future (Piore and Sabel, 1984, p. 206). The challenge now is 'to see how flexibility – until now confined to a relatively small segment within the mass production system – can be extended throughout the economy' (Piore and Sabel, 1984, p. 258). These national developments are likely to produce a new international division of labour. As mass production economies of scale become irrelevant, 'the more likely each nation would be to produce a wide range of products on its own' (Piore and Sabel, 1984, p. 277). Elsewhere Piore and Sabel envisage that mass production will migrate to the LDCs while the advanced countries specialize in high tech, footwear, garments, and machine tools.

Making distinctions

It is now time to turn from exposition to criticism, and our criticism begins by considering the basic opposition between two types of production; mass production relying on special purpose product-specific equipment and semi-skilled workers to produce standardized goods *versus* flexible equipment and skilled workers to produce customized goods. Does this opposition provide a secure foundation for a large superstructure of meta-history? Our answer is that the opposition is not up to the job. Piore and Sabel never develop criteria for identifying instances of mass production and flexible specialization in a way that is intellectually satisfactory. The identifications that Piore and Sabel do make are, in our view, arbitrary and unjustified.

This issue has already been raised in our exposition. We noted then that Piore and Sabel fail to state criteria of dominance which would allow us to determine whether and when one form of production comes to dominate a given area thereby creating a distinctive regional or national economy of the mass production or flexible specialization type. Worse still, our argument below shows that it is very difficult to identify particular enterprises or industries as instances of mass production or flexible specialization. At a conceptual level, the opposition appears clearcut. When there are national differences about the organization of the labour process, there are only three invariant dimensions of difference between mass production and flexible specialization. These differences concern the dedication of equipment, the extent of product differentiation, and the length of production runs. They are summarized in Figure 5.1.

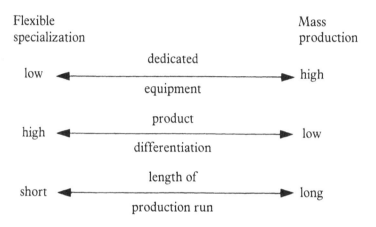

Figure 5.1 Distinctions between mass production and flexible specialization.

The problem of identification arises because, in most instances, a specific enterprise or industry cannot be neatly situated at one pole of variation (on the far left or right in Figure 5.1) in all three dimensions. It is certain, for example, that many enterprises and industries which Piore and Sabel would classify as mass production do not use completely dedicated equipment to produce a single standardized product. The car industry provides some obvious illustrations of this point.

Many significant items of equipment in car factories are not dedicated. Consider, for example, the large hydraulic presses which have been used for more than fifty years in car factories to produce steel body panels. Such presses have a working life of approximately thirty years and a high rate of throughput (Hartley, 1981, p. 29). A modern car firm would not keep one model in continuous production for the life of the press and, at any one moment in time, the press will be used to produce a variety of panels for one or more models. Different panels are obtained by changing dies and the press is simply equipped with a new set of dies when models are changed over. As so often in the production of consumer goods, the tooling is dedicated and model specific but many items of capital equipment are re-usable. Does that make the car industry less of a mass-production industry or not a mass-production industry?

As for product differentiation, the output of major firms does not usually consist of a single standardized product which stays in production for decades. The Ford T and the Volkswagen Beetle are exceptions. Other car producers have increasingly imitated the General Motors strategy of providing a range of differently priced models. And, in the European car business, differences in size have always been important. This kind of mass production differentiation is disparaged by Piore and Sabel, who observe that GM's models shared many components and were only 'presented as different' (Piore and Sabel, 1984, p. 51). But that disparagement is unjustified when Piore and Sabel provide no criteria for discriminating between fundamental difference and trivial styling variation which they admit is commonplace in both flexible specialization and mass production.

The conclusion must be that dedicated equipment and limited product variety are not unproblematic characteristics which can be used to differentiate the mass production enterprises and industries from the rest. In this case, does length of production run provide an empirical yardstick which can be used to identify mass production and corroborate the meta-history? It would, for example, be significant if Piore and Sabel were able to present statistical evidence which showed that, in the consumer durables industries, production runs had grown dramatically shorter over the past fifteen years. But in a 300-page book, there is no statistical evidence at all on production runs for any product of the nineteenth or twentieth centuries. Even if evidence were to be supplied, that would of course raise a whole series of questions about how short a production run has to be before we cross the Rubicon from mass production to flexible specialization? This key question is not posed or answered in *The Second Industrial Divide*, where the deficiencies of the argument are covered up by a regression into circular argument and self reference. If we ask how long is the production run of a mass-produced piece of string, Piore and Sabel's answer would be that the production run of craft string is shorter.

If each dimension of difference between mass production and flexible specialization turns out to be problematic, the difficulties of identification are compounded if we consider the way in which the dimensions of difference are articulated together. As Figure 5.1 shows, the simple Piore and Sabel opposition presupposes a par-

ticular pattern of joint variation in all three dimensions of difference. A (every?) mass-production enterprise will combine limited
product differentiation and long-run production runs. But it is fairly
easy to show that at an enterprise level some 'mass producers' of
differentiated goods can sustain long runs while others do not.
Japanese majors in consumer electronics can achieve long runs
because they have a high share of a protected home market and
export successfully to the rest of the world. Thus in the late 1970s,
cumulative volume per TV chassis type was 1.2 million in Japan,
compared with an average of 400,000 in Europe, and just 150,000
in the UK, whose national producers did not export and were losing
share of their home market (Magaziner and Hout, 1980). In this
instance, differences in the size of the available market determined
massive differences in production run for enterprises producing
similarly differentiated products.

Nor can the existence of a wide range of choice be used to identify
an area where flexible specialization is necessarily making ground.
Under free trade conditions, mass production now invariably
provides a bewildering choice; British consumers can choose
between more than thirty brands and around twenty different makes
of washing machines from British and European factories (*Which?*,
1986). If that choice does not amount to very much then that is
because one product type (the front loader) dominates the European
washing-machine market.

The implication of our argument is that mass production and
flexible specialization cannot be satisfactorily identified in particular
instances, even at the enterprise and industry level. This weakness
must undermine much of Piore and Sabel's argument that mass
production did displace flexible specialization in the nineteenth
century and that flexible specialization can now displace mass
production. After all, if we cannot identify instances of mass production or flexible specialization, how can we determine that one
type of production is displacing the other?

Challenging the meta-history – the case of Ford

The general problem with meta-history is that it tries to stuff too
much into the same bag. This is inevitable when any long and
complex historical experience is summarized with the aid of a simple
framework which identifies only a couple of stages (or divides). This
produces certain characteristic effects – some processes and episodes
will be misrepresented because the interpretative presuppositions of
the framework have to be satisfied, while other processes and
episodes will vanish because they cannot be handled within the
framework. When Piore and Sabel are so economical with the

concepts and assertive about the connections, it would be surprising if they avoided these problems in their meta-history of manufacturing since 1800. And the issues here are best approached by examining the crucial case of Henry Ford and the Model T. If we except a rather curious attempt to represent the $5 day as a primitive policy for boosting demand, what Piore and Sabel say about Ford is fairly orthodox. Thus, they note two points which are emphasized in the existing secondary literature: first, Ford's process innovations lowered the price of his product and thus extended the market (Piore and Sabel, 1984, p. 51): second, Ford was able to finance his company's expansion without public sales of equity and bank loans (Piore and Sabel, 1984, p. 70). What they do not pause to consider is that these points raise fundamental questions about whether the Ford case contradicts their meta-history and, more specifically, their grand theory of technical change. In our view it does so and this is the theme which we now wish to develop by counterposing Ford's achievement and Piore and Sabel's meta-history.

It is necessary to begin by clarifying the issues. We would not wish to argue, following Chandler (1964), that the triumph of mass production was an inevitable response to the potential mass market which the railways created in the United States. Ford's success with the Model T depended on a variety of technical prerequisites including product innovations like the robust and easy to use gear change of the T. Nor would we wish to argue that Ford's process innovations had any 'unique' or 'intrinsic' superiority in all circumstances (see, e.g., Piore and Sabel, 1984, p. 40). The Ford T succeeded in particular circumstances when the preconditions for a mass market had been established. This point is proved by the sales success of the T in its early years before the most important process innovations had been introduced. Sales increased tenfold to $42.5 million in the years 1908 to 1912 (Nevins, 1954, p. 645; Hounshell, 1984). The question is why mass production triumphed over craft production in these particular circumstances. Piore and Sabel's general theory of technical change asserts that choice of productive technology is settled by the exercise of political and financial power and that seems to imply that the balance of economic advantage is fairly even.

Ford made radical process innovations in the 1912–13 period by combining technical elements which already existed and applying them to the mass production of a complex consumer good including numerous components and sub-assemblies. There were three key technical elements. The first element was the use of interchangeable parts which had already been pioneered in car manufacture by Cadillac (Nevins, 1954, p. 371). This directly reduced the labour requirement and was a prerequisite for the development of the assembly line. The second key element was the layout of machines in shops according to the sequence of process operations. As a Ford engineer argued, this again reduced labour requirement by eliminating unnecessary internal movement of parts and work in progress (Bornholdt, 1913, p. 277). The third and final element was the introduction of the moving assembly line which had originally been applied to the stripping of carcases in the meat trade. When applied to the key operation of assembling the chassis of a light touring car, the results were dramatic. In August 1913, 12.5 man hours went into assembling the Model T chassis; by April 1914, after the assembling line had been introduced, the labour requirement was reduced to 1.5 man hours (Arnold and Faurote, 1972, pp. 136–9).

All this required an increase in capital investment, but the reductions in labour input were so large that Ford dramatically reduced costs of production. The benefit was passed on to the consumer in the form of lower selling prices, as Table 5.1 shows.

The Ford T was a keenly priced, bottom-of-the-market motor car when it was introduced in 1908. But, by 1916, in real terms allowing for inflation, the price had been quartered. This was not at the expense of Ford Motor Company's profits, which increased from $3 million in 1909 to $57 million in 1916 (Nevins, 1954, p. 647).

One further crucial point is that the success of the Ford Motor Company was not politically sponsored or supported by financial institutions. Of the $100,000 initial capital, over half was credited to Form and Malcolmson for machinery and patents; only $28,000 was paid in cash. The eleven original backers who put in money were small businessmen, a brace of lawyers, a carpenter, and an office worker (Nevins, 1954, p. 236–7). These men were not Rockefellers

Table 5.1 Selling price of the Model T touring car

	US$
1908	850
1909	950
1910	780
1911	690
1912	600
1913	550
1914	490
1915	440
1916	360

Source: Nevins (1954).

and they did not have a direct line to John Pierpoint Morgan. Equally, none of Ford's backers would have been *persona grata* at meetings of the executive committee of the bourgeoisie. The inescapable conclusion is that political and financial sponsorship was unnecessary because, in the particular circumstances of the time, Ford's combination of process innovations had an overwhelming economic advantage over the 'craft methods' of production which had been used hitherto to make cars which were toys for rich men.

All the rhetoric about 'branching trees' and openness covers one central deficiency in Piore and Sabel's account of mass production *versus* flexible specialization at the first divide; they never present any evidence on the cost of producing cars, or any other complex durable, by alternative methods. The case of the Ford T suggests there never was a choice because there was not a viable craft alternative to mass production of complex consumer durables. That explains why Piore and Sabel are unable to cite any examples of successfully surviving craft production in the key industrial areas where mass production developed. In industries like cars, craft producers only survived precariously by moving up-market and meeting the small-scale demand for high-priced luxury alternatives to mass-produced manufacturers.

Challenging the meta-history – mass production after Ford

The case of Ford and the T shows how our meta-historians can ignore crucial cases which contradict their meta-history. We now wish to turn to make the rather different point that Piore and Sabel's account of subsequent mass production fails to register distinctions and differences which are important but do not exist within their framework. In their meta-history mass production is always the same, and the inevitable outcome, after the triumph of mass production, is a history where nothing really happens except for 'regulation crises'. In an earlier text, Sabel accepted the logic of the position and proposed the concept of 'Fordism' as a kind of shorthand for mass production; 'I will use Fordism as a shorthand term for the organisational and technological principles characteristic of the modern large scale factory' (Sabel, 1983, p. 32). When adequate criteria of instances are never elaborated, it becomes possible to see Fordism everywhere in manufacturing over the past sixty years. Against this we wish to argue that Ford's innovation of the assembly line factory had a limited field of application and Ford did not provide a strategic model which his successors imitated. Ford's production techniques only had an overwhelming cost advantage in the production of complex consumer durables, initially cars and electrical goods, and subsequently in the field of electronics where the products included consumer and producer goods. That gave mass production a substantial field of application; in a recent survey of British manufacturing, 13 per cent of the plants in the sample produced products which contained more than 1,000 components (New and Myers, 1986, p. 6). But for simpler consumer goods, like clothing and furniture, mass-production techniques had a limited advantage. Meanwhile the capital-intensive process industries, like steel and chemicals, went their own way before and after Ford. It is therefore quite understandable that most plants in the advanced economies do not contain assembly lines; the survey of British manufacturing which we have already cited shows that 31 per cent of plants in the sample used assembly lines and only half of those were mechanically placed (New and Myers, 1986, p. 31). Ford's innovations may have been important but they are hardly responsible for the whole trajectory of development in the advanced economies. Rather they created what Mitsui aptly calls assembly industries. Even within this field, Ford did not provide a model which his successors imitated and for that reason alone the concept of 'Fordism' is seriously misleading. As we have already noted, Ford's successors did not generally imitate his product strategy of relying on one long-lived model. Most assemblers succeed by making families of interrelated models which are changed over fairly regularly. Equally important, Ford's successors did not aspire to become fully integrated producers who carried out all the operations necessary to production in their own factory. The 'classic' integrated Ford plants of the 1920s and 1930s like Highland Park, Dagenham, and Cologne are not typical mass-production factories. Ford's successors ran assembly factories whose internal process operations were fed with bought-out components. In most European car factories since 1945, bought-out components account for half the cost of the finished motor car. These crucial variations on 'Fordism' had important repercussions for the composition of assembly output and for the organization of production in the assembly industries.

After Ford, assembly was associated with volume and variety at the enterprise level. This was technically possible because assembly lines can be run productively and profitably at relatively low model volume. That point was demonstrated by the way in which Austin and Morris were able to adopt Ford's innovations and achieve significant cost reductions when supplying the relatively small British market for cars in the 1920s and 1930s. Much of the history of mass production in Europe between the wars was one of the adaption of mass production to lower volume. The next major turning point came after the early 1960s with Japanese innovations in cars and electronics. This showed how the objective of greater variety could be achieved by mass-production enterprises which also chased volume increases. Enterprises like Toyota have developed the use of 'mixed lines' where two or more models are assembled on one line, pressed through inventory reduction through the Kanban system and 'just in time' parts delivery, and also dramatically reduced change-over and set-up times on equipment like power presses (Schonberger, 1982). The Japanese have demonstrated that productive and marketing advantage can be obtained cheaply because assembly line factories can be used much more flexibly than in most western countries.

As for the organization of production, the assembly industries created opportunities for large, medium, and small-scale enterprises which can be connected in a variety of different ways in input–output terms. Piore and Sabel's treatment of these issues is confused and confusing. They distance themselves from 'the popular view that increasingly associated large plants with mass production'. But they generally treat the survival of something other than large-scale production in the mass production industries as evidence of the deficiency of mass production and relate the survival of small firms in that sector simply to the requirements of Fordist firms for specialized equipment to build their standardized products. Against this, we would argue that it is the requirement for components which creates the main market opportunities for small firms. These opportunities are substantial, even in the case of sophisticated products like VCRs where the assembler naturally monopolizes the technically difficult high-volume process work of head production (Mitsui, 1986). Small or medium firms can also prosper in final assembly if component semi-manufactures are being produced in volume by large-scale enterprises. This is one pattern in areas of electronics where there is large-scale production of commodity semi-manufactures like TV tubes, transformers, and silicon chips. One of the more eccentric aspects of Piore and Sabel's book is that they effectively identify mass production with the production of final products for the consumer.

The discussion so far has emphasized some of the differences and distinctions which Piore and Sabel neglect. The concept of Fordism should clearly be rejected because it elides too many differences and establishes an uninformative stereotype. Furthermore, any notion of a generic modern system of mass production should be treated with great caution because there are many different ways of organizing production, even in the assembly industries. It would be intellectually interesting to analyse these differences, but until that analysis is provided it would be foolish to produce substantive work where mass production is a central organizing concept.

If the criticism so far has focused on differences and distinctions which Piore and Sabel neglect, it is appropriate finally to examine

the one difference which they do recognize. Culturally and historically determined differences in labour control figure in *The Second
Industrial Divide* as the main explanation of variation in the national
experience of mass production (Piore and Sabel, 1984, pp. 162–4).
This position rests on a misunderstanding about the general importance of labour in the production process.

As we have argued elsewhere (Williams *et al.*, 1987), labour
control is a managerial obsession which attracts attention in a way
which is disproportionate to its real significance. If Piore and Sabel
accept managerial pre-occupations too readily, that is because they
believe that 'wages are the major component of costs' (Piore and
Sabel, 1984, p. 84). But modern manufacture since the industrial
revolution has been a system which takes labour out; more specifically, Ford and his successors were successful in so far as they took
labour costs out without incurring anything like the same capital
costs. If that yields a microeconomic advantage, it is also crucial to
the macroeconomic process of economic growth which is all about
product output growing faster than production inputs, especially
labour. One measure of the proportion of total costs in manufacturing, inside or outside the 'mass production' industries (the
New and Myers survey of British manufacturing plants which we
have already cited), shows that in their sample, direct labour
accounted for an average of just 18 per cent of total production costs
(New and Myers, 1986, p. 7). What's done tactically with the
labourers who remain is much less important than what is done
strategically about taking labour out. Although tactical decisions
contribute to, they do not determine, the strategic outcome which
depends on decisions about such matters as investment strategy and
marketing. As we have argued in the case of Austin Rover, no
amount or variety of labour control can produce viability if management makes major mistakes about investment and marketing
(Williams *et al.*, 1987). Much the same point could be made about
the defeat of Ford and the Model T in the American car market of
the 1920s. Labour control was irrelevant because Ford could never
win with the T when the market increasingly preferred closed cars,
and second-hands supplied the basic transport market.

Mass production is presented by Piore and Sabel as a form of
production with a technological-cum-market core plus a variable
institutional armature. However the main emphasis then falls on
labour control which is the one national difference which Piore and
Sabel consolidate into their scheme. We have already argued that
this variable cannot explain much and we would finally add that
other variables can explain more. If the aim is to explain differences
in manufacturing performance, it would be more instructive to
examine the role of the Stock Exchange or the lending criteria

applied by different national banking systems. We have shown else-where (Williams *et al.*, 1983) how both conditions influence the performance of British manufacturing. If Piore and Sabel represent a variant of institutionalism, this is an impoverished institutionalism with little explanatory power.

Are mass markets breaking up?

Piore and Sabel argue that mass production has reached its limits when the markets for mass produced goods are saturated and break-ing up because consumers are now demanding more differentiated goods. If the level and composition of demand necessary for mass production cannot be restored, in Piore and Sabel's framework we are at a 'second industrial divide' and the only way forward is through a revival of flexible specialization which was marginalized at the first divide. This section of our criticism will examine the *Second Industrial Divide*'s interpretations of current market trends. Our conclusion is that Piore and Sabel's account of the market arises out of conceptual confusion and does not rest on any hard evidence.

Piore and Sabel's argument about saturation is focused on the older consumer durables (cars, washing machines, refrigerators) which are mature products with high levels of market penetration. But that does not in every case prevent substantial growth in volume and value of sales. The market for colour TV sets in Britain has more than doubled in size to 3.7 million sets over the past ten years because households now buy small-screen TVs as second sets (*British Radio and Electrical Manufacturers' Association Yearbook*, 1985). Value of sales is buoyant when three-quarters of a million teletext sets were sold in 1985 and satellite dishes and high definition TV are just around the corner (*BREMA Yearbook*, 1985). TV shows that the most boringly mature product can be re-invented and repackaged to win extra volume and value. In other areas, where the identity of the product is more stable, volume increases are hard to find because market penetration is high. But, for exactly that reason, a huge replacement demand exists. In white goods, for example, 12 million washing machines and 15 million domestic refrigerators are sold in Europe each year. In the new car market, the dominance of replacement demand is associated with cyclical fluctuation as consumers bring forward or postpone their purchase; in most white goods and brown goods the pattern is quite different because replacement demand is extremely stable.

Replacement demand for mature products is not enough for Piore and Sabel, who assume that volume increases are necessary for mass producers who seek to move down a long-run average cost curve by realizing ever greater economies of scale at higher levels of output (Piore and Sabel, 1984, p. 52). This is formulated by means of a schematic diagram and it is all very hypothetical because a great deal of empirical evidence suggests that the average costs of large firms are often constant over large ranges of output. Even if cost reductions can, in principle, be obtained as output increases, expansion is a risky strategy because it involves fixed investment in capacity increases which will only be profitable if the enterprise and the industry correctly predict the increased size of the future market. There is no good reason why enterprises and industries should not make steady and less risky profits by meeting a large and stable replacement demand which does not tempt producers to invest in over-capacity. If mass production existed, it could be a stable state rather than a trajectory.

In any case if enterprises in consumer goods want increases in volume and value, they can always obtain them by introducing new products. It is salutary here to list some of the new durables which are now being sold in volume in Britain although they did not exist as mass-market products ten years ago. In brown and white goods the list would include video cassette recorders, new format cassette players like the 'walkman', compact disc players, microwave ovens, dishwashers, and food processors. Most of these new products are complementary from the producer's point of view; they can be put together on new lines in existing factories and are sold through existing distribution channels. The development of new products by existing producers is completely ignored by Piore and Sabel. On the issue of new products, Piore and Sabel's one argument is that computers and home entertainment have failed to become mass production industries because their products are insufficiently universal (Piore and Sabel, 1984, pp. 204–5). These industries do not produce something like the T which is 'a machine for everyone and everything' (Piore and Sabel, 1984, p. 202). This nonsense is the bizarre result of projecting the shadow of Ford on to the reality of modern industry. VCRs are the products of large-scale Japanese assembly factories and are sold in mass markets around the world, even if they are not universal audio-visual pleasure machines like Woody Allen's 'orgasmotron'. Indeed, it is not clear why Piore and Sabel do not follow the logic of their own argument and decide that the T was not a true mass market product because Ford failed to produce a 'travel centre' which was capable of flying and crossing water as well as travelling on and off road.

Even if the mass market is not saturated, it is still conceivable that mass markets are breaking up because consumers demand more differentiated products. With the Piore and Sabel framework, market break-up is a much more significant development than market saturation. A problem about a saturated market would in itself only create a 'regulation crisis' of the kind which mass production has solved before through reconstructing the institutions which secure a workable match between supply and demand. But problems about market break-up would create a much more fundamental kind of crisis and an industrial divide if markets were breaking up in a way which creates patterns of demand which mass production cannot cope with. The argument of the next couple of paragraphs is that markets may be breaking up, but not in a way which is really threatening.

The orthodox mass producer survives by producing a family of interrelated models. And in the case of the major durables it is unusual for consumers to demand more than a handful of product types. In the case of cars in the European market, demand has converged on to four distinct product types. The demand is for small, light, medium, and large cars which Ford of Europe meets with the Fiesta, Escort, Sierra, and Granada. In every major European national market, except West Germany, 80 per cent plus of sales are taken in the three lower classes where the major manufacturers have similarly packaged lookalike models. Volume car firms can no longer survive by making one or two utility models as some did in the 1950s and 1960s, but four basic models is all that is required for the current European car market. Variants like 'hot hatchbacks' or coupés can be easily produced by feeding different components on to the main lines or by setting up lines for 'new models' which simply package components from the enterprise parts bin in a slightly different way. Such competition only threatens those manufacturers who cannot find volume sales and decent runs and thereby cover development costs.

Length of production run will depend on how the enterprise is advantaged or disadvantaged by the parallel process of market fragmentation which has occurred generally in the consumer goods markets of all advanced countries (except Japan) over the past twenty years. With the increasing interchange of manufactures over this period, the area of trade has widened in most product lines and the number of brands and models represented in any one market increases. As the importers move in, they claim volume and the domestic producer (or producers) with market leadership lose market share. In the British case this has been the fate of Austin Rover, or of Hoover, Hotpoint, and Morphy Richards who had a dominant position in the supply of many kitchen durables in the 1960s. The British problem is that in many product lines, producers have failed to compensate for the inevitable loss of home sales with a sufficiently large expansion of exports. That explains why Austin Rover, which is pinned down on its home market, is currently making less than 150,000 units each year of the Metro which is its best selling car. Most mainland European producers in cars or white goods also lost output at home, but market fragmentation was not an insuperable problem for them because they won back volume with increased sales to near European markets. Volkswagen, for example, prospers with less than 30 per cent of the German market because it takes 5 per cent or more of every other major international market. On this basis, VW makes more than 800,000 units of its best selling model the Golf each year. In any process of market fragmentation there will be trade winners and losers; enterprises or national industries which lose will be marginalized and possibly forced out of business. But that process does not threaten the system of large-scale production, any more than the fact of bankruptcy threatens capitalism.

If Piore and Sabel believe mass markets are breaking up that is because they are conceptually confused about what is going on and crucially fail to draw the distinction between simple product differentiation and market fragmentation which has quite different consequences. Equally clearly their position on 'the break up of mass markets for standardized products' (Piore and Sabel, 1984, p. 18) does not rest on any sound empirical basis; as we have already noted they provide no statistics on length of production runs and no criteria for discriminating genuinely different products. There is one empirical test of their position on market crisis. It is asserted that difficulties about the market are reflected in a reluctance to undertake fixed investment. In a discussion of the shocks of the 1970s,

Table 5.2 Gross fixed capital formation in manufacturing (constant prices)

	1970	1975	1983
USA	100	117.3	134.8
UK	100	84.1	57.7
Japan	100	101.6	181.7
W. Germany	100	59.1	80.3[1]
France	100	103.7	128.6[2]
Italy	100	91.1	96.0[3]

Source: United Nations Annual Accounts.
Notes
1   West German figure is for year 1982.
2   All French totals include mining and quarrying as well as electricity and gas.
3   Italian figure is for year 1981. All Italian totals include mining and quarrying.

Piore and Sabel claim that such shocks 'reduced the portion of demand that employers saw as sufficiently long run to justify the long term fixed capital investment of mass production' (Piore and Sabel, 1984, p. 183). No statistics are cited to support this claim about inhibited investment. The available evidence on capital formation shows that, if this effect operated in the mass production sector, it was not sufficiently strong to depress the level of gross fixed capital formation in all advanced countries.

As Table 5.2 shows, the real manufacturing investment levels of 1970 were effectively maintained or surpassed in 1983 in four of the six national economies. Two economies, West Germany and Britain, show a sustained fall in real investment levels. If the German record is anomalous, the decline in British manufacturing investment can be fairly easily explained when this country was a trade loser which suffered progressive de-industrialization. The evidence of healthy investment elsewhere is not explained by, but is broadly consonant with, the evidence which we have presented on market opportunities in the assembly industries of cars and consumer electronics. Piore and Sabel's intimations about market-led collapse in these industries appear to be exaggerated melodrama.

The message of new technology

Even if Piore and Sabel are wrong about market demand, they may be correct about the potential of new technology which, on their account, facilitates the resurgence of flexible specialization. They argue that dedicated equipment and inflexible automation is being superseded by a new generation of microelectronically controlled machines which allow efficient production in smaller batches. Piore and Sabel take a very definite position on the capability and salience of computer control, but here again they present no solid evidence. Crucially, their book never examines the costs and output potential of specific items of new technology in particular industrial contexts. To redress this absence, we will present some evidence of our own. In modern manufacturing, enterprises are increasingly buying computer integrated manufacturing systems. And we will analyse two cases of such systems: robotized body-building lines which are used in the car industry; and 'flexible manufacturing systems' (FMSs) which are usually used for metal machining. With robots, the issue is how new technology changes conditions of production in an industry which has been a central redoubt of volume production in long runs. FMSs are more usually installed by capital goods producers and the question here is how new technology changes the economics of batch production.

Commentators like Altshuler *et al.* (1984, p. 12) and Jones (1985)

have recently argued that a new productive flexibility is transforming the economics of the cars business (see also Piore and Sabel,
1984, p. 248). Their position is summarized by Jones who, like
Altshuler, relies on asserting the fact of flexibility and provides no
evidence about costs.

> The introduction of computer controlled production lines plus
> the introduction of much more flexible automation involving
> robots, automated handling, machining cells etc., have changed
> the economies of scale in production drastically. The use of
> robots instead of dedicated multi-welders, for instance, gives
> these plants a greater degree of flexibility to switch models in
> response to demand and reduces the cost of introducing new
> models and variants . . . A full range of cars can now be
> produced in one or two plants at a much lower total volume and
> at a cost which is competitive with much larger producers.
> (Jones, 1985, pp. 151, 152)

Against this we would argue that the new productive techniques are
much less flexible than Jones supposes and the scale economics of
the car business have not been fundamentally changed by the new
techniques.

There can be no doubt that the process of car body building has
been transformed by robots. It is now commonplace for 90 per cent
of body welds to be made automatically and, in a modern car
factory, most of these welds will be made by robots which are also
extensively used in spraying. That explains why in most of the
advanced countries, 50 per cent of industrial robots are installed in
car factories. These robots are much more flexible than an earlier
generation of dedicated jig multi-welders which could only weld one
panel of a specific shape. The costs of multi-welders could only be
covered on long runs and in Europe only VW (with the Beetle) built
whole bodies with multi-welders. Ford and Fiat used them for
'structural' components like floor pans which were not changed
whenever models were face-lifted. Robots can be set up to perform a
variety of spot welding operations on differently shaped panels for a
set of models. Every European volume car manufacturer, even little
Austin Rover, now operates robot body lines which can produce an
output of 200,000–350,000 shells for two models and several
variants on those models if the manufacturer so requires. But a
substantial commissioning cost (for software, tools, and fixtures) has
to be incurred before a robot line is brought into use; one recent
estimate suggests that 60 per cent of the cost of a robot system is
accounted for by commissioning cost (see Williams *et al.*, 1987).
Most of this commissioning cost is model generation specific. When
a new generation of models is introduced every five years or so the

panel geometry will be different and, if the old robots are retained, they will have to be expensively recommissioned. Robots cannot be re-programmed for new models by pressing a few buttons. That is a myth.

It is also certain that the introduction of robots in body building has not transformed the scale economics of the cars business. More flexible automated technology does not allow the smallscale producer to become more cost competitive than in the previous era when such firms relied on manual welding and spraying and dedicated automation was the preserve of the Americans and VW. When the commissioning costs of body building equipment is high, the large-scale producer with long model runs retains an advantage when it comes to using and re-using body lines. Furthermore body building is only one process in the manufacture of motor cars and throughput requirement remains high in several other processes. Robots are being increasingly used in the final assembly of engines, but engines are still produced on transfer lines dedicated to the production of one engine type for a long period at a rate of 300,000 units per year or more. For the forseeable future, small firms in the European volume cars business will buy in engines which they cannot produce at a competitive cost. Even if new technology did change the balance of productive advantage between large and small firms, the large firm would still obtain a general advantage from its ability to spread development costs over longer runs. Because of inability to cover development costs, small car manufacturers always risk being demoted to assembler status.

The case of FMS is inevitably different in detail but it again serves to illustrate the basic discrepancy between reality and the romance of computerized flexibility. A 'flexible manufacturing system' exists where there is computer co-ordination of two or more manufacturing cells, each of which would normally contain several machine tools; the cells will be connected by an automatic transport system which moves pallets, workpieces, and tools between machines and to and from workpiece and tool storage; the whole is co-ordinated by a DNC computer which integrates all operations according to a master programme (UN, 1986, p. 13). At first sight, the literature on FMS endorses the same *doxa* as the literature on car body building. The UN survey asserts that 'mass production as a concept is becoming more and more a thing of the past' (UN, 1986, p. 2), while there are familiar claims about added flexibility.

In mass production environments, computer controlled machines will make it possible to add flexibility to the production system in the sense that the system can be used to manufacture several different product variants with minimal set up times. This opens up important potentials, for dividing large scale production into many smaller batches with the obvious purpose of reducing in-process inventory and achieving a faster adaptation to consumer preference. (UN, 1986, p. 2)

But this literature is more sober, because it is not claimed that the availability of FMS changes the economics of the business of metal machining by tilting the balance of advantage against large-scale production undertaken by the medium- and large-sized firm. That claim would be implausible because, as the survey evidence shows, FMS systems are expensive, deliver limited variety, and have to be utilized at high volume. On our interpretation, FMS is a way of putting medium-volume batch production on a capital-intensive basis and therefore represents only a new twist on the old post-Fordist story of volume and variety.

FMSs are not cheap. The most comprehensive available survey by the UN covers 339 FMSs worldwide. In this sample, 45 per cent of Japanese systems, 46 per cent of European systems and 82 per cent of American systems cost over $3 million. Inevitably, therefore, most FMSs are bought by medium and large firms who can afford this kind of expenditure. A large investment in FMS is only sensible if the enterprise has a substantial work load which offers a combination of the variety necessary to use the technical capability of the system and the volume necessary to secure high levels of capacity utilization. This is another constraint on the adoption of FMS by medium- and small-sized firms. As the UN survey argued, 'for small and medium sized companies it is often difficult to find a large enough product family in terms of the number of parts and the volume per part which over a long period of time will ensure a sufficiently high degree of utilization of FMS' (UN, 1986, p. 55). Smaller firms are also disadvantaged because they will usually lack the necessary in-house expertise to develop and run a sophisticated custom-built system.

The amount of variety delivered is very variable and quite obviously relates to the different requirements of particular enterprises and industries. For obvious reasons, most large firms who buy and use FMS do not want a machine which delivers industrial pump pistons this week and auto clutch components the next. Width of product envelope is built in at the design stage and usually determined by upstream and downstream process requirements. All the surveys show that Japanese FMSs deliver substantially more variety than western FMSs. The UN survey showed that 49 per cent of Japanese FMSs were able to produce more than fifty 'variants' of a product; the comparable European and American figure was 17 and 37 per cent. Jaikumar (1986) has shown that FMSs in American factories are used for longer runs than in Japanese factories. The implication is that western firms are installing expensive over-sophisticated equipment which is not necessary for their business strategies and the end-user requirements in the markets defined by those strategies. Variety of output is not an end in itself and many western users of FMSs are incurring hidden costs because they are buying facilities whose full potential will never be exploited.

Whatever variety is planned for and delivered, it is absolutely essential to obtain volume which guarantees high rates of utilization. In this respect the crucial consideration is not batch size but the cumulative volume of all the batches produced through the year. And this cumulative volume is always high; in Jaikumar's (1986) survey, US FMSs delivered an average of 17,000 parts per year while Japanese FMSs delivered an average of 24,000 parts per year. When fixed costs are high, an FMS must be driven intensively near to the limit of capacity if payback in three to five years is to be achieved. This is always achieved in Japan where two-shift working is the norm and where nearly one-third of the sixty FMSs in Jaikumar's survey were being operated on a continuous three-shift basis. As a western observer reported after a tour of Japanese FMSs, 'in all factories, the large product volumes and high throughputs were particularly impressive' (*FMS Magazine*, April 1986, p. 69). By way of contrast, the British financial experience of operating FMSs is disastrous; in the New and Myers survey, more than half of the sixty-four plants which had installed FMSs reported losses or no pay off. British production managers lack the technical ability to use even mundane metal-working machinery in an intensive way (Daly *et al.*, 1985). And many British firms have a proven inability to find volume which is as necessary for FMSs as for other more traditional forms of capital intensive process equipment which produces less variegated output.

We do not pretend to know the truth about new technology. We doubt whether there is one message in this bottle. If technological change is uneven in its nature and effects, it is unlikely to offer the same benefits to all enterprises and industries. But, in this context, our evidence does cast doubt on the universal validity of Piore and Sabel's over-confident assertions. And, whatever new technology does offer in the two cases which we have considered, it is not going to inaugurate a new era of flexible specialization which restores those craft methods of production that lost out at the 'first divide' (Piore and Sabel, 1984, p. 5, see also p. 17). New generations of computer controlled equipment may deliver a more varied output but they do not restore an economic system based on redeployable productive resources and low fixed costs. That is a world which we have lost. When robot bodylines or FMSs do not change the economics of the business in which they are installed, this new technology is likely to be controlled by medium- and large-sized firms who will not use it to create a workforce of independent craftsmen.

Piore and Sabel's vision of an artisan future is, like so much else in their book, plausible in some respects. If new technology has one general effect, it is to reduce the relative importance of semi-skilled direct labourers in the manufacturing workforce. In a company like Austin Rover, for example, only half the workforce in 1985 consisted of direct workers of the traditional blue collar kind. But that does not require any return to polyvalent craftsmen who have independent control over entry and the prospect of short-term job security through work sharing (Piore and Sabel, 1984, p. 116). These elements of the 'craft model of shop floor control' are not going to be re-created by the modern corporation. The intentions of British managers are disclosed by their interest in, and enthusiasm for, the Atkinson (1984) model of labour control. In this schema, enterprises create an elite of multi-skilled workers whose training and skills are enterprise or plant specific and whose privileges as 'core workers' are granted and can be taken away by the company. The extent and significance of such labour central strategies remains to be investigated. Meanwhile, Piore and Sabel's schema is unhelpful because here again we have an instance where they simply project a stylized shadow of the past on to the present in a way which confuses our understanding of what is going on.

The benefits of flexible specialization?

We cannot accept Piore and Sabel's diagnosis of what has gone wrong in the advanced economies. The notion of a crisis of mass production must be rejected for two reasons: first, it is based on a concept of mass production which is probably incorrect and certainly elides too many differences; second, it is contrary to the available evidence on market trends and new technology. But it must be admitted that the advanced economies are not prospering and it is conceivable that flexible specialization might provide a basis for industrial regeneration. This last section considers what flexible specialization can deliver and comes to the conclusion that it is less than Piore and Sabel promise.

When the preconditions for a revived Keynesianism cannot, in Piore and Sabel's schema, be met, flexible specialization is an attractive way forward. Flexible specialization does not depend on a functioning national or international economic order which delivers a particular level or composition of demand. If flexible specialization is to maintain technological dynamism, according to Piore and Sabel it does require an integration of production into the local community. But this could be managed on a regional or local basis. If neither family nor ethnic identity provide suitable principles of integration in the modern advanced economies, the necessary integration could be provided by municipal or regional government. Within this framework, flexible specialization provides a simple universal rule for choice of strategy at the enterprise and industry level. On Piore and Sabel's account, if new technology has one message and if there are general trends in the market place, then for enterprises and industries there can only be one correct strategy of flexibility. Piore and Sabel do not formally draw this conclusion, but it is the logic of their position. In this context it is significant that in their long book there is not one case where they commend inflexibility as an appropriate and effective contemporary business strategy. Our question must be what can strategies of flexibility deliver?

Any simple rule which says 'the more flexibility, the better' would not always produce sensible results for the enterprise and the industry. In multi-process activities like steel making or car manufacture, the impact of technological change is almost always uneven and flexible automation is not the invariable correct answer to every question about the design of process technology. Best practice Japanese factories typically use a mix of dedicated 'hard' automation and flexible 'soft' automation. Leading Japanese automation experts like Makino insist that 'hard automation will always be very important' and cost effective because many process functions do not change frequently. In other cases, where flexible technology can be applied across a range of processes, it is impossible to produce the whole of an industry's output using flexible technology. For example, as long as steel mini-mills are scrap-charged, they can do little more than fill a niche in international markets where most of the output is produced in large-scale basic oxygen converters; the price of scrap would go through the roof if all the advanced countries used it as the basic raw material for steel production.

At an enterprise level, choice of technology depends on the costs of available process technologies, the product strategy of the enterprise, and the markets which are available within the limits of investment in distribution. Enterprise calculation is about making an appropriate choice within these parameters. And the choice which is correct for one enterprise will not necessarily be correct for another enterprise. This point is demonstrated by the contrast between VW's success at Wolfsburg with dedicated automation which is used for Golf body building and final assembly, and Austin's failure at Longbridge with the same kind of automation which is used for Metro body building. In both cases, choice of dedicated technology was consistent with the company's product strategy of producing a long-life model with few variants. But the market position of the two companies was very different and dedicated equipment which could be intensively used by VW was under-utilized by Austin Rover. The strength of VW's European distribution is such that the company can sell 750,000 Golfs each year while Austin Rover, which is pinned down on its home market, has difficulty in selling 150,000 Metros. With this kind of volume, it would have been more sensible for Austin Rover to choose a more flexible line where two or more different models could be built in whatever proportions the company preferred.

The contrast underscores the importance of executing strategy, and making choices work. If choice of technology should be related to the market, when technology has been chosen, execution is about ensuring the right level and composition of demand by managerial (and maybe political) action. This is an area where the British always do badly. We have elsewhere criticized 'giantism' in British nationalized coal, steel and cars where enterprises naively pursued economies of large-scale production (Williams et al., 1986; Chapter 4 of this book). In all three cases massive investment in modernization only became totally disastrous when projected demand failed to materialize and the nationalized enterprises faced problems about the under-utilization of newly constructed capacity. The problem was not that the strategies were inherently absurd, but that they were executed ineptly because managers and politicians failed to secure the market that was necessary if the new large-scale facilities were to run profitably. That adjustment of the market could have been made in at least two of our three cases. Austin Rover's managers could have invested in overseas distribution and the government could have given some preference to British manufactured cars. If that intervention was politically problematic, ministers could have easily prevented the CEGB from forcing down the price of power-station coal which is the main product of British Coal.

From our point of view, the weakness of Piore and Sabel's position is that it virtually abolishes the role of enterprise calculation which, in their schema, must become a matter of identifying the particular implications of universal trends in technology and the market. As our examples show, this is an inadequate way of conceptualizing the choices and opportunities which face enterprises and industries in the advanced countries. Institutional conditions ensure there are substantial differences in national ability to exploit such opportunities (Williams et al., 1983) and the resulting differences in performance create further difficulties. Trade in manufactures between the advanced countries is zero sum game, and, in an open international economy, successful manufacturing countries like Germany and Japan gain trade share at the expense of unsuccessful manufacturing countries like Britain. The migration of manufacturing output and employment to the more successful advanced countries is a reality which Piore and Sabel avoid by positing the possibility of a future world where all can succeed through flexibility.

If Piore and Sabel exaggerate the benefits which can be obtained from flexibility, more fundamentally they exaggerate the benefits which can be obtained from the regeneration of manufacturing. Their book is an argument about the possibility of a prosperous future based on manufacturing. But any regeneration of manufacturing in the advanced countries is unlikely to solve problems about the distribution of social welfare which are becoming ever more acute. Piore and Sabel cover up these problems in their concluding chapters by putting before us a vision of industrial districts spreading out to create a new republic of craftsmen and smallholders. Against this, in our view, institutional forces and free trade are likely to create regional and national islands of prosperity and to sustain substantial wage differentials between manufacturing workers and the rest – even within the islands of prosperity.

The most unsuccessful advanced economies like Britain contain regional islands of prosperity. As Hyman (1986) points out, the Thames valley in Britain provides a model of prosperity built on a diversified base of high-tech manufacturing and services. Piore and Sabel attach special significance to those industrial districts like Prato and Emilia Romagna whose prosperity is supposedly built on a foundation of flexible specialization. If national prosperity built on flexible specialization is to materialize, then it would be necessary for these islands to expand so that they dominate the whole of the national economy. Before we could determine whether that outcome is plausible, we would need to know the proportion of national employment and output which these districts account for at present. Typically, Piore and Sabel provide no information on these points. In only one case are we given any figures, and these relate to performance rather than extent; in Emilia Romagna all we are told is that wage levels and income per capita are rising relative to the rest of Italy and unemployment rates are falling relative to the rest of Italy (Piore and Sabel, 1984, p. 227). Such information does not allow us to determine whether industrial districts of this type are filling in occasional niches or can colonize the whole economy. In effect Piore and Sabel can only provide homiletic examples of flexible specialization's supposed success in regional economies. The Italian regions are like Samuel Smiles' heroes; they show us all that, with the right kind of effort, it is possible to rise above the disadvantage of humble origins.

Where manufacturing succeeds (with or without flexible specialization), that success only directly benefits a minority of the population. As Hyman (1986) points out, in all the advanced countries two-thirds to three-quarters of the workforce is outside the manufacturing sector. In most of these countries the proportion employed in manufacturing is in relative decline and in unsuccessful manufacturing countries there are large absolute declines in numbers employed; the numbers employed in British manufacturing have declined by more than two and a half million in the past fifteen years (Cutler *et al.*, 1986; Chapter 4 of this book). Steady secular increases in labour productivity have been sustained in manufacturing since the industrial revolution and the expansion of manufacturing output has never required a commensurate increase in manufacturing employment. To make this familiar point in a slightly different way, any increases in manufacturing (net) output are typically appropriated through rises in real wages rather than increases in employment (see Williams *et al.*, 1987). The mechanics of appropriation ensure that the manufacturing sector is always a high wage sector in the advanced countries. Redistribution to the unwaged and to the low paid outside manufacturing will be necessary and such redistribution is most easily carried out by central government which in all the advanced countries has a dominant role in taxation and in secondary income redistribution through social security. That suggests the limits of the Piore and Sabel model of locally guaranteed prosperity. The dynamism of flexible specialization might be secured by the integration of production into the local community. But there are clearly limits on what municipal action can achieve. Most municipalities and regions lack the powers of taxation to achieve social objectives like a substantial redistribution of income.

Conclusion

In conclusion we have demonstrated that Piore and Sabel's basic opposition between mass production and flexible specialization is unworkable because empirical instances cannot be identified; their meta-history is contradicted by the case of Ford and suppresses the subsequent history of the assembly industries; their analysis of market trends and new technology is unconvincing; and their view of where flexible specialization can take us is incurably romantic. Why, then, has this mix of futurology and meta-history been represented as providing a serious and reliable guide to the modern industrial world, despite its manifest conceptual and empirical weaknesses? Part of the answer lies in the fact that everywhere it strikes comforting and responsive chords. Thus in Britain Piore and Sabel's work provides a rationale for the local initiatives and plans for socialism in one municipality which have been increasingly popular over the last decade. The reception tells us more about the critical standards of this audience than about the real merits of the text.

References

Altshuler, A., Anderson, M., Jones, D., Roos, D., and **Womack, J.** (1984), *The Future of the Automobile; the Report of MIT's Automobile Program*, London, Allen & Unwin.

Arnold, H.L. and **Faurote, F.L.** (1972) *Ford Methods and the Ford Shops*, New York, Arno Press (reprint, original 1915).

Atkinson, J. (1984) *Flexibility, Uncertainty and Manpower Management*, Institute of Management Studies Report, 89.

Bornholdt (1913), 'Placing machines for sequence of use', *The Iron Age*, vol. 92.

BREMA *Yearbook* (1985).

Chandler, A. (ed.) (1964) *Giant Enterprise: Ford General Motors and the Automobile Industry*, New York, Harcourt, Brace.

Cutler, R., Williams, K., and **Williams, J.** (1986), *Keynes, Beveridge and Beyond*, London, Routledge & Kegan Paul.

Daly, A., Hitchens, D., and **Wagner, K.** (1985) 'Productivity, machinery and skills in a sample of British and German manufacturing plants', *National Institute Economic Review*, February.

FMS Magazine (1986), April.

Hartley, J. (1981) *The Management of Vehicle Production*, London, Butterworth.

Hounshell, D. (1984) *From the American Systems to Mass Production 1800–1932*, Baltimore, Johns Hopkins University Press.

Hyman, R. (1986), 'Flexible specialism: miracle or myth', paper to EGOS AWG, Warwick Colloquium on Trade Union Research, June, University of Warwick.

Jaikumar, R. (1986), 'Post-industrial manufacturing', *Harvard Business Review*, November–December.

Jones, D. (1985) 'Vehicles' in C. Freeman (ed.), *Technical Trends in Employment, 4, Engineering and Vehicles*, Aldershot, Gower.

Magaziner, I. and **Hout, T.** (1980) *Japan's Industrial Policy*, London, Policy Studies Institute.

Mitsui, I. (1986) *The Japanese Sub-contracting System*, Komazawa University Press, Tokyo.

Murray, J. (1985), 'Benetton Britain'. *Marxism Today*.

Nevins, A. (1954) *Ford: the times, the man and the company*, New York, Charles Scribner & Sons.

New, C. and **Myers, A.** (1986) *Managing Manufacturing Operations in the UK, 1975–85*, London, British Institute of Management.

Sabel, C. (1983) *Work and Politics*, Cambridge University Press.

Schonberger, R. (1982) *Japanese Manufacturing Techniques*, New York, Free Press.

Tolliday, S. and **Zeitlin, J.** (1987) *The Automobile Industry and its Workers: Between Fordism and Flexibility*, Cambridge, Polity and Blackwell.

United Nations (1986), *Survey on Flexible Manufacturing Systems*, Geneva: UN (OECD).

Which? (1986). London Consumers' Association, May.

Williams, K., Haslam, C., Williams, J., and **Wardlow, A.** (1986) 'Accounting for failure in nationalized enterprises' *Economy and Society*, vol. 15, no. 2 (Chapter 4 of this book).

Williams, K., Williams, J. and **Haslam, C.** (1987) *The Breakdown of Austin Rover*, Leamington Spa, Berg.

Williams, K., Williams, J. and **Thomas, D.** (1983) *Why are the British Bad at Manufacturing?* London, Routledge & Kegan Paul.

6
Overseas investment and left policy proposals

Allin Cottrell

Abstract

This chapter examines and extends the debate over Roy Hattersley's proposal for a tax on the earnings derived from overseas investments of UK residents. Two frameworks are employed to analyse the issue, loanable funds theory and a modern macroeconomic approach stemming from Buiter and Miller. It is concluded that such a tax could be effective in lowering the domestic interest rate and stimulating domestic investment, depending upon the circumstances of its imposition, but that it will also be likely to reduce net exports. Questions are raised concerning the desirability of such a policy if there is no longer a net outflow of loanable funds when a putative future Labour government reaches power.

There appears to be a fair degree of interest on the British left at present in some form of control on foreign investment, as a component of the economic strategy of a future Labour government committed to raising investment and employment in the UK. Roy Hattersley has proposed a scheme which essentially involves a tax on the returns from foreign asset-holdings (speech to Teeside Fabians in January 1985[1]) which was shortly afterward apparently endorsed by Neil Kinnock. This scheme was subjected to critical scrutiny by Hugh Stephenson (1985a, 1985b) then subsequently defended by Hattersley (1985a). Such proposals should be seen in a double context. On the one hand they can be seen as a reaction to the 'massive outflow' of funds following the abolition of exchange controls in 1979.[2] There is at least a *prima facie* case that domestic investment could have been substantially higher in the absence of such outflow. On the other hand, these proposals can be related to the currently rather cool attitude within the Labour Party towards nationalization of financial institutions. Policies to reduce the incentive for private UK financial institutions to carry out overseas portfolio investment can be presented as a 'more practicable' alternative to large-scale nationalization – see for instance Paul Smith (1985), who explicitly defends controls on capital export in these terms against the claims of Coakley and Harris (1983) that only national-ization will permit a significant redirection of flows of investable funds.

The object of this chapter is to take up the arguments mentioned above while introducing to this debate a greater degree of economic rigour. The contributions cited above contain rather a high pro-portion of assertion and counter-assertion – perhaps a necessary consequence of their polemical and largely non-technical nature – yet the issues at stake are sufficiently important to warrant a more formal and careful examination. The general perspective of this chapter is pragmatic; the writer has no particular ideological objection to controls on foreign investment (either 'from the right' on the grounds that the market always knows best, or 'from the left' on the grounds that only nationalization can be effective). But pre-cision is lacking at present on these questions: What exactly is it that such a policy is supposed to achieve? How exactly is it supposed to achieve the desired aim? And at what cost?

First, let us take stock of the stated case for and against controls on foreign investment somewhat more fully. As I read it, the general objectives to which the Hattersley tax proposal is seen as contri-buting are:

1   to raise employment in the short run, by raising aggregate
    demand in the domestic economy; and
2   to raise domestic capital formation.

These two objectives are closely related, but analytically separable. The specific contribution of the proposal in question, as claimed by its supporters, is that it will lower the domestic interest rate, and make it easier for the government to borrow to finance industrial interventions. In addition, Paul Smith argues that the increased availability of funds in the home economy is likely to raise domestic stock prices, hence encouraging private-sector investment financed by new stock issues. Against this, Stephenson has argued that the Hattersley proposal offers no substantial benefits, and that the *only* possible function of any type of exchange controls is to influence the *exchange rate*. Such controls, it is claimed, are 'irrelevant to decisions about investment and job creation' and the whole scheme is condemned as unwonted '*dirigisme*'. Coakley and Harris, on the other hand, argue that capital outflows have not significantly reduced the availability of funds in the domestic economy, and that even if such flows were interdicted, the funds would still not go into domestic industrial investment in the absence of a thorough re-structuring of the financial system under nationalization.

First response: I fully accept the objective of raising aggregate demand and hence employment in the UK economy. There is ample evidence that the current rate of unemployment in the UK is not the so-called 'natural rate', and therefore that a stimulus to demand could significantly reduce unemployment. It is doubtful, however, whether policies to reduce the incentive for overseas investment *per se* will raise aggregate demand. It will be argued below that they are likely to substitute domestic investment for net exports, leaving aggregate demand broadly unchanged.

Second, the objective of raising home *investment* in particular has to be argued for in its own right. As a component of aggregate demand, investment is basically at par with consumption, government current expenditure, and net exports. As a source of future income for today's savers (the channelling of whose saving is at issue) overseas investment may be argued to be 'just as good' (if not better) than home investment. This is after all the basic argument of the portfolio managers who have been carrying out the large-scale foreign investment of recent years. So what is the special virtue of domestic capital formation? The standard argument here is that domestic capital formation raises the domestic capacity output and the productivity of labour, offers the prospect of increased international competitiveness, and therefore contributes to longer term prospects for employment, real wages, and living standards in the home economy. If it is not the business of private financial institutions to calculate in these terms, it is the business of government to do so, and government should arrange market incentives such that private financial institutions are led to fall in line with 'national' objectives.

It is not my intention to reject this case altogether, but one must not be too uncritical in assessing it. There is plenty of evidence that an inadequate *volume* of investment as such has not been the main factor in contributing to the relatively poor performance of the UK economy. The adverse consequences of the conjunctural collapse of investment in the early Thatcher years should not obscure this point. With a longer perspective we can see that it is the *efficiency* of investment in the UK rather than its volume which has been substantially out of line with the more economically-successful OECD nations. Non-residential investment as a fraction of gross domestic product has been consistently higher in the UK than in the USA over the whole period since the 1950s (although slightly lower than in France and Germany), while the incremental capital output ratio has been much higher in the UK, and the index of output per unit of capital much lower, especially in manufacturing. In addition, the rate of return on capital stock has been substantially lower in the UK than in the USA, West Germany and Japan, at least since the 1960s. (Detailed substantiation of these points can be found in the

OECD *Economic Survey of the UK*, January 1985). All of this is not to suggest that there would be no benefit from raising the rate of industrial investment in the UK, only that it is misleading to place undue emphasis on the need for a volume increase at the expense of investigating the factors which have made investment substantially less productive in the UK.

Having made this point, however, let us concede that an increase in the rate of domestic capital formation is arguably an important component of a strategy for future employment and competitiveness, with the proviso that the investments be well-chosen and that the conditions for increased efficiency of investment be seriously examined.[3] The question then is whether controls on foreign investment (and I take the idea of a tax on foreign investment returns as the example here) are likely to contribute signficantly to this aim, without imposing disproportionate costs in other respects.

To answer this question at more than the level of assertion, we need to use some reasonably precise analytical framework. Unfortunately, there is no uniquely 'correct' framework available, and this paper offers two complementary perspectives on the issue, utilizing two different models of financial markets and interest-rate determination. The first perspective is that offered by the 'loanable funds' theory of the interest rate, which is implicitly appealed to in most of the contributions cited above, while the second utilizes the insights of Buiter and Miller (1981) into the short-run behaviour of asset markets.

Loanable funds

The loanable funds theory offers a conception of the financial system as a mechanism for collecting flows of funds from savers and channelling those flows to borrowers. On this view the interest rate (or vector of interest rates, but we simplify by assuming there is only one rate) is the factor which balances the desired flow-supply and flow-demand for funds. The conception was, of course, challenged by Keynes, who argued that it is the level of aggregate income which adjusts to equilibrate desired saving and investment (or, more generally, borrowing), while the interest rate plays the role of equilibrating the demand to hold money with the stock of money in existence. In the 'classical' theory which Keynes was attacking, income is not free to move to equilibrate supply and demand for loanable funds since it is assumed that a freely operating labour market will ensure continuous (or almost continuous) full employment, so that aggregate real income is 'pinned down' at its full employment level. Neither can the interest rate equilibrate money demand and money stock since it is also assumed that the demand for money is not responsive to the rate of interest. Keynesian and 'classical' theory in their full forms are clearly inconsistent but none the less, as D.H. Robertson (and later Leijonhufvud) showed, it is possible to marry loanable funds analysis with a broadly Keynesian orientation to the working of the economy, i.e. one which assumes neither continuous full employment nor that the demand for money is simply a fixed percentage of nominal GNP. This point will not be developed at length here (the interested reader is referred to Leijonhufvud, 1981, Ch. 7). We simply note that when we utilize loanable funds analysis within a 'non-classical' context we have to be sensitive to the possibility of:

1 shifts in the supply of funds schedule due to changes in aggregate income; and
2 non-equivalence between 'saving' and 'supply of loanable funds' whenever agents wish to alter their holdings of money balances over time.

The following loanable funds analysis rests on these simplifying assumptions.

1 The exchange rate is freely floating. There is not direct government intervention in the foreign exchange market in the form of purchases or sales of foreign currency.
2 Capital is perfectly mobile internationally. In the absence of government intervention there is therefore one world interest rate, which is determined in the world market for loanable funds at the point at which supply and demand balance.
3 The domestic economy is so small in relation to world financial flows that it faces the world interest rate as a *datum*, i.e. variations in domestic financial flows have a negligible impact on the world interest rate.

While the world interest rate is determined on the world financial market, we can construct supply and demand schedules for loanable funds for the domestic economy, showing the volume of funds which would be supplied or demanded at various possible interest rates (but at a given level of income) by residents of the home economy. The intersection point of the latter schedules determines the interest rate which *would* clear the domestic loanable funds market *if* the domestic economy were closed to international borrowing and lending. This latter interest rate we denote by r_d, while the world interest rate is denoted by r^*. This set-up is shown in Figure 6.1.

Figure 6.1 is constructed in such a way that if the domestic economy were closed to international financial transactions the equilibrium interest rate would lie below the world rate ($r_d < r^*$). Correspondingly there is an excess flow of loanable funds over

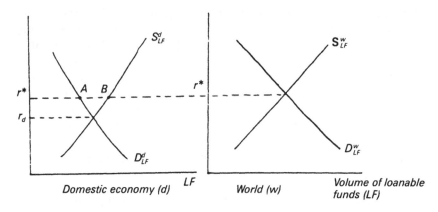

Figure 6.1

domestic demand (shown by the distance *AB*) in the home economy at interest rate $r^\star$. This 'excess supply' represents the net outflow of loanable funds from the home economy. And since the balance of payments account must sum to zero, this net capital outflow must be associated with a surplus on the current account of the balance of payments. By shifting the D^d_{LF} and S^d_{LF} schedules we could show situations in which r_d equals $r^\star$ (zero net capital outflow; current account balance of zero) or r_d lies above $r^\star$ (negative capital outflow; current account deficit).

We can now use this geometric apparatus to analyse the effect of placing a tax on the returns from foreign investments, starting from the position shown in Figure 6.1 with positive net capital outflow. The world interest rate $r^\star$ is not itself affected, but the return available to domestic residents from investing abroad is reduced, to $(r^\star - \tau)$ where τ is the rate of taxation on foreign investment earnings. We assume, however, that domestic residents are still free to borrow from abroad at $r^\star$. The situation is then as shown in Figure 6.2.

The domestic supply and demand schedules are not shifted by the imposition of the tax, but the interest rate charged on loanable funds in the domestic economy falls from $r^\star$ to r_d. To see why this is so we should notice that the 'effective' supply of funds schedules from the viewpoint of domestic borrowers is given by the line *ABCD*. No funds are available below the rate $(r^\star - \tau)$ for although domestic savers are willing 'in principle' to supply a certain volume of funds for less than that rate, there is no reason why they should lend *any* funds for less than the return available on foreign investment (unless considerations of risk enter their calculations; we abstract from that possibility here as it does not affect the main line of argument). Over the range *BC* an interest rate in excess of $(r^\star - \tau)$ is required to induce domestic savers to supply additional funds, but from point *C* onward domestic borrowers have unlimited access to funds at the world rate $r^\star$, hence there is no reason why they should pay any higher rate to domestic lenders. (Again, relaxing this assumption would not materially affect the argument.) The point, then, is that the interest rate r_d equilibrates the domestic demand and the 'effective supply' of funds. (Note that in Figure 6.1, by contrast, the effective supply of funds to domestic borrowers is simply a horizontal line at the level $r^\star$.)

Within this theory, therefore, taxing the returns on foreign investment does indeed lower the home interest rate. This will then, *ceteris paribus*, stimulate domestic private-sector investment (and/or make it cheaper for the government to borrow to finance domestic investment). There is another effect, however. Referring back to Figure 6.2 we can see that the domestic demand for loanable funds will expand from the level associated with point X to that associated with point Y, while the domestic supply will shrink (from C to Y). The excess of domestic supply of loanable funds over domestic demand therefore disappears. Net capital export has ceased and therefore the current account balance must also be at zero.[4] In other words the rise in domestic investment is at the expense of a fall in net exports of goods and services.

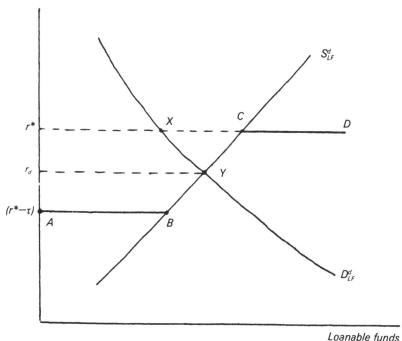

Figure 6.2

The actual mechanism whereby net exports of goods and services are displaced involves movement of the exchange rate. As capital outflow falls, the flow demand for foreign currency falls, causing the domestic currency to appreciate. This appreciation reduces exports and raises imports. This argument suggests that home country GNP will be broadly unaffected; the investment component of aggregate demand rises while the net export component falls.

There may, however, be some secondary effects here which lead to change in domestic GNP, if the multiplier effect of investment differs from that of exports. This point is examined by Thirlwall (1980) who constructs estimates of the differential multiplier effects of the various categories of 'autonomous expenditure', based on the different import components of these categories (the higher the import component of a given class of expenditure, the less the multiplier impact of a change in that class of expenditure on home country GNP).

Thirlwall's figures, calculated from the 1971 *Input–Output Tables for the United Kingdom*, show a slightly lower import coefficient for investment as compared to exports, which suggests that the displacement of a given volume of exports by an equal volume of investment would result in some positive impact on GNP, as the positive multiplier on the change in investment would outweigh the negative effect of the export reduction. In the present context, however, this result is at best suggestive, for two reasons. First, we cannot take it for granted that the relative magnitudes of the import coefficients on investment and exports have remained the same since the compilation of the 1971 *Input–Output Tables*.[5] Second, the displacement effect described above is not one in which investment replaces an equal volume of *exports*. Rather, currency appreciation will tend to reduce exports to some degree while also raising the propensity to import (raising imports relative to GNP): it is *net* exports which will, in the model given above, fall to the same extent that investment rises. Hence while some secondary effect on GNP is quite possible, it is hard to produce a compelling argument as to the direction of the effect.

Note that it is crucial to the argument above that the domestic economy starts out with a net outflow of capital. This can be seen by considering briefly what happens if we start out with a net capital inflow, as shown in Figure 6.3.

Figure 6.3 shows the case where initially r_d lies above r^*, that is, the domestic demand for loanable funds exceeds the domestic supply at r, so there is net capital *inflow*. Once again, the 'effective' supply of funds to home borrowers becomes $ABCD$ after tax is imposed, but this time there is no effect on the domestic interest rate or investment. Both before and after the tax, the domestic demand for

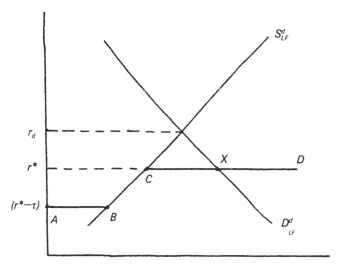

Figure 6.3

loanable funds is that associated with point X while the operative interest rate is r^*. Net capital inflow both before and after is represented by the distance CX. The point is that the domestic suppliers of funds can still earn the rate of return r^* by lending to domestic borrowers, whose demand exceeds the domestic supply. The benefit, if such it is, of switching interest-responsive domestic expenditure for net exports by means of taxing the returns on foreign investment appears (within this model at any rate) to be available only to an economy which starts out with a net outflow of capital.

This last rather striking result is, however, sensitive to the assumption of *perfect* international mobility of capital. The assumption that domestic and foreign financial assets are perfect substitutes in investors' portfolios is surely too strong. Yet if these assets are not perfect substitutes, our loanable funds analysis becomes rather more complex. Consider the flow supply and demand for *domestic* financial assets; the domestic flow supply of these assets, S_a^d (which we take as equivalent to the flow demand for loanable funds) will be a function of the yield on these assets, which we denote by r_h, and other variables such as the expected profitability of real investment projects:

$$S_a^d = S_a^d \left(\bar{r}_h, \ldots \right)$$

where the negative sign over r_h indicates that the supply of domestic assets is inversely related to the yield on those assets. The flow demand, which is the sum of the demands originating from domestic

and foreign savers, will in turn be a function of the yield on the
domestic assets, r_h, the yield on foreign assets, $r^\star$, and other factors.
Among these 'other factors' we find portfolio considerations. Let P
denote the proportion of domestic assets held in savers' portfolios;
then if the two classes of assets are not perfect substitutes, we would
expect the flow demand for domestic assets to be, *ceteris paribus*, a
declining function of P. We then have:

$$D_a^d = D_a^d(\overset{+}{r}_h, \bar{r}^\star, \bar{P})$$

as our representation of flow demand. We can now set out the flow
equilibrium condition for the market in domestic financial assets:

$$D_a^d(\overset{+}{r}_h, \bar{r}^\star, \bar{P}) = S_a^d(\bar{r}_h, \ldots).$$

This condition may be shown graphically as in Figure 6.4. The
slopes of the supply and demand schedules are reversed in Figure
6.4 simply because we are expressing the analysis in terms of supply
and demand for *assets* rather than for loanable funds as such. We
can see from the diagram that if $r^\star$ were to fall this would shift the
demand for domestic assets to the right, leading to a fall in the yield
on those assets, r_h.

Now recall that the D_a^d schedule represents the sum of domestic
and foreign demand for domestic assets. The *domestic* component
of this demand will be additionally influenced by our tax rate τ: a rise in
τ will reduce the net return available to domestic savers from acquiring
foreign assets. It will therefore act in the same direction as a fall in
$r^\star$, leading to a fall in r_h. This time notice that this effect is *not*

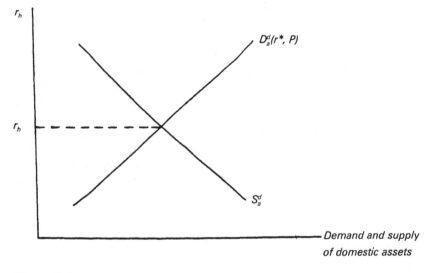

Figure 6.4

dependent on the domestic economy starting with a *net* capital outflow. We only require that domestic savers were previously acquiring foreign assets to some degree, and that the reduction in return on those assets causes substitution towards domestic assets.

If portfolio proportions do play a role, an additional point emerges. Consider an economy which has been experiencing large-scale net outflows of capital, such that the proportion of foreign assets in domestic savers' portfolio has been expanding (P falling). We should expect this process to be self-limiting. As P falls, the demand schedule for domestic assets gradually shifts to the right, reducing r_h and stimulating the supply of domestic assets (i.e. domestic investment) while the rate of acquisition of foreign assets falls. The purely theoretical model given above does not tell us how fast or how strong this effect is likely to be, but it does suggest that we should not expect indefinite continuation of the large-scale net capital outflows from the UK which began in 1979.

The model utilized above is highly simplified, to be sure, but it does make possible some useful observations on the debate. First, Hugh Stephenson seems to be wrong. The foreign investment tax does not merely affect the exchange rate alone, but will also effect the domestic interest rate. Then, unless domestic investment is totally unresponsive to the interest rate, Coakley and Harris (1983) will also be wrong: we do expect some effect on domestic investment. Second, however, the proponents of such a policy (Hattersley, Smith) should notice that the effect on the domestic interest rate and investment is not *guaranteed* to be significant. Our 'perfect substitutability' loanable funds model showed no effect on the policy unless the country starts from a position of net capital outflow, and while that result is questionable it may still be the case that the degree of effectiveness of the policy depends upon the initial state of capital flows. As a practical matter, we should ask how likely it is that a future Labour government will inherit a situation of net capital outflow. Taking a longer perspective, the more typical problem for the UK – and one which is likely to re-emerge with any attempt at macroeconomic expansionism – is that of limiting the current account deficit. Suppose that the tax policy were effective in switching domestic investment for net exports even under conditions of net capital inflow – is it then desirable? The proponents of the policy have not really addressed the consequences of the reduction in net exports which it is likely to entail.

Short-term dynamics

The loanable funds theory utilized in the previous section has some insights to offer, but it is not an appropriate means of analysing the possible short-run dynamic effects of imposing a tax on foreign investment earnings. Loanable funds theory focuses on *flow* equilibrium and is not very useful for assessing stock adjustment effects. We therefore complement the foregoing with an analysis in the manner of Buiter and Miller (1981), which enables us to take into account the possible consequences of forward-looking behaviour on the part of asset-holders while the domestic price level is 'sticky' and takes time to adjust to any change in economic conditions. Presumably it is important to check whether the imposition of a foreign interest tax is liable to give rise to any nasty short-run surprises.

The model to be used here is essentially the same as in Buiter and Miller, except for the deletion of a number of exogenous variables which are not relevant to the present discussion. It is given by the following equations:

$$\text{(1)} \quad y = -\gamma(r - \dot{p}) + \delta(e - p) \qquad\qquad \gamma, \delta > 0$$
$$\text{(2)} \quad m = ky - \lambda r + p \qquad\qquad\qquad k, \lambda > 0$$
$$\text{(3)} \quad \dot{p} = \phi y + \pi \qquad\qquad\qquad\qquad \phi > 0$$
$$\text{(4)} \quad \dot{e} = r - (r^\star - \tau)$$

The variables are defined as follows:

y = log of real domestic output
r = nominal domestic interest rate
p = log of domestic price level
$\dot{p}$ = time rate of change of log of price level, i.e. inflation rate, dp/dt.
m = log of domestic money stock
π = trend or 'core' rate of inflation
$r^\star$ = return on foreign investment
τ = rate of taxation on foreign investment returns
e = log of the exchange rate (domestic currency price of a unit of foreign currency)
$\dot{e}$ = time rate of change of log of exchange rate, $de/dt(e > 0$ implies depreciation)

The variables m, π, $r^\star$ and τ are taken to be exogenous.

Equation (1) is a log-linear *IS* schedule, according to which current output is a decreasing function of the real domestic interest rate and an increasing function of international competitiveness. Equation (2) represents the condition that money stock equals money demand, which is a function of real income, interest rate, and price level. Equation (3) represents a 'Phillips curve'; inflation departs from its trend or core rate, π, as current output departs from its 'full employment' level. Units are chosen such that full employment income equals 1, so that its logarithm equals zero. Equation (4) is a simple but analytically powerful representation of *stock* equilibrium in the foreign exchange market. The rate of depreciation of the domestic currency equals the interest differential in favour of home financial assets, so that there is no net gain or loss from holding home as opposed to foreign assets.[6]

Two additional variables are defined: l denotes the 'state of liquidity' in the home economy, and is set equal to $m-p$; while c denotes the degree of international competitiveness and is set equal to $e-p$. Buiter and Miller show how this model may be analysed formally and we shall not repeat the intermediate mathematical steps here. We move straight to the reduced form equation for the evolution of liquidity and competitiveness over time, $\dot{l}$ and $\dot{c}$ respectively.[7]

$$(5) \quad \begin{bmatrix} \dot{l} \\ \dot{c} \end{bmatrix} = \frac{1}{\Delta} \begin{bmatrix} \phi\gamma & \phi\lambda\delta \\ 1 & \delta(\phi\lambda - k) \end{bmatrix} \begin{bmatrix} l \\ c \end{bmatrix} + \begin{bmatrix} 0 \\ \tau \end{bmatrix}$$

where $\Delta = \gamma(\phi\lambda-k)-\lambda$, which is *a priori* ambiguous in sign but is assumed to be negative. A negative vale for Δ is a necessary and sufficient condition for dynamic stability of the system and for an increase in aggregate demand to have the effect of raising domestic output at a given state of competitiveness. Equation (5) is a re-statement of Buiter and Miller's equation (7), with all exogenous variables except τ set to zero for simplicity, since τ is the variable upon which the present argument is focused.

Now in steady state equilibrium, both domestic liquidity and competitiveness must remain constant over time, i.e. $\dot{l} = \dot{c} = 0$. The next analytical step is then to derive from (5) the loci in l, c space along which $\dot{l}$ and $\dot{c}$ are zero. The LL locus along which liquidity is unchanging is given by

$$(6) \quad \phi\gamma l + \phi\lambda\delta c = 0$$

which implies that $\dfrac{dc}{dl}\Big|_{\dot{l}=0} = \dfrac{-\gamma}{\lambda\delta} < 0.$

Similarly the CC locus along which competitiveness is unchanging is given by

$$\frac{1}{\Delta} l + \frac{\delta(\phi\lambda - k)}{\Delta} c + \tau = 0$$

which implies that

$$(7) \quad c = \frac{1}{\delta(k - \phi\lambda)} l + \frac{\Delta}{\delta(k - \phi\lambda)} \tau$$

For 'relatively low' values of ϕ (i.e. deviations of output from its full employment level do not cause large movements of inflation away from its 'core' rate), $\delta(k - \phi\lambda)$ will be positive, in which case

$$\frac{\mathrm{d}c}{\mathrm{d}l}\Big|_{\dot{c}=0}$$

is also positive. We choose to illustrate using this case, although $\delta(k - \phi\lambda) < 0$ would not alter the qualitative results, provided that Δ is still assumed to be negative. We also, then, have

$$\frac{\mathrm{d}c}{\mathrm{d}\tau}\Big|_{\dot{c}=0} < 0$$

The phase diagram showing this set-up is given in Figure 6.5.

The phase diagram shows the 'saddlepoint' property of the model. Starting from any point to the left or right of the LL locus there is a tendency to move towards that locus. To see why, suppose that c is held constant while, starting from a point on the LL locus, we arbitrarily increase l (move to the right) by raising the money stock. This rise in liquidity will then lower the interest rate, stimulating aggregate demand. This will cause output to rise above its full employment level which in turn will speed up inflation. As the price level rises, liquidity falls and we return towards the LL locus. By contrast, if the system starts from a point above or below the CC locus it tends to move away from that locus. Suppose l is held constant while, starting from the CC locus, we arbitrarily increase competitiveness by depreciating the currency (move vertically above CC). The increase in competitiveness will stimulate income, which in turn raises money demand, and puts upward pressure on the interest rate. But then the domestic interest rate moves above the foreign rate $r^\star$, and to maintain stock equilibrium in the foreign exchange market the domestic currency must depreciate over time; competitiveness increases further and we move further away from the CC locus.

There is therefore a unique trajectory, shown by SS, which leads in towards the steady state A: if the system 'starts' at any point off this line it will fail to converge upon A, as shown by the arrows of motion in Figure 6.5. If traders in financial assets realize this (and we assume that they do) then the system will always 'jump' on to the convergent SS locus whenever the steady state is disturbed. Notice, however, how this 'jump' must occur. Since the money stock is exogenous and the price level of domestic output is sticky, the state of liquidity, l, is *not* a variable capable of jumping at a point in time. The exchange rate, on the other hand, is free to move at any point in

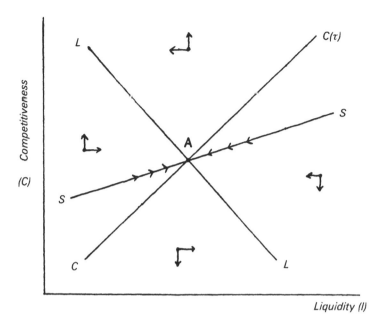

Figure 6.5

time, hence it is the exchange rate which will 'jump' to take the system on to the *SS* locus.

We are now ready to consider the effect of an increase in τ within this framework. As can be seen from equation (7) and the following discussion of the algebraic signs of the coefficients in that equation, an increase in τ will reduce the level of competitiveness, *c*, consistent with the condition that $\dot{c} = 0$, for any given value of *l*. In other words, the *CC* schedule is shifted downwards. This is shown in Figure 6.6, from which we can see that the new steady state, *B*, occurs at a lower level of competitiveness and higher level of liquidity than the original steady state, *A*. The reduction in the net return on foreign assets, $r^*-\tau$, requires a corresponding reduction in the domestic interest rate, while this reduction in *r* in turn is associated with a greater demand for real balances, $m-p$. As in the loanable funds analysis given earlier, the net effect of the rise in τ is to increase domestic investment (this will be stimulated by the fall in *r*) at the expense of net exports (which will be reduced by the fall in *c*).

By reference to Figure 6.6 we can also discuss the short-run dynamics resulting from the imposition of τ. Given that liquidity is not free to jump, the initial impact must be to move the system to point *X*, which lies on the convergent path *SS* at the original level of

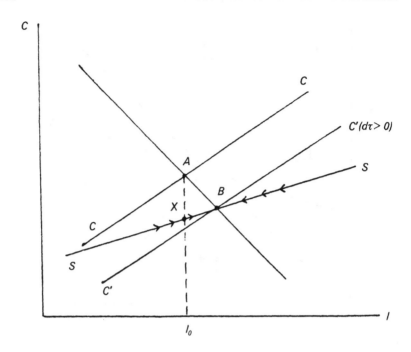

Figure 6.6

liquidity, l_0. Note that at point X competitiveness lies below the new steady state level. That is, the exchange rate initially 'overshoots' (over-appreciation of the domestic currency) then gradually moves towards its new steady state level as domestic liquidity adjusts. The intuition of what is happening is as follows; $(r^* - \tau)$ falls immediately upon the increase in τ, but r cannot fall immediately to its new steady state level since it is playing the role of equilibrating domestic money stock and money demand. The temporary divergence between $(r^* - \tau)$ and r (with $r > r^* - \tau$) must therefore be 'bridged' by a period of depreciation of the domestic currency. But this requires that the domestic currency initially appreciates beyond its new steady state level.[8]

This in turn will mean that domestic output falls below its 'full employment' level initially, since competitiveness is down while the stimulus to investment due to a lower domestic interest rate is not yet fully operative. In a word, the imposition of τ causes a temporary domestic recession before investment takes the place of the lost net exports.

This argument suggests that a Labour government would have to be careful in imposing such a tax lest it have a short-run depressing effect on domestic output. There is, however, a potential way around the problem. It was stated that the liquidity variable was not free to jump to its new steady state value. This is true in so far as private agents cannot effect such a jump when the price level of goods is 'sticky'. But the monetary authority could perhaps put matters to rights, by 'jumping' the value of the *nominal money stock* upward when τ is imposed. This would permit the step increase in liquidity which would be required to move the system straight to point B, obviating the recessionary interlude. Obviously, there may be practical problems with such a move. If such a policy were interpreted as a general slackening of monetary policy it could have inflationary repercussions. The point remains that in the absence of such monetary accommodation the imposition of τ could indeed generate a nasty short-run surprise.

Conclusions

The intention behind the arguments presented here is not to dismiss the Hattersley proposal. Indeed, such a proposal makes good sense when:

1 the economy is experiencing substantial net capital outflow in conjunction with a surplus on the balance of payments current account; and
2 a high priority is placed upon raising the rate of domestic investment.

Hugh Stephenson goes too far in dismissing the proposal. None the less a number of critical points must be made. First, focus on the need for a higher rate of domestic investment should not be allowed to obscure the point that inadequate efficiency of investment may be a more serious problem in the UK. Second, we have to take carefully into account the 'side effects' of the tax proposal. While it is obvious to all that one effect must be to reduce the income from overseas investments, if it reduces their volume – and the proponents of the policy are content to live with this – it has not been made clear that we can also expect currency appreciation and a loss of net exports. In the same context, the possible adverse short-run dynamic effects have to be considered, along with complementary policies which might reduce or eliminate these effects. Third, we have to ask whether the situation which the policy is designed to ameliorate (i.e. large-scale net capital outflow) is likely to persist much longer anyway. To reiterate, the main international economic problem confronting a future Labour government pursuing expansionary macroeconomic policies is more likely to be that of preventing excessive capital outflow. This is not to say, however, that the Hattersley proposal would be irrelevant in such a context. A full discussion of this point goes beyond the scope of this paper, but a brief comment is in order. It is arguable that the short-to-medium term effects of exchange rate changes are asymmetrical; while an appreciation of the domestic currency will reduce the volume of net exports, a depreciation may tend to aggravate inflation more than it improves the net exports position.[9] In that case a Labour government pursuing an expansionary domestic policy may believe it important to arrest any depreciation caused by such a policy rather than, à la Barber, relying upon depreciation to balance the current account. In its role as a disincentive to the gross acquisition of foreign assets, the Hattersley tax proposal may have a useful part to play here.

Notes

1. The text of this speech was subsequently published in *Fiscal Studies* (see Hattersley 1985b).
2. Over the period from 1981 till the first half of 1984 UK gross private investment overseas proceeded at an annual rate of over £10 billion. Meanwhile overseas investment in the UK private sector fluctuated between £3.1 and £4.7 billion per year. Adding in overseas investment in the UK public sector, we get a figure for inward investment flow fluctuating between £3.4 and £5.4 billion. Net acquisition of foreign assets proceeded, therefore, at an average rate of well over £5 billion per year over the period. (Figures taken from *Economic Trends, Annual Supplement*, 1985 edition, CSO.)
3. This is easy to say, of course. In practice what it means is that investments should not be directed largely towards shoring up industries which are long-term losers in the changing pattern of international division of labour, and that management and labour practices have to be questioned rather than just relying upon an infusion of funds to raise competitiveness.
4. If τ were smaller, such that $r^* > (r^* - \tau) > r_d$, then the domestic interest rate would not fall all the way to r_d, but only to $r^* - \tau$. In that case although the domestic 'excess supply' of funds falls it does not fall to zero. Still, reduced capital export would be associated with a reduced positive current account balance.
5. Particularly since the difference between these import coefficients as calculated by Thirlwall was rather small in the first place: 0.210 for investment *versus* 0.229 for exports.
6. Strictly, the formulation given in equation (4) implies perfect foresight on the part of asset holders. This assumption could be relaxed by introducing a stochastic element and substituting rational expectations for perfect foresight, but this would complicate the analysis unnecessarily.
7. Briefly, equation (5) is derived by taking the basic equations for l and c (i.e. l $m - p$ and $c = e - p$) and inserting the information on $\dot{p}$ and $\dot{e}$ given by equations (3) and (4). Equations (1) and (2) are then solved for y and r and these solution values are substituted in the l and c equations. Matters are simplified if we assume, as do Buiter and Miller, that $\pi = \dot{m}$, i.e. that the 'core' inflation rate equals the rate of growth of the money stock.
8. In a rational expectations context, anticipation of the imposition of τ would be likely to cause appreciation. In this respect the Hattersley tax proposal differs from standard quantitative controls on the volume of overseas investment.

Agents anticipating the re-imposition of the latter type of control might carry out a pre-emptive burst of acquisition of foreign assets, leading to a sharp depreciation of the currency. But it would not be rational for agents anticipating a tax on the earnings from their overseas asset holdings to do this.

9. This argument rests partly on asymmetrical behaviour of the domestic price and wage levels, which may be flexible upward yet 'sticky' downward. Also, if non-price competitiveness is important to international markets, a depreciation may do little to expand the market share of UK products considered relatively undesirable on non-price grounds.

References

Buiter, W.H. and **Miller, M.** (1981) 'Monetary policy and international competitiveness: the problems of adjustment', in W.A. Eltis and P.J.N. Sinclair (eds), *The Money Supply and the Exchange Rate*, Oxford, Clarendon Press.

Coakley, J. and **Harris, L.** (1983) *The City of Capital* (1983) Oxford, Basil Blackwell.

Hattersley, R. (1985a) 'Investing in Britain', *New Statesman*, 22 February.

Hattersley, R. (1985b) 'A new exchange control scheme', *Fiscal Studies*, vol. 6, no. 3, pp. 9–13.

Leijonhufvud, A. (1981) *Information and Coordination*, Oxford, Oxford University Press.

Robertson, D.H. (1940) *Essays in Monetary Theory*, London, Staples Press.

Smith, P. (1985) 'UK financial institutions, financial crises, and nationalization', *Economy and Society*, vol. 14, no. 1, pp. 55–76.

Stephenson, H. (1985a) 'There are better ways to catch a cat . . .', *New Statesman*, 1 February.

Stephenson, H. (1985b) 'Where lending is harder than borrowing', *New Statesman*, 8 February.

Thirlwall, A.P. (1980) *Balance of Payments Theory and the UK Experience*, London, Macmillan.

Name index

Subject index

Note: All references are to the United States unless otherwise specified.

For Product Safety Concerns and Information please contact our EU
representative GPSR@taylorandfrancis.com Taylor & Francis Verlag GmbH,
Kaufingerstraße 24, 80331 München, Germany

Printed and bound by CPI Group (UK) Ltd, Croydon, CR0 4YY
01/05/2025
01858392-0001